GOOD FOOD,
GLUTEN FREE

GOOD FOOD,

GLUTEN FREE

HILDA CHERRY HILLS

KEATS PUBLISHING, INC., NEW CANAAN, CONNECTICUT

Mrs. Hills will be happy to answer inquiries or requests for copies of her gluten-free diet sheet provided the writer send an international reply coupon to cover postage and a self-addressed envelope. Her address is 20 Convent Lane, Bocking, Braintree, Essex, England.

GOOD FOOD, GLUTEN FREE
Published in 1976 by Keats Publishing, Inc.
By arrangement with the Henry Doubleday Research Association

Copyright © 1976 by Hilda Cherry Hills

Library of Congress Catalog Card Number: 75-10538

ISBN 0-87983-103-0

Printed in the United States of America

Keats Publishing, Inc.
27 Pine Street (Box 876), New Canaan, Connecticut 06840

Dedicated to

the memory of Sir Robert McCarrison, the great physician who taught that good health demands good food, and what good food really is.

Also to the future good health of anyone going on a gluten-free diet prepared to follow his advice, as expanded in this book to meet their special needs.

CONTENTS

A Medical Appraisal of This Book
by Laurence E. D. Knights, F. R. C. S. xi

Foreword by Jean A. Monro, M.D. xv

Preface xvii

1. Why This Book Has Been Written............... 1

2. A Short History of Celiac Disease and Its Treatment 9

3. Other Conditions Apparently Linked with Celiac Disease: Diabetes, Skin Disease, Milk Intolerance..... 17

4. Other Diseases Which May Benefit from a Gluten-Free Diet: Multiple Sclerosis, Schizophrenia, Rheumatoid Arthritis, Regional Enteritis and Autism.... 22

5. The Aims and Methods of a Gluten-Free Diet and Results to Be Expected........................ 44

6. Feeding the Celiac Infant and Young Child........ 65

7. In the Kitchen: Recommended Good Foods and General Hints.................................... 78

8. Children's Parties; Eating Out; Packed Meals; Picnics; Traveling Abroad; Menace in Menus; Menus for One Week: Spring, Summer, Autumn, Winter; Minimum Trouble Menus 84

9. Recipes: Biscuits, Breads, Breakfasts, Cakes, Candies, Cookies, Desserts, Drinks, Fish, Meats, Miscellaneous, Salads, Sauces, Soups, Spreads, Vegetable and Fruit Cookery, Vegetarian Dishes 105

Recipe Index 227

General Index 237

A MEDICAL APPRAISAL OF THIS BOOK

This outstanding book, written very much in the spirit of Sir Robert McCarrison to whom it is dedicated, successfully seeks to provide an understanding of the basis of good food, that is, food that does you good and meets the body's nutritional needs, and at the same time provide recipes and menus for the many celiacs for whom a cereal-derived factor, namely gluten, can cause severe and protracted illness. Celiac Disease (C.D.) is really a collection of symptoms presenting usually in childhood, but sometimes in later life, associated with changes in the small bowel mucosal lining and responding to removal from the diet of gluten found mainly in wheat and rye. The opening chapters give a succinct story of C.D. and a brief account of conditions apparently linked with it or likely to benefit from the diet. Informed understanding and comment are backed by good references to the medical and scientific literature.

These apparently completely diverse diseases have this too in common; they are diseases of our affluent society and therefore of the Western world in particular. They include diabetes, the commonest metabolic disorder, multiple sclerosis, the commonest disease of the nervous system, schizophrenia, the commonest mental disorder, dermatitis herpetiformis, a not uncommon skin complaint, regional enteritis, an increasingly common disease of the bowel. For none of these diseases is the real cause known. Gluten is not a direct poison to the bowel lining, and why it causes trouble is unknown. It is thought that it may invoke an immunological reaction which is the body's second line of defense to get rid of what it does not like, or that the bowel lesion may result from lack of a necessary enzyme or chemical messenger so that even if the

right components are provided, the production-line is halted
through lack of control.

C.D. is not as usually stated an inherited disease in the
sense that it is genetically determined with the implication
that little can be done about it. If it were, identical twins
would both suffer, but this is not necessarily so. What may be
inherited is a predisposition, but more important are environmental factors before and after birth, i.e. nutritional factors in
mother and child.

The clinical course of C.D. is very variable and bears little
relation to the degree of bowel involvement. The only reliable
diagnostic feature is the response to a gluten-free diet; the
proof of the pudding is the *not* eating. This rightly is Mrs.
Hills's thoroughly practical approach.

All disease manifestations are an adaptation to an un-
friendly environment. If food is wrong, is not mixed properly
with the digestive ferments or the ferments are deficient (as
in fibrocystic disease of the pancreas), or nature's mechanical
arrangements are upset by removal of stomach or small bowel
or by short-circuit operation, or finally there is a defect in
bowel mucosa, then absorption of the products of digestion
goes wrong. Needed food factors, whether proteins, fats,
minerals or vitamins, will be passed out often noticeably as a
fatty diarrhea and lost to the body's economy. Not only so,
but the environment of helpful protective and vitamin-making
organisms lower down the bowel is altered. Thus the malabsorption syndrome presents in many ways. Fats, the only
product of digestion insoluble in water, are especially affected. Through loss of fat and protein which may be con-
siderable, there is failure to thrive. Loss of vitamin D leads to
bone changes and rickets. Loss of vitamin A to poor vision in
dim light, dermatitis in babies and chest trouble in children.
Loss of vitamin E removes a co-enzyme of essential fatty
acids. Loss of vitamin B-12 and folic acid may lead to a pernicious type of anemia. Loss of riboflavin causes soreness of the
tongue and of the corners of the mouth. Loss of iron, an iron
deficiency anemia. Loss of calcium may lead to tetany. Multi-

ple sclerosis and conditions associated with C.D. all have nutritional determinants and in some there are known to be malabsorption defects. The "good food" regime is good for any man for the very factors that are ill-absorbed in C.D. are those that tend to be deficient in the population at large thanks to our over-processed, nutrient-lacking, convenience food. So *Good Food, Gluten Free* goes far to provide the body's requirements for internal self-renewal which is the basis of health.

LAURENCE E. D. KNIGHTS
FELLOW, ROYAL COLLEGE OF SURGEONS

FOREWORD

The advice in this book combines the benefits of a gluten-free diet with the principles of good nutrition.

It is becoming increasingly acknowledged that there are many diseases of the Western world which are due to faulty diet; obesity, diverticulitis of the bowel, cancer of the colon and coronary artery disease are but a few. Often the factor implicated is the over-use of refined foods, sugar and refined flours which have been promoted largely because of their long shelf-life. Advice is here given about the use of foods which should overcome the problems of over-refined products.

A gluten-free diet is essential for people with celiac disease and dermatitis herpetiformis. Its value for other conditions is under investigation.

Because the medical profession is obliged to use great caution in advocating new techniques of treatment, before doctors can claim that a gluten-free diet is beneficial, its efficacy in these other conditions must be established. However, doctors are free to use new therapeutic measures if there is hope of regaining health or alleviating suffering, and in the postulated benefits of a gluten-free diet there are scientifically established facts, many of which have been reviewed in this book. In each condition considered there are many factors responsible for the production of the disease, and gluten may be one of them.

It should be emphasized that if there were any risk of harm to anybody from a gluten-free diet then it should not be recommended by anyone. However, there can be no harm from the diet itself, only perhaps inconvenience, as it is not in common use in the Western world. In the East, millions live healthily on a gluten-free diet.

It is very difficult for someone who is not a doctor to survey the medical literature as intensively as Mrs. Hills has done, and she deserves great credit for her perspicacity and success.

This book is the culmination of thirty years' study of nutrition applied in particular, recently, to Mr. Lawrence Hills's condition. For this combination many of us will have cause to be thankful, and I would like to express my personal gratitude to Cherry Hills for whom I have the deepest respect.

JEAN A. MONRO, M.D.

PREFACE

All that follows has been written to help adults and families going on a gluten-free diet with knowledge that will reduce anxiety, and help them to understand why it is so important to keep within the limitations it imposes. Though the main object will be to alleviate the condition of one member of the family—such as a celiac child or a husband in a wheelchair with multiple sclerosis—when it is adopted by the whole family for simplicity in the kitchen, all gain not only better food but even better health than average by going without refined carbohydrates.

This restriction sounds unpalatable and monotonous to those who are used to conventional menus, but offers adventures in eating and cookery that are rewarding in themselves, as anyone trying the many recipes from many countries in my book can prove for themselves. I hasten to add that except for the simpler recipes, few of these are all my own work. The more elaborate ones have been freely borrowed, although many have had to be altered and adapted to meet the special need to exclude wheat, oats, barley and rye. Most of the people of this world live on gluten-free rice, corn (maize) and millet, so there is nothing impossible about this unconventional cookery.

First and foremost I would like to thank Dr. Jean Monro who wrote the Foreword, read the Ms for medical accuracy, and gave me the help and encouragement from her special knowledge of the conditions that a gluten-free diet can benefit, without which I would never have dared to write this book. Then I would like to say "thank you" to Mrs. Lore Birkenruth for the very many recipes from Continental experience, especially those using millet, which she gathered with so much trouble for me to share with those I want so very much to help.

I would like to express my gratitude to the authors of many standard works for their permission to use not more than five of their recipes. Because their books should be on every kitchen bookshelf I give the book I used and its author, so that at least readers can get them from their library and see just how many more gluten-free recipes they can find if they look hard enough.

So "thank you" for helping me help others to Adelle Davis for *Let's Cook It Right*, Beatrice Trum Hunter for *Natural Foods Cookbook*, Ursula Cavanagh for *Wholefood Cookery Book*, Veronica Vezza for *Vegetarian Cookery Made Easy*, Jean Hewitt for *The New York Times Natural Foods Cookbook*, Lydia Chatterton for *Modern Cookery Illustrated*, Ruth Bircher for *Eating Your Way to Health* and Doris Grant for *Dear Housewives*.

I would also thank Bon Viveur, Elizabeth Ray and many others for single recipes and ideas that I have borrowed and adapted. Finally I would thank the Members of the Henry Doubleday Research Association, and the multiple sclerosis sufferers who sent the donations that made it possible to print this book, [the original English edition—ed.] from which I shall take no royalties, for these will go to further research on helping the "incurable" with good food gluten-free.

HILDA CHERRY HILLS

PREFACE TO SECOND EDITION

The success of the first edition of this book was not only measured in sales, but in readers who are walking again. One of the latest of these is reported in Chapter 4, from a patient who is walking normally after eight years in a wheelchair, who has been on the diet for only a year. I would stress that this diet excludes refined carbohydrates as well as gluten, but includes sunflower seed oil. I would also draw the attention of all readers to the improved whole rice and soya bean loaf in the recipe section. My husband says that this recipe alone makes it worth buying the handmill to grind the grain fresh.

HILDA CHERRY HILLS

1

Why This Book Has Been Written

My husband is a celiac. This means that in digestion he cannot absorb the protein (gluten) in barley, oats, rye or wheat. Therefore, he has been on a special diet, unfamiliar to most people, for eight years and must remain on it for life. That is why I have written this book. We want to help the increasing number who are faced with coping with a similar situation either for themselves or for a member of their family. I hope to show that this is not as difficult as it may at first appear, and to point to a way in which it can be carried out to maximum effect with results which can be remarkably rewarding, as in the case of my husband, whose physical and mental energy and capacity for hard work today at the age of sixty-three, puts many a younger man to shame.

He has given me permission to relate some of his life-story as a practical way of encouraging others to collaborate over the necessary change in food habits as he has done, with never a grumble or a sigh.

He was a sickly child from birth and was not expected to survive infancy, continually harassed by attacks of intractable diarrhea which reduced him to skin and bone. This chronic condition of crippling ill-health continued throughout his childhood making it impossible to go to school, and he spent his days in a wheelchair. Fortunately, his father was a brilliant teacher with a science degree who was also an inventor, and his devoted and intelligent mother kept him supplied with a vast variety of books to fire his vivid imagination and quick wits over a wide field so that his education was exceptional if not orthodox, while an emaciated and frequently bedridden body could do nothing to keep down a soaring spirit.

1

There was a welcome pause at puberty when his condition improved considerably so that he was able to give up the chair. But he was still seriously ill at intervals and a wise physician, although unable to diagnose or improve his condition, told his anxious parents that his only hope of survival lay in an outdoor life. So he was apprenticed into horticulture. Hindsight shows that the prediction was in essence correct for it meant that he was getting plenty of life-saving vitamin D, which would not have been available in any indoor occupation.

But the constant and unremitting struggle against illness went on as he worked, with many a change of job into different fields of horticulture as he returned to normal life after yet another spell in hospital. This pattern continued right through the three and a half years he spent in the Royal Air Force which he passed into by tactfully keeping his mouth shut. When he was finally invalided from the service on D-Day 1944, he went back into horticulture when fit enough. But yet another serious bout of the illness that dogged his days forced him to decide that he could no longer carry on this work. In Service hospitals he had written many articles and the first of his ten books on horticulture to be published; now he turned to free-lance journalism and the writing of more books. Out of this grew the Henry Doubleday Research Association which he founded and called after a worthy Quaker, and all that the Association stands for now, some twenty years later.

He still suffered from the recurrent bouts of prostrating fever and diarrhea that left him weak and more emaciated, if possible, than ever. But somehow he persisted in carrying on with his writing commitments, even if this meant dictating to a typist sitting by his sick bed, either at home or in hospital. For however bloody the battle, he kept his head unbowed, his spirit unbroken, and his range of interest ever widening.

Then in the early spring of 1964 the break came at last. He was admitted to the Royal Free Hospital, the long overdue diagnosis of celiac disease was made, and he was put on a gluten-free diet. This diet, begun in hospital, was followed when he returned to the home he shared with his mother, and for the first time in his life he began to put on weight, not to lose it. Even the great hollows in his cheeks filled out; his life became less of a battlefield. Early that summer he had a couple of relapses owing to eating some oat-cakes on a short Scottish holiday, when his supply of gluten-free bread failed to arrive because of the postal strike, and this landed him again in the Royal Free Hospital. But by the time we got married, at the end of September 1964, he had begun to get the better of his lifelong invisible enemy, and it became my dearest ambition to make it a complete and resounding victory. And (under God) I think we can claim to have achieved this.

Since then his only relapses have been due to inadvertently eating something (when I, the watchdog, have not been present) pressed on him by a kind hostess, quite unaware that even a home-made delicacy invariably results in a serious reaction if it contains any of the forbidden wheat, rye, oats or barley. On one occasion, the trigger was a plate of oxtail soup eaten when lunching as a guest at a high-class restaurant, in the innocent belief that it was thickened, as at home, with onions and butter beans. Of course the restaurant soup came out of a package and these invariably contain that cheapest of thickeners and fillers, white wheat flour, which is, of course, forbidden food.

Obviously, my campaign for feeding him better had to be carried out with tact. So for a few weeks I toed the shortest possible stretch of the hospital prescribed dietary line, by giving him all the most nutritious and enjoyable foods I could at meals, and restricting his gluten-free flour to a couple of thin slices of bread at tea time. However, the loaf made with this flour remained so unpalatable, in spite of being improved in taste and texture when I substituted 25 percent home-ground brown rice, that he made no objection when I absolutely refused to fill him up with it for breakfast and supper or to serve gluten-free biscuits and cakes for the mid-morning snack or tea. Nor would I use this special gluten-free flour for coating fried fish or thickening gravies and sauces. Yet all this processed carbohydrate is recommended to patients medically diagnosed as celiacs and given a prescription for the gluten-free flour under the National Health Service in Britain.

Those who dutifully follow this advice believing, quite erroneously, that this specially supplied gluten-free flour must have some *healing virtue*, very quickly find that it puts on weight. Of course it does. But who wants to acquire the burden of obesity? Certainly, we did not. What I wanted was to replace the fat that had already accumulated on my husband with good solid muscle. This we triumphantly did. How we did it will I hope become clear from the chapters that follow.

With these changes well established and also well enjoyed by my guinea pig in human form, we took what I regard as the last vital step for those with the courage to take it. We cut out *all gluten-free flour altogether! No more such bread at all!* Here I have to confess that I had continued to eat two slices of delicious home-made whole-wheat bread at tea-time, as I have for many years. But in November 1971, I gave this up and went on exactly the same completely gluten-free diet as my husband. Not only am I quite content on it, but it makes me feel more justified in telling other people who are obliged to stay on it, that this need cause no sense of deprivation once one gets used to it.

Perhaps the first and most important result of his eating *none* of the *second best foods* but only the *best* (because most nutritious) foods, and consenting to take brewer's yeast with each meal and yogurt daily, was that my celiac decided, off his own bat, to give up smoking! He felt so much better that he no longer needed the help of endless cups of highly sweetened tea and a cigarette to keep him going. After being a pack-a-day man for over twenty years that took some doing. But he stuck to it, and how I rejoiced. It had always distressed me to see the harm he was doing to himself, though I could understand his need for a crutch of some sort over the years of hard struggle with his complaint. Furthermore, I am supersensitive to smoke myself, and suffer both at the time and for many hours after, when I have to share a confined space with a smoker.

His reward, and it certainly meant self-denial at first, was that the improvement that had already begun on our better food went on increasing steadily from this moment. His breathing gradually slowed and deepened, flabby fat (being given no fuel) was ousted by firm muscle, his general vigor improved amazingly without the signs of severe nervous strain of earlier days, and he no longer wanted to smoke at all. To-day he gets younger and more energetic every week. As he needs to be, for his work in every field goes on increasing and he has more and more to cope with.

Of course a one-time sufferer from chronic ill-health wanted to share this way to optimum health with all other celiacs, and I always intended to write a small booklet on the subject for which I had been collecting the material for many months. But researching for and writing not only an article for each issue of our quarterly Newsletter, but a rather ambitious book on do-it-yourself ecology, there seemed to be no time or opportunity for doing this. Then suddenly the opportunity—if not the time—was irrevocably thrust upon me, and I had to get to work to get something down on paper at last.

On 21st November 1971, the *Observer* published the report of a journalist that a medical student at Bristol University (now a qualified doctor) had made a special study of the fingerprints of celiacs and found them missing. This had aroused the interest of the police, who were concerned that there should exist in Great Britain 25,000 people without fingerprints, and therefore presumably potentially about to commit crimes with impunity. At once the celiac in our house decided that he was called upon to take action and this letter from him appeared on the following Sunday in the *Observer*.

As one of the 25,000 celiac disease sufferers referred to in your "missing fingerprint" news story (21 November) may I point out that oats, barley and rye—and not only wheat—

contain the gluten and produce the effect. Maize [corn], rice and millet alone are safe. I have kept fighting fit for seven years by sticking to a diet which excludes the nutritionally inferior and unnecessary gluten-free flour supplied for our special use. Details of the cheaper and simpler diet that I use will gladly be sent on receipt of a self-addressed envelope.

That evening he left on his way by plane to Stockholm on matters connected with sewage, etc., and there I was next day, alone on a limb, with all the H.D.R.A. correspondence plus a flood of letters from celiacs pouring in and, needless to say, not a word written of the leaflet we had promised to send! By the time he returned at the end of the week, there had been well over two hundred applicants and I had spent most of my time sending individual replies to the very large numbers who asked a great many questions at great length. Many seemed very upset and confused as to why they, or one of their children, had been put on this outlandish diet with such unpalatable, or even *vile* bread, as so many called it. Others were heartily sick of keeping to a diet on which they still felt so weak, etc., or wondered why they had improved so little when they never touched wheat bread but only ate Ryvita or oats porridge, quite unaware that these also are now forbidden to celiacs, and so on and so on. Among them, too, were those who asked whether there were some book that could be recommended which they could read in order to understand rather more about their condition and its treatment by this special diet. I had to reply that as far as I knew no such book yet existed, and it became obvious that the expanded booklet would have to meet all such questionings if it were to be of real help to people.

Many notable nutritionists, doctors, dentists, biochemists, dieticians, agriculturalists and others have contributed to the modern knowedge of nutrition and of the effects for good or ill of food on those who eat it, and that means all of us. Let us make better use of this knowledge revealed in the books and scientific papers where it lies unheeded by the vast majority living their daily lives.

It is hoped that what began as a mere revolt in our small kitchen may grow by nothing but the most peaceful means into a great revolution in all those kitchens throughout the world, which cater and cook not only for celiacs, but for all those who may derive benefit from following this unfamiliar diet. Then, indeed, we may rejoice that not only will they be given as a matter of course the freedom from gluten which is required, but also the highly nutritious good food which they can, and should have, if they are really to reach the full potential of their powers to enjoy useful and healthy lives to the full.

My title perhaps needs a little preliminary explanation, as it may puzzle some people who will ask, "What is meant by the 'good food' referred to?" and "Why gluten-free?"

Good food means foods that provide better materials than the average to enable our bodies to carry out their various functions better, so reaching and keeping to a higher level of health and mental and physical capacity for work and enjoyment of life. No creature can create its own energy. This must always be derived from food as fuel, and foods which are just not good enough fail to give us enough fuel or enough nerve or muscle power to work at maximum efficiency. So for all of us good food means foods chosen according to the known principles of good nutrition, uninfluenced by advertising, indolence, custom or any other reason.

No one deliberately buys shoes with cardboard soles for bad weather. Why, then, do we spend money on inferior foods which can deceive the eye and tongue, but can not deceive the bodily systems which function well or badly, according to the quality of the foods we supply them with? Superior foods exist side by side with the rest, but we need some knowledge to make the right choices. Those who want to feed their families so that they can make the best use of themselves and lead the fullest lives can acquire this information as it is presented here, instead of in some scientific journal where it is only read by specialists in the academic world.

As for the puzzling "Gluten-Free," this is important for the minority for whom this book has been written. We all know that everyone must eat, but not everyone knows that not everyone can eat everything. For increasing hundreds of thousands all over the world, but especially in the Western world, among all ages from infants to the elderly, and among males and females, there is one item in ordinary foods which is *toxic* and therefore *taboo*. This means not only absolutely forbidden, but subject to very heavy penalties if this rule is broken by disobedience. This forbidden item is called gluten, and the first medically established condition in which it must not be eaten is now called the celiac disease or condition (pronounced "*see*leack," and spelled "coeliac" in Great Britain), and those who suffer from it are called celiacs. Exactly as for alcoholics for whom there is no medicine and no recovery possible, except by sticking to the rule of NO ALCOHOL, so for any celiac there is no medicine and no recovery possible, except by sticking to the rule of NO GLUTEN. This must be absolutely understood and absolutely accepted. There are no exceptions to this rule. The food eaten in all these cases must be gluten-free since gluten must never be eaten again, and this requires accurate knowledge as well as faithful perseverance. It becomes all-important to know not only what gluten is, and in what foods it occurs so that it can be entirely excluded, but how best to build up a satisfactory daily diet without it. All this has been established after much patient research and will be referred to later. Meanwhile, we shall take a look at the history of celiac disease and its treatment in a short summary.

2 A Short History of Celiac Disease, and Its Treatment

Although it is generally considered by the medical profession that cases of what appear from descriptions of the symptoms to be celiac disease have occurred from the earliest times, its documented history in Great Britain seems to have begun with a report in 1888 from St. Bartholomew's Hospital, London, by Samuel Gee, after whom the disease was first named. There has been clinical interest ever since in this wasting disease, first recognized in infants, which in the years before the toxic factor of gluten for these individuals was realized, led at best to a short life of chronic invalidism, and at worst to an early death.

Some years after Gee's death, it was re-christened celiac disease, meaning relating to the belly, on account of the abdominal distension and pain, which with diarrhea are among the most obvious symptoms. After it became clear from the characteristic profuse, fatty and offensive stools that fats and fat-soluble vitamins were not being absorbed, a fat-free diet was often recommended. Yet such a diet causes further deficiencies,[1] and has in fact been found conducive to the formation of ulcers because foods leave the stomach so rapidly that the walls are exposed for long periods to strong hydrochloric acid.[2] Furthermore, it is now known that while solid fats are not well absorbed by celiacs, liquid oils which contain far more of the essential fatty acids necessary for all human nutrition, are well absorbed.[3]

For others, low residue diets were prescribed, i.e. with all the natural fiber, the so-called roughage removed. These were equally ineffective and harmful because they actually removed a valuable element in food, but left untouched the gluten which had not yet been proved to be the toxic factor.

9

These diets were based on the erroneous assumption that coarse foods injure the stomach linings of human beings. But, as those eminent clinicians and researchers over many years, Dr. T. L. Cleave and Dr. G. D. Campbell, have so very forcefully pointed out, these coarse foods "no more injure the lining membranes of the stomach than they do the lining membranes of the mouth, and, provided they are properly masticated are on the contrary very safe foods, because of their high buffering (protective) action."[4] In fact, this remains one of the main arguments against the use by anyone of any of the refined carbohydrates (starches and sugars), which is discussed in later chapters.

A third approach was to consider that all carbohydrates, with the exception of bananas, were injurious, and were severely restricted. This had rather better results since the exclusion of wheat and other grains could indeed allay the symptoms and gradually restore the health. Also, bananas have been found to be very good sources of magnesium,[5] which is a frequently found deficiency in these cases, and of which celiacs may excrete four times more than their intake.[6]

But it was not until 1950 that the reason for this favorable reaction to starch restriction was clearly shown, when a Dutch investigator, W. H. Dicke, published his doctorate thesis on celiac disease.[7] After many years of research and experience, he was able to demonstrate that the deleterious factor was not in fact in the starch as had been supposed, but in the protein in wheat and rye, bearing the name gluten, which can be washed out from the kneaded flour by a special process.[8] Further investigations by others revealed that analogues to gluten, i.e. substances with the same function but a different structure, are also present in oats and barley, and these are therefore also forbidden, although rice, corn, millet (and sometimes buckwheat) are well tolerated.[9] (Note: The celiac in our family is intolerant to buckwheat, which is not unusual.)

Some years later, biochemical investigators were able to demonstrate that the toxic constituent was only present in the gliadin, and not the glutenin fraction of the gluten, so further pinpointing the offender to be avoided.[10]

Modern techniques using a tiny biopsy* capsule at the end of a rubber tube which is swallowed by the patient, have since revealed what actually happens down there, out of sight in the small intestine of anyone who suffers from celiac disease, or malabsorption, as the end result of eating gluten.[11] The masses of minute waving hairs covering every inch of the walls of the small intestine, which are called "villi," club together, flatten out and even disappear entirely. This means that the absorption of food, which is their function in life, practically stops, causing gassy distension and pain in the abdomen, with pale frothy evil-smelling stools, and varying degrees of diarrhea. There are serious losses of fats, fat-soluble vitamins, water and water-soluble vitamins and minerals with emaciation which may be severe, and there may also be a kind of eczema, known as dermatitis herpetiformis, which burns and itches. It is hardly necessary to point out that the owner of such abnormal tissues is seriously ill although, most fortunately, removing all gluten from the diet alters all this very rapidly, in most cases. It does *not* mean that such patients should be fasted in the mistaken hope of stopping the diarrhea by this means. On the contrary, it has been found that fatalities occurred if the acute stage was treated by starvation, for of course, severe malnutrition already existed.[12]

A new era opened for celiacs in the 1950s, for Dr. Dicke's work firmly established the validity of a gluten-free diet as the one and only essential treatment, and this has been prescribed ever since. The effects are heart-warming and can appear miraculous. Generally, in a mere matter of days there is a cessation of diarrhea, a decrease in the abdominal distension and pain and other symptoms, with some return of physical strength. As the appetite is regained, improvement continues, weight is put on, hollow eyes and cheeks fill out, and any psychological difficulties fade out.[13] These healing results also

---

* Diagnostic alternative is remission (abatement of the symptoms) on a gluten-free diet and relapse on a gluten-containing diet.

occur in adults with conditions labeled "idiopathic staetor-rhea," "non-tropical sprue" and so on, now generally recognized as phases of the same illness as celiac disease, who are also put on a gluten-free diet. But it is still stressed by the experts that, although normal health may appear to have been restored, the gluten-free diet must not therefore be given up, because there can be a para-anaphylactoid response (severe shock reaction) in children or adults on eating any gluten after being on a gluten-free diet.[14] This appears to take place because although the absorptive cells, the villi, look normal to the eye under microscopic examination, they still allow incompletely broken-down gluten products to be absorbed into the bloodstream, and it is supposed that these are toxic. In fac, earlier experiments had shown that if ten grams of gluten (not of wheat flour as such) were added to each meal of "healed" celiacs, the villi showed damage at the tips after three days, and in six days there was as severe damage apparent in the surface epithelium (skin) of the intestine as in an untreated celiac.[15] But providing no more gluten is eaten after the first reaction, the villi recover more or less promptly and absorption returns to normal. Moreover, the salutary lesson has been driven home that gluten must at all times be avoided.[16]

Why is it that increasing numbers of ill people today respond favorably to gluten-free food? Why is gluten poison for them, though not for others? Why is it that for celiacs there is no treatment except never to touch gluten? Does the fault lie in the person, or the protein, or both?

These questions, and many others relating to the etiology (causation) of gluten-induced illness in celiacs have occupied the attention of many medical and other scientific minds for many years.

As early as 1950 a family predisposition had been suggested.[17]

In 1951 it was reported from Canada that "an adverse condition favoring the development of celiac disease, was an unfavorable uterine environment, and that there was a high incidence of diabetes among celiacs and siblings, i.e. during pregnancy, suggesting a congenital origin."[18]

A British investigator in 1956 referring to this paper stated, that of the eighty-eight patients attending the Clinic for Celiac Disease at Great Ormond Street Hospital, London, no effects of maternal age, birth order or social class had been found, but there was definite evidence of other celiacs among near relatives of the patient, suggesting a genetic origin.[19]

Indeed, the most widely held view in the United States and Great Britain which has persisted is that it is due to a defect of genetic origin.[20]

One investigator has described this as a basal metabolic fault since as he states, "it is clear that the celiac handles gluten differently from the normal" while supporting the hypothesis that the necessary enzyme is lacking and suggesting that the presence of Giardia intestinalis, a parasitic organism in the intestine, may have a bearing on the disease.[21]

The hypothesis of a missing intestinal enzyme, still current in Britain in 1971,[22] had been supported by Italian investigators in 1970 carrying out a general survey of cases, including one case report. They stated that in their view celiac disease was due to enzymatic changes.[23]

However, this view had been disputed by others in the United States and in 1962 di Sant Agnese and others reported that they had seen many children later disagnosed as celiacs who had shown the same symptoms before getting any gluten at all. They also claimed that there was evidence that there was a basic metabolic defect in many Dutch children which lay dormant during the war years when they went short of food, but showed up as celiac disease when wheat was introduced again, and that severe cases of celiac disease in children and adults had become rare in the United States and Europe in the last few years.[24] (Incidentally, this opinion is hardly borne out by the figures recently quoted for Britain of an estimated 25,000 diagnosed cases, and an unknown number still undiagnosed.)

Nevertheless, four years later an investigator surveying

adult celiac patients at the Veterans Administration Hospital, Nashville, N.C., commented that although others attempted to account for the gluten sensitivity by calling it a genetic effect, out of the thirteen cases surveyed, ten first showed symptoms after the age of sixty years, and it seemed unlikely that such patients could have had a genetic fault of a defect in mucosal (lining membrane) enzymes, for presumably the majority would have experienced stresses before that age likely to uncover latent celiac disease.[25]

But other workers in the same year pointed out that present work showed that the enzymatic digestion of gluten is impaired in adult celiac disease, but returns to normal when successfully treated by a gluten-free diet. This conclusion does not support the hypothesis that celiac disease is due to the absence of an enzyme normally concerned with the digestion of gluten.[26] On the other hand, other workers have stressed the fact that in children a lack of the clinical symptoms of relapse does not exclude a response to the reintroduction of gluten, although this may not appear for six months to a year.[27]

Current research is also concerned with the possible role of immuno globulins[28] and the compatibility (agreement) of the immunologic and enzyme defect theories has been pointed out.[29] As far back as 1967, a report appeared from St. Thomas's Hospital, London, that out of fifty-four patients on a gluten-free diet, there were all degrees of failure in 30 percent of the cases. There was a mortality rate of 17 percent, and all the failures had Paneth cell deficiencies, whose role is as yet unknown (Dorland's Medical Dictionary, 20th edition, suggests that they are concerned with the elaboration of an enzyme); it was stated that this required further investigation.[30]

REFERENCES

1. *J.A.M.A.* 1960. Editorial. 173: 1141.
2. Robert, A., et. al. 1958. *Proc. Soc. Exp. Biol.* 98:9.
3. Fernandez, J., et. al. 1962. *J. Clin. Invest.* 41:488.
4. Cleave, T. L. and Campbell, G. D. 1966. *Diabetes, Coronary Thrombosis, and the Saccharine Disease.* Bristol, England: John Wright and Sons. (The "ine" in the title is pronounced like *Rhine* and has nothing whatever to do with the artificial sweetener, but means "related to sugar.")
5. Balin, J. A., et al. 1961. *New Eng. J. Med.* 265:631-633.
6. Goldman, A. S., et al. 1961. *Pediat.* 29: 948-952.
7. Dicke, W. H. 1950. *Coeliake.* M.D. Thesis, University of Utrecht.
8. _____. Jan. 1953. *Acta Pediat.* 223-231.
9. Van de Kamer, J. H. 1959. *Acta Pediat.* 44:465.
10. Beckwith, A. C., et al. 1966. *Arch. Biochem. and Biophys.* 117:239-249.
11. Anderson, C. 1963, *B.M.J.* 21.9.
12. Anderson, D. H., et al. 1953. *Pediat.* vol. II, 3:207.
13. Reed, L. S. 1970. *New York State J. of Med.* vol. 70 (16), 15.6.
14. *Ibid.*
15. Bayless, T. M., et al. 1964. *J. Clin. Invest.* 41:1344.
16. Creamer, B. 1968. *Trans. Med. Soc.* London. vol. 85.
17. Ebbs, J. H. 1950. *Am. J. Dis. Child.* 79:930.
18. Thompson, Margaret W. June 1951. *Am. J. Human Genetics.* vol. 3, no. 2.
19. Carter, R. C., et al. July 1956. *Ann. of Human Genetics.* vol. 23, part 3, 266.
20. Boyer, P. H., et al. 1957. *Am. J. Dis. Child.* 91 (2), 131. Sheldon, W. Jan. 1959. *Ped. J. Am. Acc. of Ped.* vol. 23.
21. Frazer, A. C. Aug. 1960. *J. of Pediat.* 57 (2).
22. Challacombe, D. N., et al. April 1971. *Arch. of Dis. of Child.* 46.

23. Bayeli, F. F., et al. 1970. *Min. Med.* 61, 53, 2925-2938.
24. di Sant Agnese, P. A., et al. 1962. *J.A.M.A.* 180:308.
25. Collins, J. R. July 1966. *Am. J. Dig. Dis.* 564.
26. Douglas, C. D., et al. Jan. 1970. *Clin. Science.* 38:11-25.
27. Shmerling, D. H. 1969. *Acta Pediat, Scand.* 58, no. 3:311.
28. McWhinney, H., et al. 1971. *Lancet.* 2, 121-4, 17.7.
29. Reed, Lawrence. 1970. *New York State J. of Med.* vol. 71 (16), 15.8.
30. Pink, I. J., et al. 1967. *Lancet.* 11.2.

3

Other Conditions Apparently Linked with Celiac Disease: Diabetes, Skin Disease, Milk Intolerance

1. DIABETES

In the past, a certain amount of attention has been directed to the question of whether there is a link between celiac disease and diabetes, and if so what the nature of the link is. In 1951, a study of 115 celiacs (65 inpatients and 54 outpatients) at the Hospital for Sick Children, Toronto, revealed a high incidence of diabetes in celiacs and their relatives, the data suggesting, though not proving, the association.[1] In 1969 investigators in Belgium pointed out that they had always stressed that the malabsorption in the diabetic child was probably not due to the coincidental development of primary celiac disease and expressed the opinion that glucose malabsorption could be the basic defect and a complication of diabetes itself.[2] But Finnish workers at the Children's Hospital, Helsinki University, reported later that among the 110 children under two years of age and 22 children over two years with celiac disease whom they had investigated, this disease was associated with diabetes more often than could be attributed to chance,[3] and the question still appears to be open.

2. SKIN DISEASE AND THE SMALL INTESTINE

Whether disease of the small intestine such as celiac may cause skin disorders or vice versa has also received much attention in recent years. Children with the celiac condition do not as a rule have eczema, and any skin trouble related to sensitivity to gluten in infants is said to be very rare. However, in adults there is a substantial incidence of itching eczema of various types, and a good deal of investigation has been carried out into one particular type called dermatitis herpetiformis, in which characteristic groups of blisters may

17

develop which tend to be lost in scratching. There are crops of itchy red papules which tend to come and go, usually on pressure areas, but they have been observed round the ankles, the back of the neck and round the chin and the backs of the knees.[4]

Some investigators, reporting in 1968, had found that following a gluten-free diet had no effect on this skin complaint,[5] but others later reported that it had a favorable effect,[6] and considered that the skin lesions were related to those of the intestine.[7]

However, yet another set of investigators reporting from Newcastle, pointed out that as one-third of patients with dermatitis herpetiformis were without intestinal symptoms, it was clearly not caused by enteropathy (disease of the intestine). Nevertheless, they concluded that all patients with this skin complaint should have the type of investigation carried out for celiac disease, but added that anyone on a gluten-free diet who suffered from dermatitis herpetiformis would still require the sulphone currently in use to control the rash for an indefinite period after the skin had cleared.[8] (Since a sulphone may have undesirable side effects and, it is stated, should have supportive supplements of iron and vitamin B complex, some sufferers may feel that they would prefer to test out whether massive doses of vitamin B complex in the form of brewer's yeast without the drug would not clear the skin as in the case of the patient [L. D. H.] referred to in the first chapter.) A later report from another investigator pointed out that in some cases the dermatitis improved, then relapsed on the eating of gluten and suggested that these studies indicated an immunological disorder that might be more general in the dermatitis than in celiac disease.[9]

Late in 1970 came the report of a case of dermatitis herpetiformis triggered by cow's milk which improved on a gluten-free and almost milk-free diet, with the suggestion that milk provided antigenic stimulation for the skin lesion in this case.[10]

3. MILK INTOLERANCE IN CELIAC CHILDREN AND ADULTS

Feeding problems with children on a gluten-free diet may in some cases be increased by an intolerance to cow's milk. A study reporting in 1962 on the blood serum of forty celiac children, claimed to show a definite relationship between intolerance to wheat on the one hand and to cow's milk on the other.[11]

Three years later came a Scandinavian study of infants, putting forward the hypothesis that an early intolerance to cow's milk may set the stage for later gluten sensitivity leading to celiac disease, although when the milk was excluded, a tolerance to it appeared, and at the age of two years gluten was well tolerated.[12] The next year came a report of investigations on a family of Mexicans where the four youngest of thirteen children were celiacs. On a gluten-free diet and elimination of milk they all showed immediate improvement, and the suggestion was made that removing the offending lactose (milk sugar) was not only therapeutic but might prevent damage of the intestinal walls leading to sensitivity to gluten.[13]

At the Children's Hospital of the University of Helsinki, forty infants were subjected to absorption tests if they had symptoms suggestive of intolerance to cow's milk or gluten. Cows' milk intolerance was verified in twelve, with eight of these also intolerant to gluten, the first symptoms appearing *before any wheat had been given,* and twenty-eight were intolerant to gluten. The response to an elimination diet was good in all cases, and the intolerance appeared to be of shorter duration than that described in older children and adults with celiac disease, but there was great variation in the period of intolerance. It was pointed out that the malabsorption of disaccharides (a class of sugars which includes lactose) is a well-documented cause of intolerance to cow's milk, although a larger amount of lactose is contained in breast milk.[14] Those on breast milk made a good recovery.

More recently there have been a number of investigations

showing that among black Americans, Chinese and other Ori-
entals, aborigines and others, there is a large incidence of lactose intolerance in adults.[15] Some later investigators have
found that the intolerance to milk may be more to the proteins than the sugar, estimating that this is true for 0.1 to 8
percent of the population and stressing the importance of
early diagnosis when available. Treatments are said to be uniformly successful.[16] It has been pointed out that intolerances
due to defects may persist into adult life, and although certain
defects may be acquired and are therefore transient both in
childhood and in adult life, adult lactase deficiency is a very
common condition.[17]

Pediatricians working in Africa have shown that Buganda
infants tended to become intolerant to lactose through losing
lactase activity in the mucosa (intestinal walls) over their first
four years.[18] Later investigators have found that tribes of
Bantu origin have a lower activity of the lactose-splitting enzyme, lactase, than other African tribes even if there was no
abnormality of the intestinal walls.[19] Other studies have shown
that when children with kwashiorkor, the protein deficiency
disease that is the scourge of lower economic groups in the
tropics and sub-tropics, are acutely ill, their absorption of
lactose is impaired, but as the disease retreats the absorption
improves. This may explain why skim milk, either fresh if
obtainable, or reconstituted, became the classical basis of modern dietary therapy for the condition.[20]

A professor of medicine in the United States publishing in
1970, has laid it down that in the early course of treatment in
celiac disease, cow's milk should be excluded in view of the
number of children with this condition who have a secondary
enzyme defect. He has stated that this exclusion is especially
indicated where there is a clear history of distension and diarrhea after two hours following the drinking of milk. He also
stresses that the diet should be rich in proteins and should
permit all other foods including fats.[21]

REFERENCES

1. Thompson, M. W. 1951. *Am. J. Human Genetics.* vol. 3, no. 2.
2. Hooft, C., et al. 1969. *Lancet.* 2, 1192, 19.11.
3. Visakorpi, J. K., et al. 1970. *Acta Pediat, Scand.* 59:273-280.
4. Wells, G. C. 1970. *Modern Trends in Gastroenterology.* 4:328-348.
5. Shuster, S., et al. 1968. *Lancet.* 1:1101.
6. Fry, L., et al. 1968. *B.M.J.* 4:702.
7. Van Tongeren, J. H. 1970. *Metab. Dermatol.* 140:231.
8. Marks, J., et al. April 1970. *Arch. Dermatol.* vol. 101.
9. Seah, P. P. et al. 1971. *Lancet.* 1:834-836.
10. Pocksteen, O. C., et al. Dec. 1970. *Br. J. Dermat.* 83:614-619.
11. Heiner, D. C., et al. 1962. *J. Pediat.* 61:813.
12. Lindstrom, S., et al. 1965. *Acta. Pediat. Scand.* 54:101.
13. Lipshitz-Fima, M.D., et al. May 1966. *Am. J. Dig. Dis.*
14. Visakorpi, J. K., et al. 1967. *Acta Pediat. Scand.* 56:49-56.
15. Cuatrecasas, P., et al. 1965. *Lancet.* 1:14; Chung, M. H., et al. 1968. *Gastroenterology.* 54.225; Elliott, R. B., et al. 1967. *Med. J. Aust.* 1:46.
16. Freier, S., et al. Aug. 1970. *Clin. Pediat.* (8):449-454.
17. Dawson, A. M. 1970. *Modern Trends in Gastroenterology.* 4, Butterworth.
18. Dean, R. F. S. 1963. *Recent Advances in Pediatrics.* P126, London.
19. Cook, G. C., et al. 1967. *B.M.J.* 1:527.
20. Brock, J. F. and Hansen, J. D. L. 1962. *Clinical Nutrition.* New York: Harper & Row.
21. Kowlessar, O. D., et al. May 1970. *Med. Clin. of N. America.* 54 (3).

CHAPTER

4

Other Diseases Which May Benefit from a
Gluten-Free Diet: Multiple Sclerosis,
Schizophrenia, Rheumatoid Arthritis,
Regional Enteritis and Autism

I. MULTIPLE SCLEROSIS

Over the last century thousands of scientific reports have been
published on multiple sclerosis (M.S.), a disease of the nervous system which is known to occur in acute and rapidly
progressive forms, or in a slowly progressive and remittent
form. It has been estimated today to occur at a rate of 1 in
1,200 in Great Britain.[1]

One of the most widely held views has been that the primary lesion (damage) lay in the myelin (marrow-fat-like)
sheaths of the nerve fibers, but today this is being contested,
and a number of differing suggestions have been made as to
the cause of the disease.

Work with experimental animals has demonstrated that a
lack of pantothenic acid (one of the vitamin B complex)
causes a loss of the myelin sheaths such as occurs in M.S., and
if there are deficiencies of the other members of the vitamin B
complex, this results in nerve degeneration.[2] Such damage in
animals can be corrected by supplying the missing vitamins,
but in advanced cases it has been held that irreparable damage may have been done.[3]

Twenty years ago an investigator carrying out extensive epidemiological (regarding diseases widely prevalent in commu-
nities) studies in the United States suggested that some internal mechanism could be responsible for the exacerbations
(flare-ups) which shorten life, but no formal conclusion as to
the cause was presented.[4] In the same year came a report
from an investigator of cases of M.S. in Norway relating the
incidence of the disease to *dietary habits*. He had found that
where fishermen living at a low subsistence level on a low income, raised their own potatoes and a few vegetables and

kept some livestock, the number of cases was low. The number of cases was four times as high on inland farms where dairying predominated and in prosperous towns. It was considered that this difference might be due to higher income levels allowing the purchase of cereals and margarine leading to the consumption of too many saturated fats.[5] (The unsaturated vegetable oils made into margarine are changed into saturated fats by the process of hydrogenation [see chapter 5]).

At a Symposium on Disseminated (now called Multiple) Sclerosis and Allied Conditions held by the Royal Society of Medicine in the 1960s, it was concluded that perhaps general immunological responsiveness should be closely examined,[6] but this does not appear to have led to any advances either in prevention or treatment.

However, later biochemical studies of the brain lipids (fats) showed that there were indeed different proportions of saturated compared to unsaturated fats in brain lethicins in cases of multiple sclerosis to that of non-neurological deaths.[7] Investigators some years later carried this work further and studied the levels of certain lipids (fats) in the serum (blood) of cases of multiple sclerosis and compared these with those of normal controls. As a result they fed the cases of M.S. with supplementary fats in the form of sunflower seed oil.[8] Summing up the situation, the editorial of a subsequent number of the *British Medical Journal* commented that they would refrain from dogmatic assertions, but as the absorption mechanism was unimpaired [sic] they would suggest tentatively that since the rate of loss or faulty utilization of unsaturated fat might be abnormally high in M.S., there would seem to be little harm in adding sunflower or corn oil to the normal diet of M.S. sufferers.[9]

This rather tepid view has been strongly reinforced in no uncertain terms by an eminent Danish neurologist in a paper entitled "M.S.: Can Wrong Diet Cause It?" He pointed out that M.S. should be attacked in infancy *before it occurs* when, with proper diet, sturdy myelin sheaths can be woven round the nerve fibers of the central nervous system. He commented that it had been established that if the diet lacked polyunsaturated fats (the best sources are breast milk and vegetable oils) the myelin sheath is poorly constructed. He made it quite clear that the best and unrivaled start in life is to be given breast milk with its content of 8–14 percent of unsaturated fats contrasted with the mere 2–4 percent in cow's milk, and suggested that if breast milk were not available, there should be an addition of 10 percent of vegetable (say corn) oil to skim milk with enough vitamin E to avoid the oxidation which destroys some of the essential fatty acids in unsaturated fats.[10]

Incidentally, these measures had been suggested three years earlier for all infants by the well-known nutritionist Adelle Davis, in her excellent guide for mothers called *Let's Have Healthy Children.*[11]

However, Dr. Clausen's statement that after the age of 15–16 years when the fatty sheath is fully formed there is little exchange of fat between the blood and brain, and that therefore adults with M.S. cannot hope, by adopting a better dietary fat, to repair the faulty nerve insulation laid down in the early years of life, seems open to challenge,* especially by one who has himself achieved this very result.[12] (See later paragraphs.)

It is known that a high level of saturated fats in the diet demands a high level of magnesium, and it has also been shown that by reducing these fats the recurrent spells of muscle spasms, twitchings and lack of bladder control in M.S. cases have improved.[13]

In fact, when a diet deficient in magnesium was given to healthy volunteers, this produced muscle weakness and spasms with involuntary twitching and an inability to control the bladder (the same symptoms as found in M.S.) but this

* In December 1972 Professor Davison (professor of bio-chemistry at the National Hospital for Nervous Diseases) speaking in the Workshop on Bio-chemistry and Mental Diseases of the Open University said that it is possible for myelin to regenerate.

quickly cleared when the missing magnesium was given.[14]

This important mineral magnesium is a component of chlorophyll, the "blood" in all green leaves. The best source is therefore green leafy vegetables. But as much of the magnesium is lost to the eater when vegetables are soaked in washing, swamped in water in cooking and then this magnesium-rich water is thrown away, it is not difficult to see why many people today may be short of magnesium even if their vegetables have reached the kitchen well endowed in this respect. There are other good reasons why we may suspect a shortage of magnesium to be widespread today. Veterinary researchers at the Rowett Rural Institute found demyelination of the nerve sheaths in lambs born to ewes maintained on soils with high levels of sulphate and molybdate,[15] and a speaker at the 16th International Veterinary Conference held in Madrid in 1959, reported that cows fed experimentally on grass fertilized for six years with ammonium sulphate or nitro chalk (an increasingly common practice) showed pronounced magnesium deficiency.[16] Furthermore, recent investigations of British soils revealed that some 90 percent of soils tested lacked magnesium.[17] In fact, a trained eye can detect visible signs of lack of humus in soils everywhere today, and this means that much of the magnesium present is unavailable to the plants growing there. This is reflected, especially in dry hot weather, in the classical signs of magnesium deficiency in the foliage of vegetables, crops and fruit trees.[18] Since the more artificial fertilizer applied the less the humus content of any soil, it looks as if there might be a general Western world-wide decrease in the magnesium content of most common foods today.

Moreover, the immense popularity among sophisticated peoples of using bicarbonate of soda in cooking vegetables, baking powder in baking cakes, and indigestion mixtures containing calcium carbonate, can give rise to magnesium deficiency as well as contribute to kidney stones.[19]

It has also been proposed that excess of certain minerals may have some bearing on the disease. In 1950, there appeared a paper on lead in relation to disseminated sclerosis, as M.S. was then called. This suggested that a high level of lead in the soil predisposes to M.S., possibly by neutralizing the beneficial action of copper and other trace elements, and pointing out that the teeth of M.S. patients contain abnormal amounts of lead.[20] This view has received support from yet another attempt to explain why people living in certain areas seem especially prone to M.S. It has been made over the years by a professor of geology at the University of California. At a meeting of the Interdisciplinary Section of the New York Academy of Science, he stated that studies of soils and vegetables grown in districts where the number of cases was abnormally high, had shown levels of copper, zinc, potash and molybdenum which were considered "as significant as those of iron, iodine and fluorine."[21] Some eight years later, he pointed out that there were excessive levels of lead and molybdenum in vegetables grown in at least 75 percent of the areas where M.S. cases are above the normal number, areas in Great Britain such as the old mining districts of South West Devon and North Wales, but also in the industrial cities of Liverpool and Birmingham.[22]

Then came a new interpretation of epidemiological studies put forward by Dr. R. Shatin of the Alfred Hospital, Melbourne, Australia. He suggested, as he had previously done in the case of celiac disease, that there was an inheritance of susceptibility and the primary lesion (damage) lay in the small intestine from intolerance to gluten, and that de-myelination of the nerve sheaths was secondary. He also put forward the hypothesis that the high rate of M.S. in Canada, Scotland and Western Ireland may be due to the predominating use of Canadian hard wheat, which has the highest gluten content of any in the world, and that the low rate among indigenous Africans living near the Equator may be related to the fact that they eat more millet and less wheat.[23]

Today, the possibility that a gluten-free diet may be effective in the treatment of M.S. is being investigated by members of the Medical Panel of the Multiple Sclerosis Society, including some tests being carried out at a London Hospital.[24]

But the present Chairman of the M.S. Society's Research Committee has been reported as saying that they "now have to sweat out the results over the next two years in the interests of humanity," and two years is a long time for sufferers to wait for an official pronouncement.

Meanwhile, the appearance of an article detailing the magnificent recovery of Professor Roger McDougall, playwright, and one-time professor in the University of California's Theatre Department on a gluten-free and refined carbohydrate-free diet, enriched by vegetable oils, has aroused enormous interest and encouraged a number of fellow M.S. cases to try to follow his splendid example of self-help and self-discipline.

Here was a man, now sixty-one, who in 1953 was admitted to the National Hospital for Nervous Diseases, London, for tests, and was diagnosed M.S. by an eminent neurologist. The different treatments tried out did nothing for him, and in fact he says one of them, using arsenic, nearly killed him. He was virtually blind and could not even recognize faces, had such difficulty in speaking that he was almost unintelligible and was practically paralyzed and in a wheelchair for about ten years. Since 1965 he has been able to drive an ordinary car, is writing plays again, and is described as bounding upstairs two at a time.

All this by going on to, and sticking rigorously to, a gluten-free and refined carbohydrate-free diet, enriched by vegetable oils. He attributes his remarkable recovery to *nothing else*. But he is anxious to point out that it was an unbelievably slow progress. Yet he never went backwards and in a disease which usually gets progressively worse (though remissions can occur), this gave him great encouragement to persevere.

In 1974 the Henry Doubleday Research Association received this report from Mrs. Margaret Hughes: "I have followed your diet for the past twelve months as I suffer from multiple sclerosis. I am delighted to report that I have had a dramatic improvement. I can now walk normally and do not use a wheelchair as I have done for the past eight years. I am a member of the Multiple Sclerosis Society and after seeing my improvement a dozen other patient members are following the diet. We all find the gluten-free flour unpalatable and I encourage them to follow my lead and follow your advice and eat only first class food."

SO GO AHEAD AND TRY IT FOR YOURSELF. There is absolutely no need to wait for any pronouncement about whether or not a gluten-free diet has worked for others. Indeed, it might well be that gluten is not the whole story, but the other two factors are equally important. Every single sufferer can start today to go on the diet and find out for himself whether he finds any improvement in his condition, and he should ask his doctor to prescribe the vitamins recommended.

Do not, however, make the mistake of expecting the really dramatic results to be seen in celiacs whose symptoms may recede in a few weeks, or even days. Cases of M.S. which have developed over many years cannot expect a rapid amelioration of their symptoms. Progress must inevitably be very slow as the disease is at first arrested and then gradually overcome, and this requires great determination and perseverance. All should ask for physiotherapy also, for this can be very useful in helping to maintain and improve function in limbs and speech. If this is not obtainable for any reason, then you must be ready and eager to exercise on your own and never give up trying to get your muscles to work for you properly again.

Help your muscles to help your diet towards recovery

A muscle unused is a muscle we lose. So besides keeping to the gluten-free diet, you must keep on making your muscles work for you by gentle exercise. *Do not push them to the point of fatigue. Work at the exercises little but often*—as often as possible during the day, in any spare moment.

However restricted you may be in movement, and however difficult it may seem, do all you can for yourself, even if it takes far longer than if some kind person were to offer to do it for you. Encouraging you to struggle is really kinder. However hard your speech may be to produce, however hard it may be to understand, do not stop talking on that account. On the contrary, make deliberate efforts to talk as well as you can to anyone who will listen, and reply, so that you can carry on conversations. If you have no one to talk to at times, talk to a dog or cat, or any other pet you may have, or repeat aloud any poems you can remember so as to keep in practice by talking.

A. If you are still able to walk

Keep on walking and getting about and being as active as you can, short of getting tired. Walk little and often, not for long periods.

B. If walking is very difficult

You must still exercise your leg, back and abdominal muscles to keep them from getting weaker, then strengthen them for walking. Do these exercises at least three or four times daily. Much more often if you can. *Between each exercise rest*, then breathe *out* and *in* twice (see Deep Breathing Exercises).

First get yourself a piece of stiff plastic or hardboard (it must be light for easy moving) about 24 in. by 18 in. Dust this with talcum powder and you have a smooth slippery surface which helps to make your movements easier.

I Leg exercises. Lying (on a firm, smooth bed or couch)

1. Place the board across the foot of the bed to extend a little farther than your outstretched heel, so that as you exercise your heel will slide along this slippery surface. As you progress in your range of movement, your sole will also slide along it as you do the exercises. Loosen or remove any restrictive garments. Lie down flat on your back with a low pillow under your head and keep your feet at right angles to the leg all the time. Slowly draw up one leg, bending hip and knee as far as you can. Stretch leg out straight again and press back against the bed to use the

muscles of the buttocks and those which straighten the knee. Repeat with other leg. Do 3—4 times.

2. Draw up leg as before. When fully bent turn it inwards, then outwards, then back to mid-position. Put your hand under the knee to support it, then stretch leg out again and press down as before. Repeat with the other leg. Do 3—4 times.

3. Draw up both legs together and repeat the first exercise.

4. Draw up both legs and repeat second exercise. Do 3—4 times.

When you can do these four exercises easily, progress to:

1. Draw up the leg in the same way but with the heel slightly raised from the bed. Stretch out leg still slightly raised, then press down as before. Repeat with other leg. Do 3—4 times.

2. Place heel of one leg on kneecap of other, then stretch out again and press down as before. Repeat with other leg. Do 3—4 times.

3. With foot at right angles to leg slowly lift leg as high as you can without bending the knee, then carry it slowly down again. Repeat with other leg. Do 3—4 times.

Sitting

1. Remove shoes and stockings if possible. Sit upright in a dining-room chair with knees well apart and bent at a right angle, with feet straight. Lift each leg alternately as high as you can and mark time on the spot. Repeat several times.

2. With feet pointing straight forward, keep the toes pressed on the floor and raise the heels of each foot alternately. Repeat several times.

3. Keep heels on the floor and raise the toes of each foot alternately. Repeat several times.

4. Curl up the toes of both feet at once so that feet shorten, then stretch them out again. Do several times.

5. With feet pointing straight forward, press down hard on

the outer edges of each foot at once, draw the heels back into place, hold, then relax. Repeat several times.

When your legs feel strong enough, progress to:

II Walking exercises

If your doctor has not got you a frame, stand between two tables or solid chairs on which to put your hands for support. Point both feet straight forward about 6 in. apart. (This gives you a wider base than if they were close, and helps you to balance.) Move one foot forward in a straight line and put the heel on the ground.

Then raise the heel of the other foot, transfer the weight to the outer edge of the forward foot and press the toes firmly on the ground.

Now bring the other foot forward in a straight line and put the heel on the ground as with the first foot.

As you progress, support yourself less and less with your hands. Then walk in this careful manner with someone at your side to give you any support you may need. If no one is available, use two sticks. *Do not overdo.* It is far better to exercise frequently with long rests between than to do too much in an over-long session carried to the point of fatigue. *Avoid this.*

III Abdominal exercises

1. Lying

Lie on the back with a small pillow under the knees and try to press back the navel against the spine without raising the ribs. Do not hold your breath but count aloud as you repeat this about 4 times. Rest, then repeat, gradually increasing the number of times.

2. Sitting

Sit upright and relax, with the hands lying loosely in the lap. Repeat the above exercise. Do this frequently at any spare moment.

IV Arm exercises

1. Lying
Lie on your back. Put the board under the upper arm, bend the elbow and touch the shoulder with the fingers. Now move the elbow as far away from the body as you can, sliding it along the board. As muscles get stronger you will be able to do this with the elbow outstretched. Then progress to doing this exercise and others while sitting.

2. Sitting
Sit comfortably upright with hands in the lap. Bend both elbows, stretch out the fingers and touch the shoulders. Now reach up to the ceiling as high as you can.

Bend elbows and touch shoulders again, then stretch and bend sideways and forwards. All without poking the head.

V Hand exercises
We all value our hands highly for what they can do, but it's a mistake only to grip with them as in writing, sewing, knitting, gardening, housework, dressing and all the other ways we use them. This can lead to contractions of the flexor muscles, keeping the hands partially closed all the time and reducing their usefulness. The extensor muscles must be given their turn to prevent this, especially in multiple sclerosis. Here is how you can do this. Soak the hands in warm water before beginning. Sit up to a table and lay your hands palm down on it. Stretch out your fingers as far as you can, flatten down the whole hand, then separate fingers and thumb as widely as possible. Turn over the hands and do the same with palms upwards, pressing back against the table to exercise the extensors, so counteracting the pull of the flexors. *Do not* knit, sew or grip anything tightly, or write, for any but short periods, till you can stretch out the fingers fully, then lift them up from the table, leaving the palms still touching it.

VI Deep-breathing exercises
Between any group of exercises, and also after any extra exer-

tion such as dressing, do some deep breathing to carry fresh oxygen via your lungs to muscles and other parts of the body. This will relax you better than any alcohol!

Sit comfortably upright, relax the chest and abdominal muscles and dilate and relax the nostrils a few times before you begin. Now drop the hands down by the sides and turn the palms forward. Breathe out slowly through the nose at the same time bending forward with the back rounded, and turning the palms till they face backwards. When you can get out no more air and are leaning as far down over your knees as you can, pause and rest quietly; then relax the chest and abdominal muscles, dilate the nostrils, then raise the body up again, beginning at the waistline and finishing with the head as you turn the palms forwards again, and at the same time breathe in gently with practically no effort as nature moves in to fill with air the vacuum you have created by emptying the lungs thoroughly. You use the muscles of chest and abdomen for *breathing OUT only*. If you empty the lungs properly, then when you relax these muscles the air will flood into your lungs without effort. Just dilate the nostrils so that it has easy access, and relax them as you breathe out. Prolonged easy yawning is a simple and very useful way of forcing your muscles to relax and expel the air from your lungs. So indulge in a good long deliberate yawn sometimes, and do not be above a deep drawn-out sigh now and then, if no one is near, for this also is good for the same purpose. Be careful never to sit with the arms crossed, as this hampers easy breathing.

C. If you cannot walk
Do the leg exercises given under (I) lying in a bath with plenty of warm water to support the limbs and make movements easier. Have someone by you to lend a hand if needed.

Medically recommended supplements

Ask your doctor to prescribe a high-potency vitamin program which would include especially the B vitamins, vitamins

C and E and some calcium pantothenate and magnesium chloride; these supplements are a vital part of your program.

2. SCHIZOPHRENIA

Mental illness causes more lost working days than influenza or colds and three times as many as strikes, announced Mr. David Ennals, director of the Mental Association of Great Britain in February 1972. It seems that in 1969 Britain lost over 36 million days' work through mental illness, and every year shows an increase in the number of days lost; although cynics have suggested that deductions should be made to allow for days off taken on account of hangovers or on the plea of depression, these remain formidable figures reflecting a widespread and distressing state of affairs.

Among those involved there are about 60,000 who are in hospitals at any one time suffering from schizophrenia, a rather loosely defined term covering a tragic and debilitating group of diseases affecting large numbers of people in all cultures which incapacitates the young, 75 percent before the age of twenty-five, but does not kill the average person or present the sad "glamour" of cancer.

It is many years since Freud, himself a neurologist, expressed the hope that the neurologic sciences would some time in the future find the effective causes of psychiatric disorder in disturbed cellular pathology, and that the treatment of neuroses by empirical methods, including psychoanalysis, would be replaced by precise biochemical techniques.[25] Today it begins to look as if the dawn of this prophetic future were on the horizon.

What have been described by psychiatrists as attempts over the past decade to implicate biochemistry in schizophrenia have led to some encouraging indications that correcting nutritional disorders may be superior to surgery, drugs or shock treatments, since such correction can have no unfavorable side effects or be irreversible, even if not wholly successful in effecting a cure. A Nobel Prize winner and eminent chemist, Linus Pauling, has argued that some mentally ill individuals may suffer from an inadequate supply of essential nutritional factors, if not in their diet, then cerebrally (in the brain) as a result of their individuality or disease and suggests that they should be provided with the right substances to bring them up to scratch.[26]

This has been accepted by some psychiatrists as an important possibility and one that is at any rate amenable to investigation, although current evidence was considered not to be substantial in 1971 and some psychiatrists still will not credit the hypothesis that biochemical malfunction is involved.[27] However, Dr. Julius Axelrod, another Nobel Prize winner and chief of the Pharmacology Division of the National Institute of Mental Health in the United States has been quoted as saying, in 1970, that "many researchers now believe that schizophrenia is due to some biochemical fault in the brain . . . and research such as this could eventually find a way to cure that fault."

Meanwhile, what has brought the most hope to schizophrenics and their families in recent years is the work of Professor F. C. Dohan of Pennsylvania University and the formation of the Schizophrenia Association of Great Britain. Dr. Dohan's work was first published in 1966 and his data was assembled and speculations made on the basis of the following assumptions: (1) that the development of the disease is basically the same in nearly all diagnosed schizophrenics; (2) that the possibility of developing the disease is inherited; (3) that the occurrence of the manifest disease depends largely, though not wholly, on environmental factors, one of the most important possibly being the kinds and quantities of foods eaten over long periods of time.

He carried out his studies because of reports that:

(a) There is a history of celiac disease in childhood appearing more often than by chance in adults with manifest schizophrenia.
(b) Psychoses occur more frequently in adult celiacs than by chance.

(c) Behavior disturbances which are common in child and adult celiacs can be produced by gluten, and relieved by a gluten-free diet.

(d) The severity of symptoms of celiac disease often occurs in association with psychic stress and acute infections and in some cases with increased severity of the symptoms of schizophrenia.

In conclusion, he suggested that the hypothesis could be tested by putting those with an initial attack of schizophrenia or an acute relapse from a relatively normal state, on a gluten-free diet.[28]

This was followed by further reports. Relapsed schizophrenics randomly selected for clinical studies were found to improve more rapidly on a gluten-free diet than on a relatively high cereal diet, and the secret addition of gluten to the gluten-free diet nullified this effect.[29]

Discussing the possibility that celiac disease is due to the pathology (morbid symptoms) of schizophrenia, he pointed out that not only all wheat, rye, oats and barley should be excluded but that cow's milk and other grains could be harmful to some.[30]

Other investigators reporting later in 1970 suggested that there were in celiac disease and schizophrenia factors common to both without implicating a primary genetic basis.[31]

Then evidence was produced and confirmed by the testimony of five other physicians practicing in other places, that celiac disease and schizophrenia appeared to occur in the same person or possibly the same family more often than by chance, and that there was an apparent increase in the frequency of both diseases appearing in the same individual.[32]

In a lecture at the Institute of Psychiatry held on June 10th 1971 at the Maudsley Hospital, London, and attended by members of the Schizophrenia Association of Great Britain, Professor Dohan stressed the fact that epidemiological studies had shown that the incidence of schizophrenia was higher in countries where wheat was the staple grain than in others, and wheat is the chief source of gluten, although analogues also occur in rye, oats and barley. If gluten was removed from the diet the malabsorption (which may be a basic feature of the disease, it was implied) cleared up as in celiac disease. It was well known that celiac children are prone to irritability and behavioral disorders and if a celiac child who had once been on a gluten-free diet was taken off it, he developed symptoms of schizophrenia.[33]

The Schizophrenia Association of Great Britain referred to is largely the creation begun in the summer of 1970 by Mrs. Gwynneth Hemmings of Llanfair Hall, Caernarvon, the Hon. Secretary, whose schizophrenic husband encouraged her to broadcast some of the facts about the difficulties and problems in the life of the schizophrenic family. It already numbers over 1,000 members, many of them the relatives of schizophrenics.

Its main aims are: (1) to press for more biochemical research, which is so tragically under-financed in England today that it is totally inadequate in relation to the numbers involved, estimated at some 3,000,000 with about 60,000 to 80,000 occupying about one-sixth of the hospital beds available; (2) to encourage open discussion of the disease, so that the present stigma attached to it in the popular mind may shrivel away until it is universally recognized not as some shame-making psychological peculiarity but as a physical disease, as clearly accepted as, say arthritis, which no one thinks twice about admitting and talking about quite openly; (3) to work for the welfare of all sufferers from schizophrenia.

It is hoped to form a country-wide network of concerned people who share these aims and are willing and able to help to carry them out, and several affiliated groups have been and are being formed, with members offering their homes as temporary meeting places until the group has grown enough to justify hiring a hall. Questionnaires, too, have been sent out to members to help researchers of different aspects to get a clear pattern of this disease. They are interested to find out what are the other diseases with which it may share a common genetic factor or be linked to in some way, and what infectious diseases or other factors have been noted as having a bad effect on schizophrenics.

Once launched, the Association quickly gained support and moved into action. A conference was arranged and held in London, the 28th and 29th of September 1971, at a joint meeting of the Canadian Schizophrenia Association, the American Schizophrenia Association and the Schizophrenia Association of Great Britain on the biochemistry, genetics and therapy of schizophrenia. Many papers were presented by eminent men and women from Denmark, Uppsala, St. Louis, Liverpool and London, and by nine members of the Scientific Advisory Board, Committee of Therapy of the American Schizophrenia Association. The proceedings were tape-recorded and all the papers are to be published. This was the first World Conference to be held on the subject of the biochemistry of schizophrenia and the repercussions have been worldwide, leading to further investigation, interest and action.

At the time of the Maudsley Meeting, Dr. Dohan went to Liverpool University. He had inquired of the Schizophrenia Association whether someone in the United Kingdom could be found to duplicate his work on the improvement of schizophrenia on a cereal-free and milk-free diet, and had been advised that there was a possibility of cooperation there. In consequence, some exploratory trials have now been undertaken at the University of Liverpool.

All schizophrenic members of the Schizophrenia Association of Great Britain have been strongly advised to try out this diet for themselves, asking their family doctors to prescribe for them the vitamins which have been found beneficial.* These are all of the B vitamins and an extra prescription for vitamin B_{12}, a substantial amount of vitamin C and a mixed mineral and vitamin supplement in addition.

They are also recommended to get from the library and read carefully, *How to Live with Schizophrenia* (Dr. A. Hof-

---

* Alteration of diet alone is not recommended by the Schizophrenia Association of Great Britain.

fer and Dr. H. Osmond, University Books, 1974 revised edition).

Warning

Since schizophrenics are advised to be milk-free as well as gluten-free, they should not use some brands of the gluten-free flour prescribed for celiacs, since these contain *powdered milk*. In cooking, etc., substitute soya milk as suggested in *Recipes* (Chapter 9).

3. RHEUMATOID ARTHRITIS

Biochemists and others looking at the proteins involved have revealed where the toxic element of gluten is to be found, and the medical profession looking at the patient has generally concentrated on the clinical aspects of the problem in celiac disease in child or adult. But Dr. R. Shatin of Melbourne, Australia, member of the Scientific Council of the International Society for Research into Nutrition and Civilization Disease, has, since 1963, been publishing reports on his treatment of cases of rheumatoid arthritis with a gluten-free, high-protein diet, with supplements, introducing his concept that in these patients, as in celiacs, the primary lesion is to be found in the small intestine.[34]

Shatin's concept rests on his view that "the domestication of cereals (wheat and later rye and oats) crucial to the development of civilization also confronted metabolism with a historical challenge." He points out that when man changed from a food-gatherer to a food-producer, epochal changes in his ecology were paralleled by similar changes in his diet. This transition from animal flesh and milk with what nuts, berries, fruits and roots were still available from the times when he lived exclusively on these, to domesticated cereals obtained by culturing and farming the seeds of grasses, could have been too sudden for the digestive functions of a significant minority to have been able to adapt adequately to such drastic changes in dietetic habits. Dr. Shatin considers that celiac disease may have been very common in pre-history, but that since it would have been lethal before the age of reproduction was reached, a partially dominant trait could in this way have become rare (as it now is) and recessive.

He presents evidence that there is also small intestine malabsorption in rheumatoid arthritis and suggests the possibility that a susceptibility to this disease exists which can be activated by gluten and other factors into a primary lesion (injury). He claims that the apparent benefit from the use of a gluten-free-high-protein diet in a few cases of rheumatoid arthritis has given him some practical support for his theoretical considerations and points out that in its medical aspects, his hypothesis has the merit of being eminently capable of proof.

Taking up this challenge came a report from Yale that on testing six arthritis patients no abnormal mucosa had been detected; in seventeen others there was no evidence of increased intestinal permeability, and in carefully controlled hospital trials on five patients a gluten-free diet had been of no value.[35] However, these are small numbers and it would be of interest and, we hope of benefit, to see what happens in individuals who put Shatin's hypothesis to the test for themselves, especially if they give themselves the added advantage of cutting out refined carbohydrates as well as adding vegetable oils to ensure adequate unsaturated fats. They could have nothing to lose but their disability. Absolute assurance can be given that the gluten-free high-protein diet detailed in these pages, could in no way interfere with any medical treatment, or possibly do anyone going on it any possible harm. After all, apart from avoiding substances against which we have been medically warned, we all have the right to choose what we eat, for better or worse. So why not plump for the better, and "give it a go," as Dr. Shatin, as a good Australian, might put it?

4. REGIONAL ENTERITIS AND AUTISM

There are two other conditions in which gluten sensitivity has been found, and although they are far less common, they cause suffering which could perhaps be alleviated if this reaction were taken into account.

These are cases of regional enteritis (inflammation of the lower bowel) and autism, an intractable and distressing mental condition in children which makes them turn away from the outside world and other people, and focus on themselves in unapproachable silence.

Recently, researchers have reported that they tested adults with a variety of diseases of the small intestine, not with adult celiac disease, and found that cases of regional enteritis all reacted adversely when given gluten, after twelve days on a gluten-free diet, but this had no effect on the healthy controls. The query they raised was whether the gliadin fraction in gluten which is toxic in celiac disease (which affects the upper bowel) could also be toxic for diseases affecting the lower part.[36]

Researchers investigating gastric disorders in autistic children found abnormal responses to gliadin (the toxic factor in gluten), underlying a cerebral (brain) defect affected by stress, diet or other chemical changes, with episodes of colic, diarrhea and intolerance of milk and other foods reported for all autistics. Histamine tests showed that these children appeared to be biologically distinct from adult schizophrenics.[37]

Dr. Pauline Ridges, a senior lecturer at Liverpool University who is a biochemist, has been collecting data relating to gluten and its effect on the different conditions (other than celiac disease), referred to in previous pages. She has recently been reported as saying that in studies of autistic children, seven of six pairs of siblings investigated had gastrointestinal disorders, and in four other families of autistic children, eleven had both autism and celiac disease and a further four had autism and associated intolerance to food.[38] Naturally, she urged that more research must be done in all these areas before firm conclusions can be drawn. But parents of any autistic child will surely feel that they might give a gluten-free diet a fair trial in any case, since it could well be helpful, and could not possibly be harmful.

REFERENCES

1. General Secretary, Multiple Sclerosis Society. 1972. Personal communication.
2. Krehl, W. A. 1953. *Am. J. of Clin. Nut.* 11:225.
3. *Nut. Rev.* 1952. 10:235.
4. Kurland, L. K. 1952. *Am. J. Med.* 12:561.
5. Swank, R. L. 1952. *New Eng. J. of Med.* 246:721.
6. Lumsden, C. E. 1961. *Proc. Roy. Soc. Med.* 54:11.
7. Baker, R. W. B., et al. 1963. *Lancet.* 1:27.
8. Belin, J., et al. 1971. *J. Neur. Neurosurg. and Psychiat.* 34:25.
9. Editorial. 1971. *B.M.J.* 5.6.
10. Clausen, J. 1971. *World Medicine.* 10.6.
11. Davis, A. 1951. *Let's Have Healthy Children.* New York: Harcourt Brace Jovanovich.
12. McDougall, Professor Roger. 1972. "Statement of Personal History." Color Supplement, *Daily Telegraph.* 10.8.
13. Krehl, W. A. 1953. *Nut. Rev.* 11:225.
14. Shils, M. E. 1964. *Am. J. Clin. Nut.* 15:133.
15. Mills, C. F. et al. 1960. *Nature.* 185, 4705, 21.
16. Simeson, M. G. 1959. *Proc. 16th Vet. Conf. Madrid.* 2:85-87.
17. Hunter's Seeds representative. 1972. Personal communication.
18. Wallace, T. 1961. *The Diagnosis of Mineral Deficiencies.* London: 2nd Edition. H.M.S.O.
19. Kushner, D. S. 1956. *Am. J. Clin. Nut.* 1:561.
20. Campbell, A. M. G. 1950. *Brain.* 73, 52.
21. Warren, H. V., et al. Oct. 1966. *Arch Environ. Health.* vol. 13.
22. ———. 1972. *Roy. Coll. of Gen. Pract.* 22:56-60.
23. Shatin, R. 1964. *Neurol.* 14:338-341.
24. General Secretary, M. S. Society. 1972. Personal Communication.
25. Campbell, D. G. Aug. 1956. *Am. J. Digest. Disturb.* vol. 1, no. 8, 342.

26. Pauling, L. 1968. *Science*. vol. 160, no. 3825.
27. Boulton, A. A. 1971. *Nature*. vol. 23, 7.5.
28. Dohan, F. C. 1966. *Acta Pediat. Scand*. vol. 42, 2.
29. _____. 1969. *Br. J. Psychiat*. 115:595-596.
30. _____. 1969. *Ment. Hyg*. 53, 9525, 9.10.
31. Lancaster-Smith, et al. 1970. *Lancet*. 21:11.
32. Dohan, F. C. 1970. *Lancet*. 897-899, 25.4.
33. _____. 1971. Lecture, Maudsley Hospital, London, 10.6.
34. Shatin, R. 1963. *Lancet*. 499, 2.3.
    _____. 1964. *Med. J. Australia*. 2, 169.
    _____. 1965. *Rhumatologie*. 17, 69.
    _____. 1966. *Rheumatism*. 48-51.
35. Binder, H. J., et al. 1966. *J.A.M.A*. 195:857-858. no. 10. 7.3
36. Rudman, D., et al. 1971. *J of Clin. Nut*. 1068-1073.
37. Goodwin, M. S. 1971. *J. Autism and Childhood Schizophrenia*, 1, 1, 48-62.
38. Ridges, P. 1972. *Medical News Tribune*. 20.11.

5

The Aims and Methods of a Gluten-Free Diet, and Results To Be Expected

One in every four people living, as so many do, on high calorie foods is more than 10 percent overweight, and many actually suffer from obesity. As every wearer of miniskirts knows, surplus fat is inconvenient, while life insurance companies, because of the added health hazard, raise their premium rates for the obese. In fact, putting on *fat* presents no problem, as every would-be slimmer is aware. Eat "refined" starches and sugar *ad lib* and up goes the weight almost visibly. This also happens with very underweight celiacs, providing all gluten is excluded, as on a gluten-free diet. But this is *not* the object of the exercise.

A rise in weight where there is emaciation can indeed be a sign that good progress is being made but what those added ounces should consist of is equally important, and here the two principal aims of a gluten-free diet should be made quite clear.

The first aim is to exclude all gluten from the food eaten. This means life-saving for every celiac, and may mean, if not full restoration, at least an improvement in health for other conditions responding to a gluten-free diet. The second aim is to feed, not to fatten. This means aiming at body building, not body bulging. How is this to be achieved?

Unfortunately, the emphasis to date seems to have been laid on the consumption of the specially prepared gluten-free flour derived from white flour. But it should be clearly understood that this gluten-free flour has in itself *no therapeutic value*. It in no way heals. The factor which leads to healing in some fashion is the lack of gluten in what is eaten. This flour only ensures that those who use it may continue to eat bread, biscuits, cakes, puddings, pastries, etc., which can be made from

44

it without the obvious harmful effects arising from malabsorption when ordinary untreated white flour is eaten. The assumption is that these are essential foods which must be eaten by everybody for the sake of health. They are nothing of the sort. There are millions of civilized people in other parts of the world who stay healthy and content with nothing but whole rice, millet and/or corn as their only forms of grain foods. Anyone on a gluten-free diet can do the same with nothing but benefit.

It shows a completely negative attitude to merely remove the basic harmful factor of gluten. What is needed is the positive attitude toward health which aims at an optimum diet. This means that only those foods should be used, as far as possible, which supply the best nutrients to replace and build up reserves to counteract the multiple deficiencies which occur in all cases responding to a gluten-free diet.

In celiacs it has been shown that these deficiencies include a lack of the essential fatty acids and the fat-soluble vitamins[1] and of most of the vitamin B complex as in all those who base their diet on white bread and white sugar.[2] Among many other deficient members of the B complex, the lack of folic acid in particular has been held responsible for the recurrent crises which are common.[3] It is noteworthy that this important vitamin is high in raw green leaf vegetables, but is lost in cooking especially when these are soaked for washing, and/or boiled overlong in too much water, which is then discarded along with other valuable vitamins and minerals.[4] Folic acid is also lost when foods are canned.[5]

A lack of many minerals has also been reported, especially of iron,[6] of calcium[7] and of magnesium where the loss may be four times greater than the intake.[8]

It has also been emphasized that the diet should be rich in proteins,[9] since a general decrease in the uptake of amino acids has been found. Others have stressed that because of the destruction of the mucosa in the small intestine there is malabsorption of all nutrients, especially the amino acid tryptophan and all the vitamins, especially folic acid.[10] A further point has since been made that celiac patients who respond only partially to a gluten-free diet may benefit from the administration of pantothenic acid. Since it is unstable and apparently requires folic acid and biotin for its utilization, it was suggested that although it is widely distributed in nature it should perhaps be given to folate deficient patients.[11]

To exclude all gluten from the diet, begin with listing and learning the forbidden foods, i.e., those which contain gluten in wheat or its analogues in oats, barley and rye. These must be strictly rejected without exception. At present there is no alternative. There are no "ifs" and "buts." This must be made absolutely clear to all concerned from the start. There must be no question of deception, of thinking "this once could not hurt," for it most certainly can, and the reaction to even a small amount of gluten in someone on a gluten-free diet has to be seen to be believed, although fortunately recovery takes place fairly rapidly, provided the rule-breakng is not persisted in. It has been noted by investigators that several children under observation developed a shock-like state after eating one biscuit which was *not* gluten-free,[12] and an earlier report had warned that as little as one gram (about 1/28th oz.) of wheat flour a day had caused a worsening of the symptoms.[13]

A. FOODS FORBIDDEN ON A GLUTEN-FREE DIET[14]

Commercial beverages and fruit juices	Ale, beer, gin, whisky, coffee essences, instant coffee, cocoa, drinking chocolate, Horlick's malted beverages, Cocomalt, Milo, Ovaltine, Postum, tomato juice.
Bread Cookies Cakes	Baking powders, all commercial breads, cakes, cookies, crackers, crumpets, doughnuts, meringues, muffins, pancakes, pastries, waffles, bagels, breadcrumbs, breadrolls, crisp-bread, matzoth, pretzels, rusks.
Candy and chocolates	All filled chocolates, toffees, fudge, caramel, marzipan, chewing gum.

Cereals	All cereals containing wheat, barley, rye, oats or buckwheat. When buying other grains, e.g., corn, it is advisable to confirm with the manufacturers that these are uncontaminated. All patent cereals, including baby cereals, are forbidden unless guaranteed gluten-free. (*Only puffed rice, rice crispies and cornflakes are safe.*) Dumplings, groats, macaroni, noodles, spaghetti, canned corn, vermicelli, semolina.
Dairy products	Synthetic cream, malted milk, cheese spreads.
Desserts and puddings	All pies, prepared mixes (unless guaranteed), blancmange powders, caramels, custard powders, instant deserts, rennet powder or tablets, mallow, lemon-pie fillings, lemon/orange curds, lemon powders, trifle.
Fats	Commercial salad dressings, mayonnaise.
Fish	Pickled fish, frozen fish, in sticks, or crumbed or caked or in fish fingers. Fish canned in sauce. Fishpaste.
Flours	All flours containing the grains of wheat, barley, rye, oats, buckwheat (kasha).
Fruit	Baby preparations, glacè fruit.
Gravies	Gravy thickeners and mixes (unless guaranteed gluten-free).
Ice cream	All cones, wafers, crumbs, powders. Health ice cream.
Meats	All commercial preparations containing fillings, e.g. sausages, stews, luncheon meats, meat patties, meat pies, meatloaf, mincemeat, frankfurters, croquettes, meat pastes. Canned meat. Cold cuts (unless guaranteed pure meat).

Sauces and condiments	Thickened sauces, bottled sauces, chutney, pickles, chow-chow, piccalilli, Chef sauce, anchovy sauce, ketchup, horseradish sauce.
Snacks	Potato chips and French-fried potatoes (*unless guaranteed gluten-free*).
Soups	All canned and dried soups, all thickened soups, all cream soups, soup powders.
Spices	Celery salt, chutney, curry powder, mustard.
Spreads	Fishpaste, meat spread, chocolate spread, cheese spreads, peanut butter (uness guaranteed gluten-free), sandwich spreads.
Vegetables	Vegetables in sauces, mayonnaise, cream. Baby preparations (unless guaranteed gluten-free). Vegetable mixes.

Exceptions to the above list of forbidden foods are any commercial products bearing the special symbol which denotes that they are gluten-free or a statement to that effect on the package.

N.B. Read all labels carefully. If in doubt if gluten-free (i.e. *no* wheat, rye, oats, barley or buckwheat) *omit item from the diet.* So many processed foods are adulterated with wheat flour or monosodium glutamate *which contains gluten*, and can be added without declaration to salad dressings.

B. SECOND-BEST FOODS BEST AVOIDED BECAUSE THEY MAKE FAT, NOT FLESH
1. Gluten-free flour
Because it is made from 70 percent roller milled, bleached white flour, which means it has had its original vitamins, minerals and proteins drastically reduced. Although there has been some addition of vitamin B_1, niacin and iron, this only represents a small proportion of those removed in milling;

there is no replacement of the vitamin E which has been destroyed,[15] nor of the unsaturated fats, which have been destroyed or perverted.[16]

2. Cornflour, white sugar, white rice and their products, or sago, and tapioca (*Sugar* includes the sugars and "secret sugars" present in ices, candies, chocolates, jams, jellies, invalid drinks and food, soft drinks (and oversweetened "health drinks"), canned fruits, fruits bottled in syrup, cakes, cookies and breakfast cereals.)

Because processing has removed all the minerals and vitamins from the first two[17] and many from the other three.[18] Custard powder (made from cornflour and white sugar) and breakfast cereals are practically nothing but starch, which steals the appetite and must itself steal vitamin B_1 from other sources in the body—and there may be none or little available—if it is to be broken down correctly into a source of energy.[19] Moreover, it has been found that eating cornflour "considerably increases gastric acidity compared with that which follows eating unrefined cornmeal."[20]

3. Gluten-free baking powder
Because it contains bicarbonate of soda which destroys vitamin B_1, also riboflavin (vitamin B_2),[22] also pyridoxin [23] (vitamin B_6) and also vitamin C.[24]

4. Strong ground coffee
Because it has no food value and can act as a stressor causing a rise in blood fats and cholesterol.[25] Instead, use dandelion coffee which has none of these drawbacks. Other substitutes and instant coffees may contain white flour and are therefore not gluten-free. (Nescafe is *guaranteed* gluten-free.)

C. BEST FOODS WHICH ARE RECOMMENDED
What, then, are the foods for an optimum diet which are recommended?

They fall into five categories: (a) Complete or whole carbohydrates, i.e. unrefined; (b) Complete proteins; (c) Fresh or frozen vegetables and fruits; (d) The best fats; (e) Useful supplements.

(a) Complete or whole versus "refined" carbohydrates

For many decades we have been warned about the serious long-term consequences of the excessive consumption in the average Western household of "refined" carbohydrates, such as white flour and white sugar and their products. In fact, the elegant term "refined" really means stripping off essential nutrients in the form of proteins, minerals and vitamins which are sold as feed for valuable stock like racehorses, or at a much increased cost as health food for humans. In addition, the fiber content is removed so that less mastication is needed, less saliva is produced, less bulk is provided, and much more highly concentrated food is eaten than the body requires or can cope with adequately.

Eminent men and women who have spent a lifetime in research into nutrition and disease, Sir Robert McCarrison (*Cantor Lectures*, 1936), Professor Mary Schwarz Rose (*The Foundations of Nutrition*, 1945), Dr. Weston Price (*Nutrition and Physical Degeneration*, 1950), Adelle Davis (*Let's Eat Right to Keep Fit*, 1954), Drs. Cleave, Campbell and Painter (*Diabetes, Coronary Thrombosis and the Saccharine Disease*, 1966), and Dr. Cleave's *The Saccharine Disease*, 1974, Professor John Yudkin (*Sweet and Dangerous*, 1972), Dr. Geoffrey Taylor, and scores of lesser-known names on both sides of the Atlantic have published undeniable evidence over the years that these foods, especially in excess, are responsible for the degenerative conditions which afflict so many of us, especially later in life. These disabilities include heart disease (the No. 1 killer in middle age or earlier), gastro-intestinal disorders, obesity, all sorts of ulcers, skin troubles, and diabetes, which is not uncommon today even among domestic pets, especially dogs, fed on sweets or other refined starches by indulgent but ignorant owners. Recently, Dr. Denis Burkitt, world famous for his work on cancer in African children, has recorded his opinion that these findings are consistent with the epidemiological and other evidence.[26]

But, as a professor of medicine has pointed out, while there is no area of research which has yielded so much for the benefit of man as the basic science of nutrition, we have not yet succeeded in putting enough of this knowledge to good use. It is surely time we paid enough attention to our choice of daily foods to ensure that we are not building our physical selves on sand. We must acquire knowledge and conviction if we are to avoid well-advertised fillers with little or no food value that can do us plenty of harm in the long run.

Now for the short-term consequences. Just try dutifully following the advice of the suggested menu list at present supplied to medically diagnosed celiacs to eat bread of gluten-free flour and cornflakes at breakfast, cookies made of gluten-free flour at coffee breaks, highly sweetened (with white sugar) puddings made of gluten-free flour at the midday meal, bread, cake or cookies made of gluten-free flour for afternoon snacks and bread made of gluten-free flour at dinner with plenty of white sugar thrown in with drinks of cocoa, coffee and tea, not to mention the use of cornflour in gravies, sauces, puddings, cakes, batters, etc.

How would it be possible to flood the body with more refined carbohydrates? Or spend a few weeks in hospital, for any reason, compelled (or else) by the nurse to swallow this huge amount of refined carbohydrates every day because these things have been specially made for you, although you are well stocked up with the fruit, cheese and yogurt you always eat at home and so much prefer. You will almost certainly put on weight. All that vitaminless, mineral-deprived cornflour and white sugar alone would produce bulges on a boa constrictor. But it is weight in the form of flabby fat. Who wants that?

Take a look at the numbers trying to take off just surplus fat and you will realize how many people have at last learned that such fat is neither desirable nor healthy, and are doing their best to get rid of it. Yet you are steadily eating in such a way as to put it on deliberately. Why do this? Why not find out what is really needed and set about getting just that? Why not choose instead gluten-free but unrefined carbohydrates to supply more energy, complete proteins to build better muscles (which are flesh, not fat) and unsaturated fats to rebuild or maintain the myelin sheaths of the nerves and contribute to the better structure of all body cells instead of saturated fats (the hydrogenated cooking fats and hard margarines) which clog the tissues and burden the body?

Why not cut down on all those slices of bread, on cookies, cakes, puddings, pastries and confectionery, and go in for more vegetables and fruit which have no such drawbacks? Why not put the time and skill involved in home baking to better use by substituting delicacies for special occasions made of ingredients which are health-giving, not health-destroying? This may cost a little more in money, but is really cheaper and much pleasanter in the long run than laying up disability and an untimely death quite unnecessarily. Where and what are they, these complete unrefined carbohydrates containing enough vitamin B_1 to break them down into energy, and the fiber needed for optimum functioning of the intestinal tract and their full content of natural oils?

Foods providing complete unrefined carbohydrates
These include whole brown, or converted, rice; whole millet; whole corn, preferably yellow; whole lentils; potatoes, parsnips; string beans, butter beans, dried peas, pumpkins; raisins, dates, figs, honey, bananas, coconuts, cashews, molasses. (See *Recipes* for how to use any of these which may be unfamiliar.)

(b) Complete proteins
Too many people eat too little protein, whether complete or incomplete. In underprivileged countries this is due to poverty and scarcity, conditions which must in all conscience be remedied, with international help. In Western countries this is

frequently due to the fact that the meat proteins, which carry a prestige value, are very expensive, less glamorous cuts are looked down on, or so unimaginatively cooked as to be unpalatable, and excessive amounts of cheaper "refined" carbohydrates are used to fill the hungry gaps. Few housewives seem to realize that it is better value in every way to provide a savory stew than mouthwatering pastries, cakes, cookies and desserts.

Complete proteins are those which contain all the eight essential amino acids (the building bricks of the proteins), which must be supplied in food as they cannot, like the other fourteen, be manufactured by the body cells themselves. They are especially important to build up wasted muscles and to replace the lacking body proteins in celiacs and others who are too skinny owing to the effects of stress actually caused by illness, although they are needed by all of us from the cot to the coffin.

The highest values in complete proteins are provided by fresh milk, cheese, eggs, meats (especially liver, kidneys and sweetbreads), fish, certain nuts, soya beans and the embryo or so-called germ of whole grains.

Prime steak and cuts suitable for roasts are expensive meats. But there are cheaper cuts that have just as good food value, and offals (organ meats) that have far better food value, which can be cooked in a number of attractive ways (see *Recipes* under Meats). The proteins of peas, beans, lentils, grains and flours with the embryo removed by modern processing methods rank as *incomplete* because they lack some of these factors, and cannot alone support health. However, if green vegetables or two or more of these incomplete proteins are eaten at the *same time* (and this is necessary) they can supply the factors lacking in the other, and so be made adequate. This is the practice followed by vegetarians and in fact some of the world's greatest thinkers and athletes have been vegetarians. But it does need far more knowledge than is common to keep such a diet in good balance.

(c) Vegetables and fruit

Meat, although a good source of protein, is a poor source of most minerals[27] but these can be readily obtained from vegetables and fruit, always providing they are not squandered in the kitchen, but prepared and cooked so as not to waste these very necessary nutrients and the accompanying vitamins. (For details see Vegetable and Fruit Cookery under *Recipes*.)

(d) The right fats (structural, not surplus or storage)

Butter is made simply by agitating milk. We learned this elementary fact early in our Argentine childhood. About halfway back from jogging along some five miles of bumpy dirt track road in a sort of open dog cart to visit the baker in the nearest village of mostly adobe houses we used to stop to pick verbenas, white, red and purple, and to drink the milk we had brought with us. Collected on the top of the blue and white enamel can, there were always tiny pats of butter floating on the surface, apparently conjured into existence. But clearly nothing had been added, and nothing had been taken away, so nothing had been harmed.

It is very different with hard margarine, that cunning copy of butter, and the cooking fats and processed cheeses and lard used everywhere today in countries where the use of oil is not traditional. The ingredients may be of animal or vegetable origin and methods of processing may differ, and so therefore may the drawbacks. But drawbacks there definitely are, and these should be more widely known. Basicaly, all these man-made solid fats are made from liquid oil sufficiently hydrogenated (hardened), i.e. saturated with hydrogen, to give a fat of the desired texture. This is done by heating them with hydrogen at high temperatures in the presence of very small amounts of nickel or some other catalyst. This process changes the essential unsaturated fatty acids known as E.F.A.s into abnormal toxic fatty acids with an anti-E.F.A. effect or else it destroys them, turning them into "empty" calories, with their health-giving value gone.[28]

As the essential fatty acids are absolutely essential, as their name implies, for the physical structure of the body and many of its biochemical processes, this in itself is highly undesirable. Worse still is the anti-E.F.A. effect, for this further accentuates the deficiency of E.F.A.s which occurs in the bleaching of wheat by chlorine dioxide to produce all-white flour, including, of course, that are used in gluten-free flour.[29]

In fact, fats are like people. They differ greatly in what they are, and what they do. It pays with either to recognize the undesirable and turn our backs on them. *The most desirable unsaturated fats* are found in whole grains and cold pressed vegetable oil, such as peanut, corn, sunflower, safflower, wheat germ, and in the oil of cold-blooded animals such as fish. Eggs (recently raised to the status of a vegetable by vegetarians) which are free range qualify, presumably because their diet has included the greenstuffs, earthworms and bacteria, etc., denied to their imprisoned brethren.

The less desirable (saturated) fats which may put solid fats on us in undesirable places including the arteries, are derived from warm-blooded animals and we eat them in the form of lard, chicken, pork, suet, meats and butter. They are also found in oils which have been hydrogenated, and the harder the product of this process, the greater the proportion of them.

The really undesirable fats are fats of any kind which are rancid, re-used or rendered overhot. Beware of these three Rs.

Rancidity, too often undetected by most people, can be avoided by not buying such things as shelled nuts, not keeping bacon fat or drippings too long unrefrigerated, keeping all oils that have been opened in the refrigerator, and so on, as common sense tells us. Re-use of oils in the home can be prevented by merely sautéing food in a small amount of oil which is used up and not deep-frying anything, and avoiding commercial deep-frying which naturally uses the oil over and over again in such things as fish in batter and French-fried potatoes. Rendering overhot need not occur if cooking temperatures are kept low and burning avoided thereby.

It should be noted that the requirement of E.F.A.s is

greatest in the male[30] and that they all facilitate the absorption of vitamin A and carotene.[31]

Clearly our continental friends who always use olive oil have the edge on us, although they, too, would do better to substitute sunflower,*[32] peanut, corn or safflower for the olive oil they habitually use (since they mostly grow it in their countries), as this only supplies 4–14 per cent of E.F.A.s and the other oils supply from 35–70 per cent of E.F.A.s.[33]

As far as multiple sclerosis is concerned, there is a moral in the story of fats, desirable and undesirable. Dr. Franklin Bicknell in 1960 pointed out that as E.F.A.s*[34] enter into the composition of the myelin sheaths of the nerves which begin to be formed in the fourth month of conception, it is important during pregnancy not to eat any of the abnormal fatty acids created by the process of hydrogenation, and furthermore, that it seems unwise for anyone with M.S. to eat margarine, cooking fats or white flour products for the same reason. This advice surely applies also to anyone who hopes for an optimum degree of health.[35]

The lesson is clear. Give all artificial fats a wide berth. Remember that they are used in most commercial cooking. Use the natural saturated fats—butter, bacon and drippings, etc. in moderation, and make sure that any lard or cheese, or even peanut butter you choose has not been processed. Turn over to pressed oils for cooking and salads, of course, and if you must use any margarine, choose a "soft" one which contains some unsaturated fats. As a rough guide to how much, take a careful look at a pack when chilled and estimate the softness. *The softer it is, the higher the unsaturated fats.* (N.B. All fats should be kept refrigerated.)

(e) Useful supplements

While all meats, cheese and eggs are expensive, there are for-

---

* It has been medically recommended that 2 oz. of sunflower seed oil should be consumed daily.

* Dr. Michael Crawford recommends grape and raisin pips as rich sources of E.F.A.s.

tunately some far more concentrated and less costly sources of complete proteins. These are: (1) Brewer's (nutritional) yeast; (2) Yogurt; (3) Powdered milk; (4) Soya beans and their products.

Using these foods makes it possible to provide plenty of complete proteins, even on a small budget, so helping the eater to keep young in heart if not in years. The cells of the body do not expect us to do their jobs but they do expect us to supply them with the wherewithal, for they can only build good health if kept supplied with good materials.

1. Brewer's (nutritional) yeast (dried powder, debittered)

This by-product of brewing, so much more valuable as a food than the end-product of beer, was chosen as an emergency ration in the lifeboats of the United States Navy, for some excellent reasons. It is a first-class booster of morale because it supplies all the vitamin B complex in concentrated form as well as first-class proteins. For all celiacs, M.S. sufferers, schizorphrenics, rheumatoid arthritics and any other persons needing to build up lost reserves of B complex and restore wasted muscles and other body tissues, it is a must. It has been usual to give single fractions of the B complex, but from animal experiments and observations on humans it has been found that the whole complex is superior therapeutically to any single fraction.[36]

It should be emphasized that this is not a medicine but a food, and should be treated as such. It can be added in discreet amounts without detection to gravies, casseroles, stews, savory rice, hamburger, meatloaf, fish kedgeree, and so on. Or it can be taken with food whipped into a glass of fruit juice, milk or water, beginning with ½ teaspoon and increasing gradually until it becomes quite familiar, but stopping short of causing diarrhea, which may occur if too much is taken in any individual case, the amount varying with the taker. Since it has a high phosphorus content, plenty of calcium must also be consumed to maintain the balance between the two. This is best supplied by fresh and powdered milk and yogurt. Those

with milk-intolerance should take calcium lactate or glu-
conate and of course, should obtain all the sunshine possible
since it supplies the vitamin D necessary for the absorption of
calcium.

2. Yogurt

Today yogurt has gained a popularity it never knew before
World War II, and this is all to the good because it is such an
excellent food assisting in the assimilation of calcium and re-
storing the beneficial intestinal bacteria which take such a
beating when antibiotics have been given and/or there is diarrhea.[37] However, there are still those who turn up their
noses at it. For such as these a little guile must be used to
make it acceptable in disguised forms. (Recipes are given for
masking it without cooking it, which is sheer waste, for this
destroys its special properties.)

3. Powdered skim milk

Another of the least costly and most concentrated of proteins.
There is practically no food to which it cannot be added with
advantage, and it provides the milk sugar lactose which is
changed to lactic acid by those intestinal bacteria which feed
on it. For those who are intolerant to cow's or goat's milk, a
vegetable milk must be substituted, or soya flour used as a
health-giving additive.

4. Soybeans and their products

These have been the staple food of millions in China for un-
told centuries and they amount to a "must" for vegetarians in
this country as they are an unparalleled source of complete
proteins. Those of us who were housewives during and after
World War II will remember that we were urged to add soya
flour to various foods, and these may have been put off by the
slighty musty flavor of it in those far-off days. Today, it has
lost this drawback and it is a far better addition to gravies
and so on than gluten-free flour or cornflour since it has not
been bleached or had its vitamins and minerals removed.

RESULTS TO BE EXPECTED

Writing in 1951 (before the discovery of the toxicity of gluten had been laid bare), Professor S. V. Haas, Fellow of the New York Academy of Medicine,[38] outlined the diet he had used and advocated, after more than thirty years of clinical experience with more than 600 cases, and a careful study of the literature.

These were the rules he laid down:

1. No carbohydrate other than that in fruits and, to a lesser extent, in vegetables, and in specially treated milk with the lactose removed.
2. No canned fruits, because of the added sugar.
3. No sugar as sweetening, or in the form of pastries or candy.
4. Potato at first excluded, but gradually introduced.
5. All forms of fish, fowl, meat, cheese, eggs and fats allowed.

Three years on this diet was found to be successful in 73 percent of his cases. Clearly this success could be attributed to the fact that all wheat, oats, barley, rye and buckwheat had been excluded rigorously, in spite of the fact that the significance of the gluten content of these grains had yet to be realized. But there is a point of greater interest even, with a moral for us all today.

Professor Haas emphatically states that these children tended to be more resistant to the minor illnesses of childhood and to be healthier in later life than those who had not had celiac disease. He draws the significant conclusion that the reason might well be that *a child on this diet never develops an appetite for sweets and bread and tends towards a higher protein intake than does the usual child.* Here is an expert with considered confirmation of the view that the misplaced emphasis on consuming so many products of gluten-free flour as bread, cookies, cakes, pastries, puddings, etc., at every opportunity robs celiacs of the chance to be superior, rather than inferior, to the average in health and energy. Furthermore, it underlines the great benefit which can be derived from sticking faithfully not only to the exclusion of gluten, but to the inclusion of unrefined carbohydrates and sugars in place of refined ones.

What, then, is the outlook if a good gluten-free diet is faithfully followed? Must it indeed be followed forever? A report on twenty-three celiac children from the University of Helsinki published in 1970 concluded rather vaguely that any persistence of mucosal abnormalities indicated the need for further gluten-free diet for "a long term."[39] But most authorities do indeed find the need for a life-long exclusion of gluten-containing foods, pointing out that the adult outlook for complete recovery is not as good as for children.[40] Furthermore, as a review of some 200 adult cases came to the conclusion that the gluten-free diet appeared to lessen the risk of malignancy, it would seem wise to take this hint and follow the diet for the rest of one's life. Other experts have stressed this point.[41]

There is no need to look upon this as a grim prospect. It does, of course, entail taking thought and care about the foods eaten, but it is high time more of us did just this instead of thoughtlessly buying and serving anything which producers and processors choose to offer, backed by seductive advertising, or following recipes more concerned with empty glamour combined with empty calories, rather than goodness as food.

Of course, many familier forms of food have to be altered to fit the special needs of celiacs and there is no getting away from this. But the less protesting about having to accept these changes, the better for all concerned. After all, it is the gift of life itself, no less, which is offered to every celiac on a gluten-free plate. Why not take it gratefully, not grudgingly? It does not mean that making the necessary changes means unpalatable food. Far from it. It can mean experiencing new and interesting textures and flavors, and there are plenty of choices left open for pleasant, if unfamiliar, foods. But we need to get accustomed to any unfamiliar food before we can really appreciate it, and most of us are undeniably slow about this, as shown by the history in Europe of such things as the potato, the tomato and the grapefruit.

Nearly two centuries after the potato was introduced from the other side of the world, Frederic the Great, during a period of near famine in Germany, sent a wagonload to the citizens of Kolberg, who promptly sent them back with this message, "These things have neither taste nor smell. Not even the dogs will eat them. What good are they to us?"

It took us about 100 years to accept the tomato as food, and 30 years before many people would eat the grapefruit which is so popular nowadays. We should be grateful for the common and familiar potato which is so easily available today to fill in the large gap caused by the exclusion of wheat, oats, barley and rye, with the less familiar whole brown rice, corn, millet and soya to act as auxiliaries.

MEETING THE SPECIAL NEEDS OF THE STRESS OF SEVERE ILLNESS

Celiacs in particular are generally extremely wasted-looking, although as children they may appear chubby from edema and have pot bellies which are signs of protein lack, not of health, because they suffer from an illness causing severe stress (as in the case of all serious illness) that leads to actual destruction of the body proteins making up the substance of the muscles.[42] A well-known American physician experienced in nutritional therapy, has taken care to emphasize that "tissues which have been depleted *need more of the essential factors in food* (author's italics) than even those on optimal diets.[43]"

All the recipes that follow (Chapter 9) have therefore been selected, adapted or designed to meet these requirements by cutting out or reducing to a minimum, all ingredients which are "empty" calories and by using methods of preparation and cooking that ensure the maximum possible retention of all the natural nutrients present. This means that foods calculated to put on surplus fat are *not* included, since an increase in weight due to this factor cannot be regarded as a sign of good progress as it tends to increase poor posture, lower muscle tone, impede good respiration, and generally slow down the activities of body and mind. Instead, the better foods recommended can and should lead to improved posture, firmer and stronger muscles, deeper respiration and increased physical and mental vigor, in anyone who eats them regularly.

REFERENCES

1. Phillips, J. F. 1970. *New York State J. of Med.* 70 (11).
2. Cleave, T. L., Campbell, G. D. and Painter, N. S. 1966. *Diabetes, Coronary Thrombosis and the Saccharine Disease.* Bristol: John Wright.
3. Bayeli, P. F., et al. 1961. *Minerva Medica.* 19, 25.
4. Herbert, V. 1963. *Am. J. Clin. Nut.* 12, 17.
5. Olson, O. E., et al. 1947. *J. Am. Dietet. Assoc.* 23, 200.
6. Benson, G. L. D., et al. 1964. *Medicine.* 43, 1.
7. Balint, J. A., et al. 1961. *New Eng. J. Med.* 265, 631-633.
8. Goldman, S., et al. 1962. *Pediat.* 29, 448-452.
9. Kowlessar, O. D., et al. May 1970. *Med Clin. of N. America.* 54 (3).
10. Hoffbrand, A. V. 1970. *B.M.J.* 10.10.
11. Monro, Jean. 1972. *B.M.J.* 14.11.
12. Van de Kamer. 1969. *S. A. Med. J.* 43 (4), 15.1.
13. French, J. M., et al. 1957. *Quart. J. Med.* 26, 481.
14. Kavin, H., et al. 1969. *S. A. Med. J.* 43 (4) 25.1.
15. Sharman, I. M., et al. 1960. *Br. J. Nut.* 14, 85.
16. Sinclair, H. M. 1956. *Lancet.* 1, 38.
———. (Ed.) 1958. *The Essential Fatty Acids.* London: Butterworth.
17. Mattice, M. M. 1950. *Bridges Food and Beverage Analysis.* London: Henry Kimpton.
18. Leonard, W. H., and Martin, J. H. 1963. *Cereal Crops.* New York: Macmillan.
19. Eddy, W. H., and Dalldorf, G. *The Avitaminoses.* London: Baillere, Tindall and Cassell Ltd.
20. *Diabetes, Coronary Thrombosis and the Saccharine Disease.*
21. Guha, B., et al. 1929. *Biochem. J.* 23, 880.
22. Elvehjem, C. A., et al. 1949. *J.A.M.A.* 135, 279.
23. Jones, W. A., et al. 1939. *Lancet.* 1073.
24. Abt, H. C., et al. 1939. *Am. J. Med. Sci.* 197, 229.
25. Selye, H. 1956. *The Stress of Life.* New York: McGraw-Hill.

26. Burkitt, D. 1970. *Lancet*. 1237-1240. 12.12.
27. Ingram, M. et al. *Int. Bull.* 6. Br. Nut. Found. Ltd.
28. *The Essential Fatty Acids.*
29. Sinclair, H. M. 1956. *Lancet*. 1381.
    Bicknell, Franklin. 1960. *Chemicals in Food and Farm Produce*. London: Faber and Faber.
30. Sinclair, H. M. 1961. *Proc. Nut. Soc.* 143, 157.
31. *B.M.J.* 1968. 17.2.
32. Millar, J. H. D., et al. 1973. *B.M.J.* 31.3.
33. Bicknell, F. and Prescott, P. 1948. *The Vitamins in Medicine*. London: William Heinemann Medical Books Ltd.
34. *New Scientist*. April 7 1968.
35. *Chemicals in Food and Farm Produce.*
36. Bursook, H., et al. 1938. *Am J. Dig. Dis.* 5, 246.
37. Gamba, J. C. 1953. *Revista Espanola de Pediat.* no. 50.
38. Haas, W. V., and A. 1951. *Management of Celiac Disease*. Philadelphia: J. B. Lippincott.
39. Visakorpi, J. K. et al. Sept. 1970. *Acta Pediat. Scand.* 59, 481-486.
40. Davidson, S. and Passmore, R. 1967. *Human Nutrition and Dietetics*. 3rd Edition. Edinburgh: E. and S. Livingstone.
41. Harris, O. D. et al. 1967. *Am. J. of Med.* 42, 899: Creamer, B. 1968. *Trans. Med. Soc.* London, vol. 85: Read, A. C. 1970. *Modern Trends in Gastroenterology*. 4, 180-193.
42. Cotin, A. 1953. *Clin. Nut.* 1, 232, 46.
43. Biskind, Morton. March 1953. *Am. J. Dig. Dis.*

6

Feeding the Celiac Infant and Young Child

The mother of an obviously ill infant probably suffering from persistent bouts of exhausting diarrhea naturally feels very anxious, wondering whether the condition can be cleared up, what form the treatment will take, and whether this will ensure the normal stools and energy that belong with good health. What are her feelings when the diagnosis of celiac is made? How should she respond to the doctor's statement that this means changing to a gluten-free diet, excluding all wheat, oats, barley and rye, and their products in any foods? What grounds has she for hope that her ailing infant will soon be on the road to recovery, and will grow up into a normal healthy child and adult?

I believe that she has reason to feel thankful for a correct diagnosis automatically pointing to the correct treatment which lies in her hands to carry out to the letter. Of course, she will encounter difficulties and problems and she will need to start out with an adaptable and hopeful outlook towards coping with a new and unforeseen situation. On this solid foundation, with the necessary knowledge and the will to follow it faithfully, she can build up the health she so ardently wishes for her child, but in doing so she must above all be careful not to imply or even allow a hint to creep in that hers is a deprived child to be pitied because he or she must follow a restricted diet. On no account must any sense of self-pity be communicated, for few things are so destructive of content or happiness.

This emphasized, what of the practical details? The ultimate aims, which include putting on weight, should be kept clearly in mind. But not in the form of fat—for only a little stored fat is desirable and any excess leads to sloth and apa-

thy—but of flesh, which is muscle tissue, of good bone development and of more blood cells which lead to activity and
liveliness.

If your baby has been put on a G.F.D. he may also have
been diagnosed as allergic to any feed based on cow's milk.
According to some authorities this sensitivity is almost always
transient, and provided the diagnosis has been made early
enough, the treatment now available (which entails changing
to milk substitutes) is said by experts to make the outcome
uniformly successful.° [1] These substitutes are of three types:
(1) protein hydrolysates; (2) soya bean; (3) meat-based
preparations. The physician will establish which you should
use. If the allergy has not disappeared spontaneously within
the expected couple of years, then the child must continue to
avoid all cow's milk. Admittedly this is an added complication. Fruit juices may be used, and you will be advised to
give tablets of calcium lactate in addition, or you may use the
excellent, but expensive, vegetable milk which has been especially designed for Vegans, who voluntarily forswear all
dairy products. In milk shakes and puddings, it may be possible to use the cheaper soya milk (which can be home-made;
see Index), masking the unfamiliar taste by flavoring strongly
with liquidized fresh fruits in season, or vanilla, orange, cinnamon, etc.

If your baby has been put on a G.F.D. but can take
preparations of cow's milk you will be able to continue with
the accustomed feed. But you must, of course, change the
cereal foods, for in future these must be made solely of rice
or millet, and instead of letting yourself feel bitter about this,
give a quick thought to the millions of mothers who regard
this as quite natural and satisfactory. Since the firms making
baby foods now supply these foods, there should be no difficulty there. But the question does arise: Are we giving these
foods too early?

° On the other hand a proportion of celiac patients diagnosed as glu-
ten-sensitive may have allergy to cow's milk, not just to lactose due to
lactase deficiency, but there are precipitins to casein in the stools of these
people.[2]

Weaning is, of course, a perfectly normal process for every baby and mother in the world, but the modern fashion of starting this at a few weeks only, seems to have nothing to commend it.

Nearly thirty years ago, pediatricians issued warnings that the early use of cereals was of questionable value, querying too, whether "bigger" really meant "better" babies.[3] This warning was repeated some years later by others, who pointed out that certain enzymes are lacking in infants who can cope with milk but not with foods dealt with easily by older children.[4] Yet the trend towards starting cereals earlier and earlier has continued, and today a number of baby food manufacturers are making and recommending cereal foods for babies to be given so young that they cannot yet have the necessary physiological equipment to deal with them. Some doctors have expressed grave concern over this and have suggested that this may be a practice actually creating the celiac condition in infancy, although in some cases this may only be temporary and the child may recover normal digestion.[5] It has been suggested therefore, that there should be a statutory requirement that manufacturers must state on any pack of such food not only that it contains gluten, but also that this can be dangerous if fed too early to *any infant*, and is definitely not permissible for any celiac.

If an infant appears to be hungry and will not settle after a bottle feed, this is not necessarily an indication that cereals should be begun. It is quite possible to provide a fully adequate diet and satisfy this hunger by increasing the amount of milk feed given daily and by fortifying it with proteins, minerals and vitamins. Raising the total daily feed by 8–16 oz. and adding 1 egg, debittered brewer's yeast (beginning with ¼ teaspoon for each bottle and increasing every five days up to 2 tablespoons for a day's total), 1 or 2 tablespoons of non-instant powdered whole milk or 3 to 4 tablespoons of instant powdered milk with 1 tablespoon or more of light cream, is the simple method recommended by Adelle Davis in *Let's Have Healthy Children*. These additions make up for

the deficiencies of iron and vitamin B complex in milk that
cereals are supposed to supply. In fact, pediatricians have
stressed for years that solids should never be introduced at
certain stereotyped ages, but only when the baby is still hungry after a fully adequate milk feed has been given, which
may occur at any age from 3—8 months.[6] It should be remem-
bered that learning to eat from a spoon or drink from a cup is
like learning to stand and should never be forced. If for any
good reason solid food must be given it can be diluted with
fruit juice or the usual milk feed and taken from a bottle with
the nipple enlarged to allow the food to pass through readily.

Even if introducing solid foods too early does not induce
the celiac condition, it does very often lead to feeding problems later on and is therefore inadvisable on this score. The
reason is plain. With little control over his tongue and with
underdeveloped throat muscles, the infant cannot swallow solids easily and promptly spits them out. This leads to fights
over foods becoming a habit as hard to overcome as any other
bad habit. Studies carried out at the famous Mayo Clinic on
668 babies, showed that whenever they were offered foods
from time to time, but were not actually fed until they
reached forward eagerly towards them, could swallow easily,
and only ate the amount they wanted, feeding problems were
almost completely averted. Although a few ate solids three
times daily at four months, the majority delayed this until
they were nine months old and nearly 100 percent of the
mothers were satisfied with the good appetite of their children. Furthermore, bottle feeds were not stopped until rejected by the babies themselves, so avoiding the struggle to force
milk into a child from a spoon or cup which tends to make
them milk-haters later on.[7]

PREPARING BABY SOLIDS AT HOME

Blenders and juicers are not cheap, but so useful that many of
us consider them a "must" in the kitchen. But there is now an
inexpensive small gadget, available in health, hardware and
some department stores called the "Happy Baby Food Grind-

er," which sieves and purees vegetables, cooked meats and fruits, to provide your baby's first solid foods. If you cook nourishing foods for all the family, then use this to blend some of it for your baby, before adding salt or other seasoning. This costs far less than canned baby foods, takes only a minute, retains more vitamin B_1, folic acid and vitamin C since lower temperatures are used in cooking than in canning, and there is no end to the range of foods, cooked or raw, which you can prepare. Not only can you be quite certain that no cheap fillers such as cornflour or white flour have been used, but you can increase the nutritional value by adding rather under 1 teaspoon of powdered milk to any green vegetables which may be too juicy alone. All vegetables should be as fresh as possible, washed quickly but well, and steamed over the minimum of water till just tender. Add a little milk to carrots and other dry vegetables, and use the water left over from steaming for moist ones. Serve at once, or store in the refrigerator. Uncooked apples, pears, strawberries, raspberries, guavas, peaches, grapes, young peas, carrots and baby turnips and beets can also be prepared in this way, as well as cooked white fish and meats of every sort, especially heart, kidney, chicken and lamb livers and brains.

Feeding like this from the family table in the old-fashioned way with due regard to the baby's need for softness and blandness can be the best way to ensure that the food is accepted and enjoyed. But coarse-textured foods such as cottage cheese curds and tiny pieces of hard cheeses should not be delayed beyond the sixth to eighth month to accustom the child to a variety of texture from his pureed one.

The conviction that a baby needs hard dry crusts of bread or biscuits between meals dies hard. Yet it has many disadvantages. Soggy morsels pulped by saliva are liable to cause choking and are always very messy, and the amount of nourishment gained is negligible; furthermore, the habit may ruin the appetite for more nutritious food. Far better to satisfy the urge to chew with something that resists all efforts to swallow it, yet is not as hard as a bone ring. Hark back to a substance,

no doubt first used by some inventive and harassed Stone Age
mother and still in use in unsophisticated countries, on which
I and my four brothers and sisters cut our teeth in the pampas
of the Argentine. Ask your butcher for the piece of thick fas-
cia—looking like india rubber—to be found running down the
flank of every beast slaughtered. Sterilize this by boiling, strip
off any meat or gristle that may be on it, punch or bore a hole
in it, and attach it to your baby's upper garment by a piece of
tape so that he can have a chew whenever he feels like it.
Later on, when he has really learned to chew, give him sticks
of raw, well-scrubbed carrot, turnip or celery, etc., to work on.
These cannot establish the pernicious habit of craving for refined starches but create a liking for far more valuable foods.

Sitting near the family table in a high chair with a spoon
tied to it which he has got used to tasting and sucking, he is
all set to be offered but not forced to eat suitable nibbles as
you eat. Later on, with a large towel firmly round his neck, he
can learn to feed himself from a warmed baby dish of the
same foods he has accepted easily while still being fed from
spoon or fingers.

Adelle Davis points out that vegetable oils (peanut, corn or
sunflower) as sources of the essential fatty acids so important
as "structural" fats, can be given largely as vegetable seasonings as soon as they are readily taken, and suggests starting
with ½ teaspoon for the first month, increasing very rapidly to
3 teaspoons daily.

Here is the Scheme for Weaning taken from the *Feeding
Charts for Children*, issued by the National Association for
Maternal and Child Welfare, adapted to exclude all gluten,
and as many refined carbohydrates as possible.

Weaning from full breast feeding to only milk mixture in
five stages. (*No alterations*).

FEEDING CHART FOR BABIES: 1st stage

6 a.m.	*10 a.m.*	*2 p.m.*	*6 p.m.*	*10 p.m.*
Breast feed or milk mixture	Rice cereal. Start with 1 tsp., increase gradually. Breast feed or milk mixture	1–2 tsp. bone soup with cooked pureed vegetables, e.g. carrots or any green-leaved vegetables. 1 tsp. gradually increasing to 2 dessertspoonfuls daily (best home-made). Breast feed or milk mixture	As at 10 a.m. To vary cereal give cornmeal cereal	Breast feed or milk mixture

Give vitamin supplements at 9 a.m. and 5 p.m.

FEEDING CHART FOR BABIES: 2nd stage

6 a.m.	10 a.m.	2 p.m.	6 p.m.	10 p.m.
Breast feed or milk mixture	Egg yolk 2–3 tsp. 3 times weekly with 1 buttered potato finger. Rice or corn cereal on other days. Breast feed or milk mixture. Reduce breast feed on the days when milk is being given with cereal	Bone broth or soup 2–4 oz. 2–3 times weekly or egg yolk or scrambled egg or bone marrow, with mashed vegetables, e.g. carrots, turnips, parsnips, cabbage, cauliflower, spinach, potatoes. Vegetables to be given daily. Rice pudding, yogurt, custard (egg), junket with pureed stewed prunes or pulped, baked or stewed apple (without skins or seeds). Only honey as sweetening. Breast feed or milk mixture	Cornmeal cereal with milk and honey. Or rice cereal with ditto. Breast feed or milk mixture	Breast feed or milk mixture

A child at this stage should be taught to drink from a cup (preferably not a silver christening mug, which tastes unpleasant).

Vitamin supplements as before.

Start ½ tsp. of oil on mashed vegetables, to be increased very gradually to 3 tsp.

Many babies can omit 6 a.m. feed by 4–6 months.

FEEDING CHART FOR BABIES: 3rd stage

On waking	Breakfast 8 or 8:30 a.m.	Midday Meal 12:30 or 1 p.m.	Evening Meal 4:30–5:30 p.m.	10 p.m.
Drink of fruit juice	Mashed potato or pumpkin with butter or drippings, egg yolk 3 times weekly. Basic rice or corn porridge on other days. Occasionally a little scraped or pureed raw apple or lightly stewed fruit. Milk mixture	Steamed liver, minced meat, simmered in milk, soup or broth, with grated cheese, or steamed fish or soft herring roes, with mashed vegetables, carrots, turnips, parsnips, cabbage, cauliflower, spinach, sprouts, potatoes. Egg custard or rice or cornmeal pudding with apple pulp, ripe banana or stewed prunes (only honey as sweetening). Milk mixture, or fruit juice if milk refused	Celery or carrot sticks with cottage cheese. Milk mixture	Breast feed or milk mixture

Vitamin supplements as before.

FEEDING CHART FOR BABIES: 4th stage

On waking	Breakfast 8 or 8:30 a.m.	Midday Meal 12:30 or 1 p.m.	Evening Meal 4:30–5:30 p.m.	10 p.m.
Drink of fruit juice	Baked potato with butter, egg lightly boiled, poached, coddled or scrambled, or chopped bacon 2–3 times weekly. Basic rice, millet or cornmeal, on other days. Occasionally lightly stewed fruit, or very ripe peach or melon pureed raw, or other fruit in season	Small amounts of beef, steamed liver, rabbit, sweetbread, chicken or well-cooked tripe simmered in milk or steamed fish, or soft herring roes, with mashed vegetables, e.g. carrots, turnips, parsnips, cabbage, cauliflower, potatoes, spinach, sprouts or broccoli. Egg custard, junket or yogurt, or rice, millet or cornmeal pudding with stewed fruit. Water to drink	Baked banana, or baked potato with butter, grated cheese or yeast extract. Milk	Milk. Some babies need the 10 p.m. feed until they are 9 months old, or until they can sleep through the night from 6 p.m. to 6 a.m.

Vitamin supplements as before. Give a drink of fruit juice or water between meals as required.

SAMPLE FEEDING CHART FOR CHILDREN FROM
1 to 2 YEARS: 5th stage

BREAKFAST	MIDDAY MEAL	EVENING MEAL
Scrambled or boiled egg Baked or steamed potato Piece of raw apple (hard) Milk	Minced lamb, mutton, chicken or ham Mashed potatoes and carrots or sprouts Stewed fruit, junket Water	Slices of raw apple with cheese Milk
Basic cornmeal with milk and honey Portion of grilled or steamed herring free from bone Steamed potato	Broth Vegetables—carrots, turnips, potatoes Stewed prunes and egg custard Water	Home-made biscuits and butter Fruit or raisins Milk
Poached egg on mashed potato Piece of apple or banana Milk	Steamed fish and mashed potato and vegetables Apple or dried apricot puree Water	Baked banana Cottage cheese Milk
Basic rice with milk and honey Fresh fruit from which seeds and stones have been removed Milk	Steamed soft roes Jacket potato, cauliflower, sprouts or cabbage Baked apple Milk pudding Water	Celery with grated or cottage cheese Fruit Milk
Basic millet with milk and honey Fresh fruit Milk	Cottage pie of fresh meat Boiled onions Milk pudding, stewed fruit Water	Potato droppies with butter or cottage cheese Fruit Milk
Portion of bacon and sautéed potato or banana Piece of raw apple Milk	Poached egg on boiled potato, spinach or cabbage Apple puree Water	Tomato between lettuce leaves Carrot sticks Milk
Basic cornmeal, rice or millet with honey and milk Fresh fruit Milk	Liver, potatoes and vegetables Stewed fruit and egg custard Water	Celery or apple with cottage or grated cheese Home-made biscuits Milk

Foods Additional to Those Above Suitable for Children from Two to Five Years

Soups and broths. Scotch broth (whole millet instead of barley), mutton broth (ditto), kidney soup, fish soup, chicken soup, pea soup, lentil soup, onion soup, potato soup, celery soup. All-in soup. Quick vegetable soup.

Fish. Fish pie, fish cakes (use rice or potato to thicken), fish and tomatoes, canned salmon, sardines.

Meat. Cold meat (ham, tongue, beef, lamb), Irish stew, boiled beef with carrots cornmeal dumplings, calf's head (sauce thickened with potato or rice).

Puddings. Apple amber, milk jelly, all varieties of rice puddings, cottage cheese pudding, fruit juice creams, cornmeal puddings, pumpkin puddings.

Cheese. Grated cheese (uncooked) is a useful addition to many dishes for young children and can be given from the age of 7 months.

N.B. Only unhydrogenated oils—corn, peanut, sunflower and safflower—should be used where possible in cooking.

If margarine is used it should be "soft" margarine, which may consist of 50 percent unsaturated fats to 50 percent saturated fats. As a rough guide to the content look carefully at the margarine when chilled (it should always be kept refrigerated) and estimate the softness. The softer the texture, the higher in unsaturated fats (E.F.A.s).

REFERENCES

1. Freier, S., et al. Aug. 1970. *Clin. Pediat.* 449–454.
2. Monro, Jean. 1973. Personal Communication.
3. Gerstley, J. R., et al. 1945. *J. of Pediat.* 27, 521-531.
4. Ross, I. D., et al. 1959. *Pediat.* vol. 23. 718-725.
5. Green, Peter. 1972. M. o. H. Herefordshire, personal communication.
6. Rowan-Legg, C. K. 1949. *Can. Med. Assoc. J.* 60, 388.
7. Aldrich, C. A., et al. 1947. *J.A.M.A.* 135, 340.

7

In the Kitchen

In schools and clinics all the hygienic campaigns in the world would not be so valuable as the teaching of good cooking and good housekeeping

VISCOUNT LYMINGTON

(*Famine in England*, Whittaby 1938)

Good cooking means conserving food values (see *Recipes*, Vegetable and fruit cookery).

Good housekeeping means choosing good foods.

RECOMMENDED GOOD FOODS

Most of the following can be bought in health stores. If you don't find them there or are not near a health store, most of them can be ordered by mail from:

> Walnut Acres
> Penns Creek
> Pennsylvania 17862

Agar-agar (seaweed product used in place of gelatin which supplies an excess of glycine)

Beans (soy, mung, lentil)

Corn for popping

Cream "Top milk" is called for in some recipes, to be whipped. This is now a rarity. Try to find fresh, raw milk in your health store or unhomogenized Guernsey from a reputable dairy. Whipping creams now sold in supermarkets contain emulsifiers and stabilizers to prolong shelf life and to reinforce whippability. These are best avoided. If the top of the milk is unavailable use the alternative frequently given—yogurt—which is just as delicious.

78

Dandelion coffee

Dried fruits

Flavorings (pure essences), *herbs and spices*

Grains and flours

Honey (tupelo is best)

Kefir grains for making kefir are obtainable, with instructions, from:

> R-A-J Laboratory
> 35 Park Avenue
> Blue Point, New York 11715

Molasses (unsulphured)

Nuts (fresh, unshelled)

Peanut butter (sometimes fresher when bought in a jar from a good supplier than when made on the spot for you at the health store from shelled peanuts which might have been around for a while), always unhydrogenated

Powdered milks

Raw sugar (turbinado). Never use white sugar.

Salt (sea-salt, containing magnesium and other trace minerals lacking in ordinary table salt)

Vegetable oils (for cooking and salads), corn, olive, peanut, safflower, sesame, sunflower, soy. J. H. D. Millar *et al*, in *B.M.J.* 3/31/73, recommends that two ounces of sunflower seed oil be consumed daily.

Yeast (for baking only) fresh from a baker, or dried granules from the health food store

Yeast (brewer's nutritional), debittered powder; a fortified yeast with magnesium and calcium added to balance the phosphorus in the yeast and make it more easily digested

Yeast extract (Marmite)

Grain Mill

The best and cheapest way to ensure freshly ground flour of whole brown rice, yellow corn, whole millet and soybeans, retaining full nutritional value and flavor and avoiding any possibility of staleness or rancidity, is to grind your own. You can order the Quaker City Grinding Mill from:

Straub Company
Cedar and Ray Avenue
Croydon, Pennsylvania 19020

A smaller mill, the Moulinex Grinder, can be ordered from Walnut Acres.

General hints

Baker's yeast (N.B. only for baking, not raw.)

Compressed fresh baker's yeast is best where large amounts are to be used. Stored in refrigerator in greaseproof paper or a screw-top jar, it keeps 10-14 days.

Dried yeast granules can also be used, using half amount recommended for fresh. Has rather strong flavor, so fresh is preferable, if really fresh.

Coating foods for sautéing, etc.

Add 2 tsp. milk and 1 tsp. oil to each egg used. Season with salt and paprika. Use powdered milk, rice, soya flour or corn-meal in place of flour. For croquettes and rissoles, use lightly beaten egg white with a little water to attach rice or corn-flour in place of crumbs.

Shredded coconut

Open fresh coconut. Pour off juice and use as liquid for fruit salad or milk shake. Cut off brown shell and cut flesh into 1 in. cubes. Shred a few at a time through the blender, or cut in pieces unshelled and shred like a carrot on stainless steel grater. Do not add sweetening. Store in glass jar with tight screw-on lid. Refrigerate. Can be kept several days.

Eggs

To test for freshness: (1) Drop in deep bowl of water. Fresh having smaller air cells, *sinks*. Older *stands on end*. Past praying for if *floats*. (2) Break and look at shape. Fresh yolk is domed on thick, compact white. Older yolks flatten and whites run.

Can keep 3 weeks in refrigerator at 45° F., or 12 days at room temperature, 65° F.

Egg whites
Adding a little water increases surface tension and they whip to a far larger volume.

Fruit rind (home-made)
Only use rinds *not* sprayed with insecticides, anti-mold preparations, colored artificially, waxed, gassed or fumigated.

Use lemon, orange or grapefruit skins. Wash and dry rinds. Cut into thin matchstick strips. Dry on baking sheet in sun or warm place. When thoroughly dry, store in screw-top jar.

Hominy grits, or samp (commercial)
These are not *whole corn*. Grits are produced from starch of the endosperm by dry milling. Samp in South Africa is the same.

Grits resemble the refined products of rice and wheat.

Whole cornmeal = 97 to 100 percent of whole grain

Decorticated meal (whole meal, germ and some of pericarp)

= 90 to 96 percent of whole grain

Degerminated corn (sieved to remove germ and most of pericarp)

= 85 percent of whole grain

To get whole grits, make at home (see *Recipes*).

Honey in recipes
Honey may be substituted for sugar, using ¼ cup less of other liquids to each cup of honey. Always bake at lower temperature, as honey caramelizes fast.

Using soya flour (full fat)
Add in small quantities to any moist food as it is very bland and does not affect taste, but adds good protein and oil, no starch and only a small amount of sugar.

Making yogurt from bought yogurt
Bring 1 pint of milk to 180° F. Cool it to about 100° F. If no thermometer, test if comfortably warm to the touch. Put in 1 tablespoon of plain, bought yogurt, mixing well and pour into chosen container. If this is a wide-mouthed thermos, cork it up and leave for several hours. If you are using small screw-top jars (1 pint fills 3), keep them in a suitably warm place for several hours to allow the culture to take. When ready it should resemble junket but is never quite so close-textured as bought yogurt. Keep back 1 tablespoonful to act as a starter for your next batch, and start again with fresh bought yogurt after about one week when you will find your yogurt getting thinner. Flavor as desired with honey and/or fruit juice, etc. Thicken with dried skim milk.

Warnings

Gluten
Everyone on a gluten-free diet should exclude all wheat (this includes all "gluten-free" flour because it contains residual gluten), oats, barley and rye.

Some people will find they cannot tolerate millet, corn or rice, either, perhaps because they may contain gluten or because their systems are temporarily sensitive to all cereals.

Basic preparation of dry soybeans before use in any recipe
Dry soybeans contain a factor, not destroyed by ordinary cooking temperatures, which blocks the enzymatic digestion of all proteins. Preparation by long soaking in cold storage will remove this factor.

Place 1 cup of dry soybeans in a bowl. Add 4 cups of cold water. Place in a refrigerator and leave for 24 hours, changing the water 4 times during this period and discarding it. Do not use the water for stock. Drain beans before use. This warning does not apply to varieties of soybeans like Kanrich or Akita when eaten green like French beans.

Sprouted wheat

It seems that certain gluten-free diets also include sprouted wheat, which indeed renders the gluten harmless, providing every grain germinates. But as every farmer and gardener knows, there is no seed which produces 100 percent germination and a few unsprouted grains would provide enough gluten to be dangerous for some people. Sprouted wheat is therefore excluded from our recommendations. This therefore applies also to ale, beer, whisky, gin, which are all made from malted (i.e. sprouted) wheat, oats, barley or rye.

Wheat germ

It is well known that the highly respected American nutritionist Adelle Davis always recommended that celiac cases referred to her should have wheat germ. (*Let's Get Well*, New American Library, 1972). Theoretically, wheat germ is indeed gluten-free, but in practice physical contamination is highly possible. We cannot therefore, recommend its use.

8

Children's Parties; Eating Out; Packed Meals and Picnics; Traveling Abroad; Menaces in Menus; Menus for One Week: Spring, Summer, Autumn, Winter; Minimum Trouble Menus

Children's Parties

Any child with a number of contemporaries can suffer badly from a surfeit of those ill-conceived feasts for the young called children's parties. If not tactfully managed, they can also be embarrassing and difficult occasions for a child on a gluten-free diet.

Generally, these parties mean a lavish spread of eye-catching concoctions full of sugars and sickliness which are undesirable for anyone, and simply ask for over-eating today to be followed by tears, tantrums and upset tummies tomorrow or sooner. But this need not be. Informed and sensible mothers have begun to break this foolish habit in a very effective way, and all mothers with a child or children on a gluten-free diet are advised to follow their excellent example and spread the idea among their circle of friends, for it can only result in benefit to all the children concerned.

Instead of the usual three to five o'clock afternoon party, which cuts short rests and rushes the extra time needed to dress up in party clothes, these new-fashioned parties consist of light lunches from, say, noon to two-thirty, so that a much-needed rest can follow the excitement, or a light supper from, say, five to six-thirty or a little later, depending on the age of the guests who will then go home to go to bed for the night.

Meals such as these make it possible to get right away from the traditional cakes and sweets which weight-conscious parents now see as inadvisable, even for their young off-spring—a point of view which has everything to commend it.

84

Suggestions for suitable foods

It is a good idea to start with some fairly strenuous party games, then sit the children down at table. This whets the appetite for food of any sort, which may be a good thing when the foods presented are unexpected and even unfamiliar to many. The best first course is a salad set out as attractively as possible in small dishes and served separately as with hors d'oeuvres. This could consist of potato salad with home-made mayonnaise sweetened with honey, and sprinkled with finely grated raw beets, plates of tomato in wedges, mild radishes, chunks of celery and cucumber, bite-sized pieces of crisp lettuce to be dunked in mayonnaise in tiny individual dishes, halved hard-boiled eggs stuck with raw carrot matchsticks, nut balls, small cubes of a mild cheese, freshly roasted and shelled peanuts, cottage cheese balls in celery boats, stuck with raisins, or sitting on dates, tiny meatballs, home-made crisps, flat potato cakes or droppies, and so on.

Drinks to be fruit juices (no fizzy or bottled drinks) and plain milk or home-made milk shakes. For the dessert course provide purees of dried apricots, peaches or prunes, in individual glasses, apple puree garnished with tinted whipped cream, small scoops of such fruits as melon, avocado, papaya, watermelon, etc., where these are easily available, raisin custards in individual molds or dishes, small reinforced junkets tinted with a few drops of beet juice, fruit salads from any fresh fruit available and chunks of fresh coconut still in the shell for ardent chewers to nibble. Finally, a large dish of freshly popped corn lightly sprinkled with salt, or roast chestnuts if in season, to be passed round instead of candy. This could bring the party to a close or to the advent of the birthday cake if the occasion is a birthday. The cake (which could be eaten by everyone if it were one of the flourless ones among the recipes) has been set with candles and kept out of sight until the children have eaten their fill of the above fare. Now bring it in with a flourish, set it on the table and light the candles. When the "oohs" and "aahs" have subsided, cut it in very thin slices with a very sharp knife and serve the minimum of cake with the maximum of ceremony.

You can rest assured that everyone at this party will have enjoyed a good meal and will have no nasty aftereffects. Whoever heard of tummyaches after, say, too many carrot sticks or lettuce, or too much pink junket? Nor does it entail arduous sessions with the oven for the mother who prepares such food for a party which is not only gluten-free, but a pleasant pointer in the right direction for the mothers of all the guests.

EATING OUT

Main meals

Choose fruit (melon, grapefruit, etc.) instead of soup or hors d'oeuvres, but avoid mixtures like Russian or potato salad, which contain mayonnaise (commercial), adulterated by wheat flour.

Choose broiled, baked, steamed, sautéed or pickled fish, or remove scrupulously any flour, breadcrumbs, batter or sauce with fried fish.

Choose broiled meats (no sausages) and roasts, stipulating no gravy, no stuffing, no sauce for meats and vegetables, no stews or dishes cooked with gravy which always contains white flour. (Avoid all velouté vegetables as this also means flour). For a change have a salad (without mayonnaise), or cheese and fruit.

For dessert, choose fresh fruit or fruit coupes or salads; or if available, the homely rice pudding, baked custards and stewed or baked apples. (Canned fruits and ice creams are not recommended because of the high content of white sugar.)

Snacks

Carry a small container with dried figs, apricots, nuts, cheese or home-made cookies or biscuits (see *Recipes*), and also small pieces of cheese, not processed, to be eaten with an apple.

PACKED MEALS AND PICNICS

Any main meal to be eaten at school, work or out of doors can be made much more tempting, less fat-making and valuable nutritionally if the idea of sandwiches is entirely abandoned. Just give bread a miss.

For hot meals: take wide-mouthed thermoses to carry a wide range of tasty and filling home-made soups, savory stews, curries (without curry powder), chicken, meat, fish or egg kedgerees, rice dishes of all sorts, potatoes roasted, sautéed, jacket and so on, chestnuts roasted and/or boiled, etc., etc. There are so many foods which can be portable in this way. Of course they need bowls and spoons, if not knives and forks. But why make such a fetish of eating with the fingers?

For cold meals: there is nowadays a great variety of opaque containers, which prevent light and air lowering the vitamin C content of vulnerable foods, in which to carry such items as cold chicken, fish, meatloaves, hard-boiled eggs, head-cheese, potato salads and salad greens of all sorts, so there is no difficulty there.

For dessert there is a wide choice of fresh fruit in season, frozen fruit or garden fruits, preserved without sugar, served with yogurt and honey, rather than canned ones which contain excessive amounts of white sugar—the more expensive grades containing the higher percentage.

For snacks: bread can easily be excluded. Starch hunger in celiacs—and any one else for that matter—can be satisfied by bananas, (fresh or dried) chestnuts, home-made potato chips, raisins, figs, dried apricots and other dried fruits, with an occasional home-made cookie or cake as an extra, not forming the bulk of the food eaten. Equally acceptable can be crisp celery, carrots, radishes, etc., with bite-sized pieces of cheese, cottage cheese balls, and so on.

Food for the baby

Take small closed containers holding home-made purees and other suitable foods suggested in Chapter 6, a thermos of boiling water and a bowl in which to heat them up to the required temperature. A simple way to provide a baby with acceptable food and drink in one is to cut a sweet eating apple in half, cut out the core, then scrape at the cavity with a teaspoon and give it to the child mouthful by mouthful.

TRAVELING ABROAD (BY SEA, AIR, RAIL AND ROAD)

Today we all travel for one reason or another. For those traveling for the first time on a gluten-free diet here are some hints which may be helpful. In connection with giving lectures, or collecting material for articles and books, or even on holidays, the celiac in this household has in the last eight years traveled by sea to Cape Town and back, to Spain, the Canaries and Denmark. By air and back to Sweden, to New York and across to San Francisco, with a number of stopovers on the way. By rail to Edinburgh, Fort William and many other places in Scotland and England, and by road about the Lake District and the West of England. So we can claim to have learned some of the ropes about being on a special diet in these circumstances.

By sea

If you are going on a long trip, it pays to write, when making reservations, to the chief stewards of the boats by which you are going to travel, and tell them you have to be gluten-free at all meals. We have found them prepared to bake gluten-free bread, if wanted, but we preferred to ask for cheese and apples at tea-time, and at all other times made a careful choice from menus, eating potatoes or rice, in place of bread and cookies, as at home. We found it helpful to have our own private supply of raisins, dried fruits, etc. for trips ashore and so on. But those who eat special cookies can, of course, take these in tins with them. For short voyages it is only necessary to pick and choose among the large number of foods provided. Ask for hot milk instead of coffee and at once make a sustaining drink in your cabin if you have had the foresight to take some carob flour with you. If you are unable to exist without any bread, take some loaves made of rice or cornmeal (see Index) with you, and get them put in a freezer or just in the refrigerator for the trip, to be doled out as required.

By air

Where there is little choice of food, and not very nice at that, it is best to stock up with one's own specials to supplement what you can eat off the menu.

By rail and road

There are such rigid limits to the food provided (for instance one can never get potatoes for breakfast in place of toast or Ryvita, etc.), and it is so increasingly expensive, that it pays on every count to take packed meals as suggested in the section dealing with these. The same thing applies to meals when traveling by road. Because breakfast always presents some difficulty when merely staying overnight at some roadside inn or hotel, I have played with the idea of taking a thermos of hot sautéed potatoes to be brought out at this meal, and stocking up with more at the next main meal, but have so far lacked the courage to take this rather startling step. But, surely, if enough people about the country began to ask for fried potatoes with their breakfast instead of toast to follow, something might be done to provide what could be a new fashion in food for the average as well as the trendy. Leftovers from dinner would do, providing the breakfast chef could bring himself to cope with them.

MENACES IN MENUS

French is the language of the menu all over the world, in sophisticated circles. The cult of cheapness rather than quality rely on traditional ingredients today, so it is as well to be on having spread even to French kitchens, however, one cannot one's guard and avoid all doubtful dishes, either at home or abroad. The following lists may be found helpful in knowing at least what to reject out-of-hand.

Containing Gluten

Beignets	Fritters or pancakes
Blanquette	White stew usually based on flour
Bouchée	Meat patties with puff pastry
Canapés, croûtes, croûtons	Fried bread, toast or pastry
Chaudfroid	Sauce served cold
Croquettes/kromeskies	Dipped in breadcrumbs
Escalope	Dipped in breadcrumbs
Financière sauce	Used for entrées
Fricassée	White stew probably containing flour
Hors d'oeuvre	All in sauce or mayonnaise
Minestrone	Macaroni-thickened soup
Meunière	Fish coated with flour before frying
Mousse (savory)	Thickened with flour
Navarin	Contains flour
Panada	Paste of flour or bread
Pâté	Meat paste or pastry
Petits fours	Tiny fancy cookies
Pot-au-feu	Meat soup over French bread
Quenelles	Forcemeat balls containing bread
Ragoût	Stew probably thickened with flour
Rissoles	Fried cakes in flour or pastry
Soufflé	Contains flour

N.B. Since no sauces can be guaranteed free of flour, avoid them all.

May Contain Gluten

Au bleu	Fish in fish stock or wine
A la crème	Should be cream but often flour
Bisque	Rich soup or sauce
Galantine	Pressed cold meat, may have flour or crumbs to eke it out
Macedoine of vegetables	Probably flour in dressing

| Marzipan | Should be almonds, may be potato, might be flour based |
| Praline | Probably burnt flour with almond essence, or burnt almonds |

Should be Gluten-free

Au beurre	Should be just butter
Au naturel	Uncooked, or as simple as possible
Bavarois	Should contain gelatin, but may be flour
Compote	Stewed fruit
Coupe	Water ice served with fruit
Mousse (sweet)	Should be gelatin based
Glacé parfait	Special ice cream
Puree vegetables	Pulped or sieved. Also fruit puree
Sorbet	Water ice
Terrine	Potted meat etc. (pâté or spread)

Abroad

Having gotten abroad, what does one do about breakfast when faced with nothing but the traditional rolls and coffee of so many continental countries outside international hotels?

In Spain and the Canaries, our method has been to get in yogurt which is sold in bars and drugstores as well as dairies and supermarkets, being careful since brucellosis is rife, to buy only the guaranteed-safe make, Danoni, and to combine this with the many kinds of fruits available. Then one is ready to enjoy the chufa nut drink (horchata) and prawns (gambas), which constitute morning snacks for so many Spaniards. If this does not appeal, take your special bread with you and eat it in place of rolls, or stay at some more Anglicized place where you will always get bacon, eggs, French fries and corn-flakes.

Fish in Spain is particularly inviting as well as delicious, for trucks rumble by through the night, bringing it sea-fresh to practically every region and village. It is usually broiled (a la plancha) as you give the order and there are a great many kinds all worth sampling at least, including squid (calamares), fresh sardines (sardinas), herrings (herenque), mackerel (escombro) and haddock (robalo). Furthermore, a freedom from sauces and breadcrumbs applied to them in cooking makes a far wider choice possible than in France where these additions are almost obligatory.

As for meat, the gluten-free eater is always safe with beef, lamb, kid, pork or chicken roasted (asado), broiled (a la plancha) fried (frito) or even stewed (cocido), as potatoes and other vegetables are used for thickening rather than wheat flour, and this also applies to rice dishes such as the famous paella, giblet stews (guiso de andrajos) and kedgerees called "in the mode of Cuba" (a la cubano).

Where eggs are concerned, omelets are always savory and safe, fried eggs (huevos fritos) and scrambled eggs (huevos revueltos) are familiar, but boiled eggs are unknown. A variety unknown to us in other parts of the world are a curious but delectable mixture of fried eggs sitting on mixed anchovies and kidneys. These are called "eggs as they come out" (huevos como salgan) and we have enjoyed them every time they have come out our way.

Except for the ubiquitous caramel cream, a tarted-up custard, puddings do not figure on menus in most continental countries. The far better custom of fruit for dessert is widespread and a wide choice is often to be enjoyed, as are cheeses of various kinds (eaten without crackers or bread on the gluten-free diet, of course), but unfortunately, these are very expensive, especially in Spain. In fact, it would pay to bring with you a good keeping kind if your weakness is cheese.

In Italy the passion for pastas, macaroni, spaghetti, tagliatelle (noodles), etc. and pizza make meals more of a problem and even uncanned minestrone soup is thickened with macaroni. However, there are always omelets with various fillings, chicken, vegetables and fruit in plenty. But meats are generally not up to par and to be avoided when they are prepared in the popular fashion of veal, egged and breadcrumbed. Best perhaps to stay at some British-run pension where catering meets more familiar tastes. However, yogurt is eaten everywhere and cheeses are good and plentiful.

Scandinavian countries, as all the world knows, go in for smorgasbord and open sandwiches of bewilderingly wide range. Since these are always on display for individual selection it is easy to choose the toppings which appeal and are permitted, such as numerous kinds of plain cold meats (but NO sausages), all sorts of fish, especially herrings and shell-fish, eggs and grated vegetable salads, while discarding the bread bases.

Furthermore, all these items can be bought ready prepared without any bread in supermarkets, and chicken, French fries, cornflakes and bacon and eggs are as readily available as any-where in Europe.

SUGGESTED MENUS FOR ONE WEEK IN SPRING, SUMMER, AUTUMN AND WINTER

It should be pointed out that there is, of course, no necessity for such elaborate and varied meals as those suggested in the following menus. They have been set out merely as guidelines for the ambitious, and are chiefly intended to show how far from monotonous a really good gluten-free diet can be if suitably selected. It is hoped they will, therefore, be encour-aging to the many facing the restrictions of a gluten-free diet for the first time. Capitalized dishes may be found in the *Index* to locate the recipe.

SPRING MENUS

	Breakfast	*Midday meal*
SUNDAY	Fresh or soaked dried fruit	Roast chicken
	or Popcorn Muesli	Roast potatoes
	Scrambled eggs	Broccoli
	Sautéed Potatoes	Pashka Pudding
MONDAY	Fresh or soaked dried fruit	Paella
	or Basic Millet	Broad beans
	Oven-friend bacon	Cabbage (outer leaves)
	Oven-Fried Potatoes	Potato Sponge Trifle
TUESDAY	Fresh or soaked dried fruit	Beef Roulades
	or Basic Polenta	Creamed Potatoes
	Baked Eggs in Jacket	Cauliflower
	Potatoes	Lemon Mold
WEDNESDAY	Fresh or soaked dried fruit	Ground Beef Stroganoff
	or Basic Rice	Broiled Jacket Potatoes
	Broiled Kidneys on Polenta	Leeks
	Slices—Fried	Rhubarb Whip
THURSDAY	Fresh or soaked dried fruit	Savory Hearts
	or Basic Millet	Carrots
	Broiled, split herrings	Cabbage
	Sautéed Potatoes (leftovers	Apricot Rice
FRIDAY	Fresh or soaked dried fruit	Chicken Livers and Rice
	or Corn Crisps	Broad beans
	(home-made)	Spinach
	Herring roe on Broiled	Spanish Soufflé
	Potato Slices	
SATURDAY	Fresh or soaked dried fruit	Broiled liver
	or Popcorn Muesli	Creamed Potatoes
	Boiled eggs	Cabbage
	Toasted Potato Fingers	Date and Rice Pudding

N.B. The ideal dessert is FRUIT—fresh, frozen or canned without sugar. The desserts suggested are second-best concessions to human frailty!

SPRING MENUS

	Afternoon tea	*Evening meal*
SUNDAY	Corn and Millet Bread and butter Piquant Spread Potato Sponge Cake	Spinach Soup Beef and Rice Loaf—cold Watercress
MONDAY	Corn and Millet Bread and butter Apple Lemon Curd Rice Sweet Biscuits	Quick Onion Soup Fish Baked in Milk Shredded cabbage salad (heart)
TUESDAY	Cheese Droppies and butter Almond Cones	Split Pea Soup Broiled fish slices Tossed spinach salad
WEDNESDAY	Potato Flatties and butter Liver Spread (or cheese) or Marmite. Lemon Kisses	Carrot Soup Omelet (filling as desired) Broccoli sprigs salad
THURSDAY	Rice Flour Bread and butter Apple Lemon Curd Peanut Butter Fingers	Quick Thick Rice Soup Broiled liver or sweetbreads Emerald Potatoes Spring onions—raw
FRIDAY	Rice Flour Bread toasted and butter Potted Meat Spread (heart leftovers) Coconut Brownies	Leek Soup Beef and Potato Loaf Radishes
SATURDAY	Millet Droppies Potted Meat Spread Fruit Fingers	Pumpkin Soup Fish and Onion Pie Watercress

SUMMER MENUS

	Breakfast	*Midday meal*
SUNDAY	Fresh or soaked dried fruit or Popcorn with milk Poached eggs on Potato and Cheese Pan Roast	Paella French beans Carrots Pashka Pudding (under cakes)
MONDAY	Fresh or dried fruit soaked or Popcorn Muesli Fried bacon with tomato or apple	Beef Chop Suey New Potatoes Baked Peas Queen's Pudding
TUESDAY	Fresh or soaked dried fruit or Basic Polenta Beef sausages with Sautéed Potatoes	Meat Kedgeree (leftovers or fresh) Cabbage Baked Apple Pudding
WEDNESDAY	Fresh or soaked dried fruit or Corn Crisps (home-made) Broiled kidneys with grilled potato slices	Braised stuffed breast of lamb New Potatoes Steamed Peas Ground Rice Custard
THURSDAY	Fresh or soaked dried fruit or Basic Rice Baked Eggs in Jacket Potatoes	Broiled Sweetbreads Creamed Potatoes French beans Fruit Froth
FRIDAY	Fresh or soaked dried fruit or Popcorn Muesli Broiled liver Sautéed Potatoes	Savory Hearts with Tomatoes Sautéed Potatoes Cabbage Queen's Pudding
SATURDAY	Fresh or soaked dried fruit or Corn Crisps (home-made) Scrambled eggs on Corn-meal Fried Slices	Golden Rice and leftovers Carrots Peas Cottage Cheese Whip

SUMMER MENUS

	Afternoon tea	*Evening meal*
SUNDAY	Light Spoonbread and butter Unbaked Fruit Cake	Pea-pod Potage Beef and Potato Loaf (cold) Tossed green salad
MONDAY	Baked Potatoes with Apple Lemon Curd Peanut Fingers	Summer Soup (cold (i)) Curried Fish Shredded cabbage salad
TUESDAY	Light Spoonbread toasted Radishes Unbaked Fruit Cake (leftovers)	Hard-boiled eggs on lettuce Potato Salad Pashka leftovers
WEDNESDAY	Millet Droppies and butter Apple or Ginger Lemon Curd Nut Toughies	Broad Bean Soup Cold Liver and Beef Loaf Cucumber Salad
THURSDAY	Rice Flour Bread and butter Kidney Spread or Marmite Ground Rice Strips	Summer Soup (cold or hot (ii)) Cold breast of lamb Potato Salad with chives
FRIDAY	Potato Flatties Piquant Spread Plain Macaroons	Fish Salad Rice Pancakes
SATURDAY	Rice Flour Bread toasted with butter Honey Almond Cones	Creamed Sweetbreads Radishes Apricot Rice Mold

AUTUMN MENUS

	Breakfast	*Midday meal*
SUNDAY	Fresh or dried soaked fruit or Basic Millet (hot) with milk Boiled eggs Toasted Potato Fingers	Roast beef Roast potatoes Cornmeal Yorkshire Pudding Cabbage Fruit Froth
MONDAY	Fresh or dried soaked fruit or Basic Polenta (hot) with milk Cold boiled bacon Jacket potatoes	Savory Hearts Jacket potatoes Broccoli Apple Crumble
TUESDAY	Fresh or dried soaked fruit or Basic Millet (hot) with milk Poached or fried eggs on Polenta Slices fried	Beef and Rice Loaf Celery cooked in milk Cottage Cheese Whip
WEDNESDAY	Fresh or dried soaked fruit or Basic Rice (hot) with milk Brains and fried bacon or tomatoes	Brain Cakes Creamed Potatoes String beans Apple Amber
THURSDAY	Fresh or dried soaked fruit or Basic Cornmeal (hot) Savory Liver Strips Sautéed Potatoes	Ground Beef with Cabbage Steamed Potatoes Apple and Rice Custard
FRIDAY	Fresh or dried soaked fruit or Popcorn Muesli Broiled herrings Steamed Potatoes	Fish and Onion pie Carrots Cabbage Date and Rice Pudding
SATURDAY	Fresh or dried soaked fruit or Corn Crisps or Popcorn (home-made) Fried bacon Cheese strips or cooking apple fried	Liver Sticks Creamed Potatoes Cabbage (red or white) Baked Apple Pudding

AUTUMN MENUS

	Afternoon tea	*Evening meal*
SUNDAY	Potato Wedges and butter Marmite Cooked Cheese Cake	String Bean Soup Headcheese Leek, Apple and Tomato Salad
MONDAY	Rice Plain Droppies and butter Honey Peanut Fingers	Meat Kedgeree (roast leftovers) Beet, Celery and Apple Salad Orange Pudding
TUESDAY	Irish Potato Scones and butter Shrimp Spread Rice Sweet Biscuits	Tomato Soup Fish Salad Jacket Potatoes
WEDNESDAY	Rice Plain Droppies and butter Apple Lemon Curd Cooked Cheese Cake (leftovers)	Scotch Broth (millet, not barley) Headcheese Onion and cabbage salad
THURSDAY	Cornmeal Quickbread (Johnny cakes) and butter Honey Coconut Pyramids	Ground Meat Sausages (home-made) Sautéed Potatoes Watercress Apple Cream
FRIDAY	Rice and Nut Droppies and butter Ground Rice Strips	Leek Soup Broiled Sweetbreads Emerald Potatoes Tossed green salad
SATURDAY	Cornmeal Quickbread toasted with butter Marmite Coconut Brownies	Split Pea Soup Malay Curried Chicken Livers (no curry powder) Instant Chutney

WINTER MENUS

	Breakfast	*Midday meal*
SUNDAY	Fresh or dried soaked fruit or Basic Polenta (hot) with milk and honey Fried bacon Mushrooms or apple slices	Roast Hearts with Nut Stuffing Emerald Potatoes Leeks Pashka Pudding
MONDAY	Fresh or dried soaked fruit or Basic Rice (hot) with milk and honey Fried eggs and Sautéed Potatoes	Irish stew Cabbage Date and Rice Pudding
TUESDAY	Fresh or dried soaked fruit or Basic Millet Broiled Kidneys Creamed Potatoes	Oriental Beef (or lamb) Broccoli Apple Crumble
WEDNESDAY	Fresh or dried soaked fruit or Basic Rice (hot) with milk and honey Oven-Fried Potatoes and bacon	Malay Curried Chicken Livers (no curry powder) Sprouts Coconut Pudding
THURSDAY	Fresh or dried soaked fruit or Basic Millet (hot) with milk and honey Boiled eggs Toasted Potato Fingers	Baked Stuffed Herrings Carrots Leeks Baked Apple Pudding
FRIDAY	Fresh or dried soaked fruit or Popcorn with milk and honey Smelts Creamed Potatoes	Kidney in Apple Juice Emerald Potatoes Sprouts Pumpkin or Orange Pudding
SATURDAY	Fresh or dried soaked fruit or Basic Rice (hot) with milk and honey Savory Liver Strips Sauté with potatoes (or scrambled eggs)	Beef and Potato Loaf Cabbage Chestnut Cream

WINTER MENUS

	Afternoon tea	Evening meal
SUNDAY	Corn and Millet Bread and butter Liver Spread Large Potato Cake	Soya Soup Meat-stuffed Apples Mustard and cress
MONDAY	Cheese Droppies Fruit Fingers	Pumpkin or Potato Soup Headcheese Onion and shredded cabbage salad
TUESDAY	Corn and Millet Bread toasted with butter Marmite Large Potato Cake (leftovers)	Split Pea Soup Fish Salad
WEDNESDAY	Rice Flour Bread and butter Apple Lemon Curd Ground Rice Strips	Parsnip Soup Potato Puffs (with meat) Winter Lettuce and Sprout Salad
THURSDAY	Rice Flour Bread toasted with butter Honey Milk Cheese Cakes	Mixed Vegetable Soup Stuffed Onions Watercress
FRIDAY	Potato Droppies and butter Piquant Spread Rice Sweet Biscuits	Scotch Broth (millet, not barley) Hard-boiled eggs with lettuce Beet and celery salad
SATURDAY	Millet Droppies and butter Apple Lemon Curd Plain Macaroons	Beef Chop Suey Watercress Cottage cheese and Apple Cream

Minimum trouble menus

There will be many facing the restrictions of a gluten-free diet for the first time either for themselves or for someone for whom they cook and/or cater, who will feel daunted at the apparent difficulty of the task. This is very natural if they think they must at once attack all the unfamiliar foods and elaborate recipes included here. But there is no necessity for this at all. This small book has been designed to be a comprehensive guide to eating, inexpensively if possible, while under the rules governing a gluten-free diet, and it is also intended for those who may be bored with the limited diet they have followed so far. It is hoped that these people will welcome the great diversity of recipes suggested for better eating nutritionally.

As for those in furnished rooms, boarding houses, hotels, studio apartments, shared apartments and so on, their needs are rather different, and the following are some suggestions for meeting their especial difficulties.

N.B. It is of course important to discuss the situation with the landlord, owner, principal of establishment, or apartment mates involved. These will usually be found willing to cooperate as far as they are able, providing too many demands for a difference are not made, and if it is clearly understood by all that the necessity is medical and essential for health, and not mere food crankiness. Here a letter from your doctor should be obtained to verify your claim.

Now for the practical details of meals, and how they can be altered and adapted.

Breakfasts

1. Point out to whoever it may concern that as you are forbidden to eat rolls or toast, and consequently you will also eat no butter or marmalade, you hope it may be possible to provide in their place plenty of potato (leftovers will do) for you to eat with the eggs, bacon or whatever—and you might even get tomatoes and apples when these are in season.

2. If you are already a muesli eater, as are so many of the trendy young today, make this for yourself with popcorn or rice flakes (from health food stores) instead of the usual wheat, oats, barley, rye or buckwheat.
3. Invest in a sink strainer and a large plastic bowl with lid to sprout whole millet to make a muesli. This is much cheaper than buying ready-made mixes which in any case are not for you as they all contain the forbidden grains.
4. Buy brewer's (nutritional) yeast, and take 1–4 teaspoons in water or milk with your breakfast, to push up your protein intake and make a good start to the day with no labor.

Morning break
Drink milk if possible instead of tea or coffee. (N.B. Instant coffee except Nestle's is *out* as it contains white flour, and all coffee served today may be taken as instant.)

Bag lunches
If you are accustomed to taking sandwiches, things are more difficult, it must be admitted. You will have to rely on nuts, hard-boiled eggs and cold meats, with celery, raw carrots, cold potatoes, tomatoes, cold rice, sweet peppers, watercress, mustard and cress, radishes, cucumber, lettuce, etc., for your main course, and such portable sweet things as fruit, figs, dates, raisins, dried bananas, etc., for dessert.

On the other hand, if you are living at home or have access to a kitchen, the outlook widens. You can buy a wide-mouthed thermos and fill it at breakfast time with leftover boiling home-made soups, savory stews, rice dishes, jacket potatoes (with butter to spread on them in a small container), any curried dish, and so on. Have an opaque closed container for any salad green leaves in season to eat with these, or take fresh fruit in season if preferred.

Afternoon break
The same as in the morning. Or pack bite-sized pieces of cheese with an apple or two and put in your handbag or pocket.

Evening meal

If this depends on someone else in the kitchen, try to arrange for large helpings of potatoes or Basic Rice (which is not too expensive, and easy to cook) to take the place of the usual pastries, bread, cakes and biscuits, for yourself, and spend a little extra on bringing home celery, radishes, etc., and all the nuts and fresh fruit in season you can afford, to vary the monotony and improve the balance of the meal. You might be able to get a reduction in what you pay weekly if you provide these for yourself. In any case you will find it money well spent.

Bed-time drinks

If you have been used to making cocoa, Ovaltine or malted milk (all of them forbidden) to speed you to bed, turn over to "Donkey's Chocolate" (see *Index*), which is very similar and which many of us prefer.

If you have an electric hot plate in your room

A splendid investment is a griddle—a sort of heavy rimless frying pan.

On this you can make a wide range of "droppies" (see *Index*), i.e. biscuits-cum-scones to be eaten either hot or cold with butter, etc. These can also be cooled and packed to replace bread and biscuits when you are away from home, anywhere.

Just a reminder

Although these things are a nuisance to do, the reward in renewed health and vigor is boundless, and will be an inspiration not only to yourself but to those about you, who will quite rightly admire your determination and applaud your results.

So go to it, and good luck to you whoever you are, and wherever you may be. You will get no medal, be sure, but you will have earned one.

9

Recipes: Biscuits, Breads, Breakfasts, Cakes, Candies, Cookies, Desserts, Drinks, Fish, Meats, Miscellaneous Salads, Sauces, Soups, Spreads, Vegetable and Fruit Cookery, Vegetarian Dishes

BISCUITS

Cheese Droppies

1 egg white	2 tbs. cornmeal or rice flour
2 tbs. milk	2 tbs. cheese, grated
	pinch of salt

Beat the egg white to a peak. Add the milk, flour, salt, cheese and beat till a smooth cream, adding a little milk if necessary to thin the mixture. Drop by teaspoonfuls on to hot griddle. Turn with spatula when golden brown. Eat hot or cold with butter.

Southern Corn (maize) Muffins

1 cup boiling water	1 tbs. butter
1 cup yellow cornmeal	1 egg, well beaten
½ cup milk	1 tsp. dried yeast
½ tsp. salt	½ tsp. raw sugar, molasses or honey

Pour boiling water over cornmeal. Beat in milk, salt, butter and egg. Finally, add yeast, previously frothed in a little warm water, with molasses or honey. Pour into well-oiled glass muffin cups. Bake 20–30 minutes at 475° F. Serve hot, Makes 9 muffins.

Millet Droppies

½ cup millet (whole)   water to cover
1 egg white   pinch of salt

Soak washed millet overnight in water. In morning drain off
liquid and set aside. Blend millet in blender. Whip egg white
with 1 tbs. of liquid set aside. Add pinch of salt. Stir in millet
to make a thin batter. Drop by teaspoonfuls on heated oiled
pan or hot dry griddle. Brown well on both sides. Eat hot with
butter and Marmite or honey.

Millet and Cheese Droppies

1 cup cracked millet   1 cup cheese, grated
1 tbs. soya flour   1 egg, beaten
3 cups stock or salted water

Blend millet and soya flour with ½ cup of liquid. Heat rest of
liquid. When boiling pour over mixture, add cheese and stir
till smooth. Cook covered, over gentle heat, in basin in pan of
hot water (or top of double boiler) till all liquid is absorbed.
Remove and cool. Beat in egg and drop spoonfuls on oiled
baking tin. Broil till brown. Turn and broil other side. Eat hot
with butter.

Rice and Nut Droppies

1 egg   6 tbs. peanuts, finely chopped
2 cups Basic Rice (uncooked) a little oil

Beat the egg lightly, combine with nuts and rice. Drop by tablespoonfuls on to hot griddle or oiled frying pan. Turn with
a spatula to brown on both sides. Eat hot with butter or any
spread as desired.

Potato Flatties

3 cups leftover mashed potato
  pinch of salt
1 egg, beaten

pinch of mixed herbs (op-
  tional)
rice flour to stiffen

Mix all ingredients well together. Shape into flat cakes about
½ in. thick. Place on hot griddle brushed with oil. Turn to
brown on other side. Eat hot with butter or cottage cheese
and chopped chives.

Potato Droppies

2 cups potatoes (raw and
  grated)
¼ cup hot milk

½ tsp. salt
2 eggs, separated

Blend potatoes, hot milk and salt. Cool to lukewarm. Add
beaten egg yolks. Mix well. Fold in stiffly beaten egg whites.
(1) Pour spoonfuls on to heated griddle or oiled pan over
moderate heat. Turn to brown other side. *Or* (2) Pour on to
heated oiled baking-dish and bake in oven at 400° F. for about
15 minutes. Serve in wedges (4–6) with (a) ¼ cup honey, ¾
cup unsweetened fruit juice, 4 tablespoons oil mixed in
blender; or (b) 1 cup molasses, 2 tablespoons oil, juice of 2
lemons—heat molasses and blend with the rest. Serve hot.

Potato Savory Droppies

1 lb. (3 medium) old raw potatoes, grated coarsely
1 lemon, juiced and strained

1 tbs. raw onion, grated
1 egg

Grate potatoes, squeeze out moisture between towelling and
cover with strained juice of lemon. Medium grate enough onion to fill one heaped tablespoon. Wring out in towelling and
put into small bowl. Break egg into this and beat together.
Heat griddle or heavy frying pan over low heat till it sizzles

when brushed with oil. Squeeze potatoes dry again and beat
into bowl contents. Drop by tablespoonfuls, wide apart on
griddle, and spread out very thin into neat rounds. When the
undersides are well brown, turn with spatula and cook to
same rich brown on other side. Serve hot dabbed with Marmite and/or butter.

Irish Potato Scones

2 cups potatoes, mashed   1 egg, beaten
   little melted butter or oil   rice flour

Bake or steam potatoes in jackets. When cooked remove skins,
mash and measure 1 lb. Add egg and oil. Mix in enough rice
flour to stiffen. Roll out and cut in rounds. Bake on hot
griddle or in oven till golden. Serve hot with butter and a savory spread.

Potato Wedges

1 egg white   2 cups potatoes, mashed
1 tbs. milk   4 tbs. rice flour
1 tsp. oil   salt (optional)

Beat egg, milk and oil, and stir in potato and rice flour, taste
for seasonings and add salt, if desired. Work in hands to make
a pliable dough, adding more rice flour if needed. Divide into
three. Flour board with rice flour and roll out dough into
large round. Cut into four quarters. Roll out and cut other
pieces in same way. Heat griddle, testing by dusting with rice
flour, which should then brown almost at once when ready.
Brush it off and lay four wedges on griddle. Cook several
minutes on both sides till dappled with brown. Cook rest of
wedges similarly, keeping rest cool and supple between folds
of clean dish towel. Serve while still warm to eat with butter.
Can be frozen and thawed quickly.

Rice Plain Droppies (1)

¾ cup rice flour
  good pinch of salt
1 egg

⅔ cup water
1 tbs. oil

Put flour and salt in largish bowl. Make a well in the center and drop in the egg. Add a little water and stir, drawing in the flour from the sides. When you have a thick cream, add the oil and beat. Then stir in more water, enough to make a thin cream. Set aside in the fridge for an hour or so. Heat griddle and sprinkle on it a little rice flour. When this colors slightly the griddle is ready. Pour teaspoonfuls of the batter on it, leaving room for each to make a separate round about the size of the top of a sherry glass. Turn with spatula when brown, and turn down heat to let biscuits dry thoroughly and brown on the other side. Eat hot with butter and/or honey.

Rice Plain Droppies (2)

4 tbs. rice flour
  pinch of salt
2 tsp. oil

Lukewarm water enough to mix (about 2 tbs.)
1 egg white

Mix rice flour, salt and oil with water to make thick batter consistency. Beat egg white stiffly and fold in. Set aside for 2 hours at least. Drop by teaspoonfuls on hot griddle or heavy frying pan, oiled. Turn with spatula when underside is brown, to brown other side. Eat hot with butter and Marmite.

BREADS

Corn and Millet Bread

½ cup cornmeal
½ cup millet flour
1 cup carrot, grated
1 tsp. raw sugar

¼ tsp. salt
¾ cup boiling water
2 eggs, separated
2 tsp. cold water

Mix well first five ingredients and add boiling water. Mix again. Beat egg yolks, adding 2 tsp. cold water, and add to mixture. Fold in egg whites beaten to a peak. Bake in oiled loaf pan at 400° F. for 30 minutes.

Light Corn Spoonbread

1 cup cornmeal
3 cups cold milk
3 egg yolks, beaten
1½ tsp. salt

1 tbs. honey
2 tbs. oil
3 tbs. soya flour
3 egg whites, beaten until stiff

Blend cornmeal and 1 cup of the milk in a pan. Add the rest of the milk and heat gently to boiling. Remove from the fire and let cool to lukewarm. Blend in all the rest of the ingredients except the egg whites. When thoroughly mixed, fold in the beaten egg whites. Turn into a greased square pan. Bake at 400° F. for 45–50 minutes. When cooled a little, cut into squares.

Cornmeal Blender Bread

2 cups buttermilk
4 eggs
2 tbs. oil
¼ cup brewer's yeast

1 tsp. salt
¼ cup soya flour
¼ cup milk powder
2 cups cornmeal

Gradually blend all ingredients in blender until batter is smooth. pour mixture into two oiled bread pans. Bake at 400° F. for 30 minutes.

Cornmeal Quick Breads
(Mrs. Johnny's Johnny Cakes, enriched)

2 cups cornmeal
1 tbs. soya flour
½ tsp. salt

3 cups water
2 tbs. powdered milk
1 tbs. oil

Make a thick mixture of cornmeal, soya flour, salt and ½ cup of water. Stir in powdered milk. Place rest of water in top of double boiler over direct heat and bring to boil. Add oil and cornmeal mixture. Continue cooking, stirring till smooth. Replace cover. Place over bottom of double boiler to which hot water has been added. Cook gently about 12 minutes. Remove, cool, and shape into flat cakes. Arrange on oiled baking pan. Bake in hot oven at 450° F. about 25 minutes until brown on both sides.

Rice and Soya Flour Bread (two loaves)

1 lb. (two cups) brown rice	1 tsp. molasses
¾ cup soybeans	3 cups warm water
2 tbs. sunflower seed oil	1-2 tsp. dried yeast

Grind rice and soybeans finely, place in a large bowl. Stir in oil. Dissolve molasses in 1¼ cups warm water in small bowl. Sprinkle yeast on surface. Leave till frothed over. Add contents to large bowl. Mix well with wooden spoon adding 1¾ cups warm water to make thick batter. Pour into two 2 lb. bread pans. Cover and leave at average room temperature till loaves almost reach the tops of the pans. Bake for 30–35 minutes at 400° F. Turn out on rack to cool. Do not eat till 12 hours old. Cut carefully with very sharp knife. Putting in a warm place to rise often results in the collapse of the middle when put in the oven.

Breadless Open and Closed Sandwiches

1. Meat Eaters
Thin slices of Meat or Liver Loaf or Headcheese spread with chopped cucumber, bound with mayonnaise or spread with peanut butter and slices of cucumber or finely chopped celery, chives, parsley, etc.

2. Vegetarians
Use thin slices of Peanut and Potato Loaf as above.

3. Anyone
(a) Use lettuce leaves in place of bread.

(b) Use thin slices of large, hard apples in place of bread.

(c) Thin slivers of Peanut and Potato Loaf spread with finely chopped parsley, blended with cottage cheese, or chopped chives or parsley with mayonnaise or any desired mixture, or savory spread.

BREAKFASTS

Baked Eggs in Potatoes

4 large potatoes, scrubbed   4 eggs
½ tbs. butter or oil   ½ tsp. salt

Steam the potatoes unpeeled until tender on piercing. Set aside. Place in oiled pan in oven to heat through. Take them out of the oven and make a cut across the center of each, enlarge into a hollow and break 1 egg into each potato. Sprinkle with salt and a dab of butter or oil and return to the oven until egg whites have set firm.

Corn Crisps (unsweetened)

⅞ cup cornmeal   2½ tbs. oil
1 cup cold water   ¼ tsp. salt

Blend the cornmeal and water in a pan until smooth. Bring gradually to a boil. Remove from heat, blend in oil and salt and pour mixture into a large shallow oiled pan, depth of ¼ in. only. Bake at 325° F. for 25–30 minutes. Cool slightly and cut into small sections. Eat as cereal with milk and raw sugar or honey.

Basic Polenta

1 cup cornmeal   1 tsp. salt
3 cups water, milk or soya milk

Blend cornmeal and 1 cup of liquid into smooth paste. Heat rest of liquid and salt in top of double boiler over direct heat. When it boils add paste and stir till quite smooth. Place over bottom of double boiler containing boiling water and cover. Cook gently till all the liquid is absorbed. Serve as porridge.

Polenta (enriched)

1 cup cornmeal
½ cup powdered milk
1 tsp. salt

1 cup water, milk or soya milk
2 cups simmering water or milk or soya milk

Mix cornmeal, powdered milk and salt with 1 cup cold liquid. Stir all the time while adding this mixture to 2 cups of simmering liquid in a pan. Stir about 5 minutes or till it thickens, lower heat and continue cooking about 15 minutes or till all liquid is absorbed. Serve hot with top milk and honey or raw sugar.

Cornmeal Fried Slices

1 cup cornmeal
1 tsp. salt
1 tbs. powdered milk
1 cup cold water

3 cups boiling water
a little powdered milk for coating

Mix a paste with the cornmeal, salt, powdered milk and cold water. Have water boiling in pan, stir in paste and cook for 15 minutes. Rinse out a 2 lb. loaf pan with cold water and pour batter into the pan. Cool thoroughly and refrigerate overnight. Turn out and cut in ½-inch slices, dip in powdered milk to coat, fry in oil or bacon fat until brown, turn and brown other side. Serve instead of fried bread with bacon.

Polenta Slices (leftovers)

Slice leftovers when cold into ¼-½-in. thickness. Brush with oil and fry in pan or cook on hot griddle until brown. Turn to brown other side. Use instead of toast under scrambled or poached eggs or instead of fried bread with bacon.

Basic Millet

4 cups water   2 tbs. oil (optional)
1 cup raw millet   1 tsp. salt

Bring water to boil. Add millet, oil and salt, gradually, so as not to stop boiling. Cover and simmer 20–30 minutes or until millet is tender. If cooked the night before, cover with a little water to prevent crust forming. Pour off before re-heating for breakfast or whatever. Eat with honey or raw sugar and milk, hot or cold. Sliced leftovers can be fried to eat with bacon and egg as with polenta.

Popcorn

½ cup popcorn   2 tbs. oil

Use large pan with tight lid. Keep heat high. Toss or stir popcorn in oil till all grains are coated. Cover. As soon as popping starts, turn heat as low as possible. *Do not* shake or lift lid to look. This can be dangerous as they fly about fiercely.

Makes a breakfast dish topped with top milk and a dash of raw sugar or honey, instead of cornflakes or rice crispies which are over-processed and over-sweet. If the popped corn is put in the blender at the lowest speed for a few seconds, it makes another delicious cereal, such as Muesli.

Popcorn Muesli

2 tbs. popcorn ground in   1 tbs. grated or chopped hazel
   blender   nuts or pecans
1 tbs. raisins   juice of ½ lemon
1 apple, grated

Mix all ingredients except lemon juice in bowl. Pour lemon juice over. Eat with dash of honey and milk to taste.

Toasted Potato Fingers
(in place of bread toast)

Wash and scrub a large, old, waxy potato. Steam till nearly tender. Drain well. Peel and leave till cold. Cut in bread-thick slices and pat dry between towelling. Toast under broiler or on wire rack over burner. Cut into fingers to be eaten with boiled eggs or anything customary with bread toast.

Basic Rice

2-3 cups cold water
1 cup brown rice

1 tsp. salt

Bring 2 cups of water to boiling point. Drop rice in slowly so that boiling does not stop. Add salt. Cover and lower heat and cook until tender, about 20–30 minutes. All the water should be absorbed. Serve hot or cold with milk and honey or use in recipes as directed.

CAKES

Cooked Cheese Cake

1 cup cottage cheese, firmly packed
½ tbs. rice ground in blender or mill
2 tbs. honey

pinch salt
2 eggs, separated
1 tsp. orange rind, grated
1 tbs. raisins
cinnamon

Mix together cheese, rice, honey, salt, egg yolks and orange rind. Beat well and add raisins. Whip whites stiffly and fold in. Pour into oiled deep cake pan, filling not more than half full. Bake in moderate oven 350° F. about 35 minutes or until firm. Turn out on to serving dish and sprinkle with cinnamon.

Milk Cheese Cakes

2 tbs. rice ground in blender or mill
2 tbs. raw sugar
½ lb. milk cheese
pinch salt

grated rind of one orange
2 eggs, separated
1½ tbs. raisins
1 tsp. sugar
1 tsp. cinnamon for sprinkling

Mix well first five ingredients. Add egg yolks and beat thoroughly. Fold in 1 egg white and add the raisins. Put into oiled patty pans, filling only halfway. Bake at 350° F. for 30–40 minutes, or until firm. Turn out carefully and sprinkle with sugar and cinnamon mixed.

Large Potato Cake

2 cups potato flour
½ lb. (2 sticks) butter or soft margarine beaten to cream

1 egg or 2 egg whites
10 drops lemon essence
1 cup raw sugar

Mix ingredients and beat thoroughly for 10 minutes. Pour into oiled pan and bake at 400° F. for 15 minutes.

Rice and Corn Cake (plain)

½ scant cup rice ground in blender or mill
½ cup cornmeal
1 stick butter or soft margarine
⅓ cup raw sugar

grated rind of ¼ lemon or
½ tsp. almond essence
2 eggs, beaten
milk to make batter

Put rice and cornmeal into a bowl. Beat butter, sugar and rind in another bowl to a cream. Add beaten eggs and then cornmeal and rice to cake batter consistency, using a little milk if necessary. Turn into oiled loaf pan and bake in moderate oven 1–1½ hours at 350° F. Turn out onto wire rack.

Sponge Cake

4 eggs, separated	⅛ tsp. salt
1 cup honey	1 scant cup potato flour
1 tbs. lemon juice	

Beat egg yolks until thick. Blend in honey, lemon juice and salt. Alternately fold in potato flour and stiffly beaten egg whites. Turn into oiled 9-inch pan. Bake at 375° F. for about 20 minutes, then raise heat to 400° F. and continue baking 15 to 20 minutes longer.

Unbaked Fruit Cake

1 cup seedless raisins, chopped	1 cup chopped, pitted dates
1 cup coconut, grated	½ cup chopped, dried bananas
2 tbs. lemon juice	enough non-instant powdered
grated rind of ½ lemon	milk to absorb moisture
1 cup nuts, chopped	

Mix thoroughly all ingredients except powdered milk. Add the powdered milk as required. Press mixture into lightly oiled loaf pan. Chill. Turn out on plate and slice very thinly with sharp knife dipped in hot water.

CANDY

Go slow on dried fruits eaten alone, and use toothbrush afterwards. About 75 percent of the weight is natural sugar, which clings to the teeth and can cause tooth decay, though not as *fast* as *white sugar* in sweets.

When making home-made candy aim at a maximum of nutrition by using ingredients such as powdered milk, honey, nuts of all kinds and especially soya "nuts" (see recipe).

Children can make most of those given here for themselves.

N.B. All candy is better given immediately after, or with, a meal. Otherwise it should be eaten with a drink to follow.

Molasses Toffee

¼ cup raw sugar
2 tbs. lemon juice

2½ cups molasses
2 tbs. butter

Put sugar in pan, pour on lemon juice and when dissolved add molasses and boil up to 247° F. Remove, add butter and boil to 290° F. Pour into an oiled shallow pan. Mark out in squares and when quite firm, turn out in sections and store in a covered container.

Brown Nougat

1⅔ cups blanched almonds or peanuts, chopped fine
1½ cups sieved and rolled raw sugar

1 tbs. lemon juice
1 tsp. oil

Dry the nuts in a slow oven without browning. Place sugar in heavy pan with lemon juice and stir with wooden spoon over slow heat until sugar dissolves, then stir briskly and bring to boil, up to 240° F. Stir in nuts and pour the mixture into an oiled shallow pan. Press down well with spatula or knife and mark in small sections. When cold, separate sections and store in a covered container.

Soya Nut Toffee

2 cups raw sugar
1 cup soya grits

2 tbs. peanuts, chopped

Heat sugar gradually in heavy pan. Stir constantly until it melts and looks golden. Stir in grits and peanuts and pour into shallow oiled pan in thin layer. Leave to cool. When cold break into small pieces with light hammer, over a clean cloth.

Walnut Wonders

¾ cup raisins
¾ cup pitted dates
¾ cup pitted prunes

2 tbs. soya flour
   (commercial, i.e. pre-cooked)
6 walnuts

Mince raisins, dates and prunes. Make into stiff mixture by stirring in soya flour and adding more if necessary. Roll into small balls and set on plate to dry, or flatten down in oiled pan and cut in squares. Press 1 piece of walnut on each.

Modelling Fondant (inexpensive)

1 medium potato
1 tsp. almond essence
2 tbs. butter

1 cup raw sugar, sieved and
   rolled
½ cup powdered milk and more
   as required

Peel, cut in quarters, steam, then sieve potato to make ¼ cup mashed potato. While warm add almond essence and butter and stir well. Sift together sugar and powdered milk and add. Chill. Then knead in enough powdered milk to handle well. Shape into miniature fruits and vegetables. Color with cinnamon or carob flour for bananas and potatoes, and beet juice for apples, tomatoes and strawberries, etc.

Fondant Nuts

½ cup finely sieved hot mashed
   potato
2 tbs. butter
1 cup raw sugar, sieved

½ cup powdered milk and more
   as required
1 tsp. lemon juice
   nuts—filbert, peanut or roasted soya nuts

Before potato cools, stir in butter. Sift sugar and milk together, and add with lemon juice. Mix thoroughly. Chill. When chilled, add enough powdered milk to make smooth pliable paste, roll into small balls. Add 1 filbert, 4 roast soya nuts or 1 peanut to each. Chill again before eating.

Fruities

½ cup fresh broken walnuts, hazelnuts or peanuts

½ cup pitted dates, raisins or dried figs; chop nuts and fruit fine and measure afterward

1 grated apple
1 tbs. orange or lemon juice
¼-½ cup powdered milk

Put all ingredients in bowl and mix thoroughly to a firm dry paste, adding a little more powdered milk if too moist, or using less if too dry. Press down firmly on small sheet of parchment paper to ½ in. thickness. Cover with another piece of parchment paper and press together. Chill. Cut in small fingers about 2 in. by ½ in. Keep in closed container. Do not keep more than a few days as they dry out quickly because of the milk powder.

Nut Crunch Fingers

1 cup peanuts (or soya nuts, walnuts, pecans or hazelnuts) lightly roasted and broken in pieces by covering with a clean cloth and tapping gently with a small hammer.

1 tbs. lemon juice
2 tbs. honey
commercial soya flour to thicken

Mix the broken nuts, lemon juice and honey well in a bowl. Stir in enough soya flour to make a thick paste. Press into a flat dish brushed with oil. Leave a few days to harden. Chill, then cut in fingers.

Nut Toffee

2 cups nuts, chopped
2 cups raw sugar

2 tbs. butter

Toast nuts lightly, then spread them over an oiled pan. Melt butter in heavy pan. Add sugar, stir over moderate heat till sugar is melted. Pour at once over nuts. Cool. Break up with light hammer.

Peanut Butter Balls (uncooked)

½ cup peanut butter (unhydrogenated)
½ cup honey
¾ cup milk powder
½ cup rice flakes

¼ cup soya beans, roasted and made into "grits"
1 tbs. Home-Made Citrus Peel, chopped finely or pulverized

Mix all together. Shape into balls. Roll in shredded coconut. ground-up nuts, or sesame seeds.

Peanut Butter Fudge (uncooked)

½ cup peanut butter (unhydrogenated)
½ cup honey

about 1 cup dried milk powder

Combine first two ingredients. Stir in powdered milk and mix well to make stiff paste. Turn on to oiled parchment paper. Press down to ½ in. thickness. Cut into cubes, or roll into finger thickness. Chill and cut in chunks. Or stuff into pitted prunes or dates. Or press between halves of dried apricots, peaches or walnuts. Or roll into balls and dust with coconut meal, or milled nuts. Flavor with lemon or vanilla or cinnamon as liked.

Honey Toffee

1 tbs. oil
1 lb. honey

a little lemon juice

Pour oil into the pan and shake to cover the surface. Put in the honey and lemon juice and cook, stirring constantly until a soft ball forms when ½ tsp. is dropped into a cup of cold water. Pour into a well-oiled pan and leave to set hard, then break into pieces using a light hammer.

COOKIES

Coconut Drops

1¾ cup dried coconut   1 egg, well beaten
½ cup raw sugar

Mix coconut and sugar thoroughly and add beaten egg. Beat
with a fork until mixture sticks well together. Drop by tablespoonfuls on oiled baking sheet and bake in moderate oven
350° F. until golden brown and firm.

Coconut Pyramids

1 fresh coconut   1 cup raw sugar
2 tbs. rice ground in blender or   1 white of egg, beaten
   mill   ½ tsp. oil to brush pan
   pinch of salt

Grate coconut finely. Mix with ground rice, salt and sugar.
Add enough whipped egg white to make a very stiff paste.
Drop in spoonfuls on oiled baking sheet and bake 15 minutes
in moderate oven at 350° F. or until golden brown.

Lemon Kisses

1 stick (4 oz.) butter   2 tbs. rice ground in blender or
½ cup raw sugar   mill
3 eggs   3 tbs. arrowroot
   few drops lemon juice   lemon curd (pumpkin or
   rind of ½ lemon, grated   apple)
                                           N.B. Occasional use only; ar-
                                           rowroot is not recommended.

Beat butter and sugar to soft cream. Whisk eggs for five
minutes. Add to mixture and beat until smooth. Add lemon
juice and rind. Stir in rice and arrowroot. Put spoonfuls of
mixture into oiled shallow patty pans and bake in moderate
oven, 350° F. for about 10 minutes. Press together in pairs
with pumpkin or apple lemon curd or butter when cold.

Apple Macaroons

2 egg whites
⅓ cup raw sugar
⅔ cup ground almonds
2 tsp. rice ground in blender or
  mill

few drops almond essence
(optional)
little cooked apple flavored
with a grating of lemon rind

Beat the egg whites until quite stiff, gently stir in the sugar, ground almonds and ground rice. A little almond flavoring can be added. Put a spoonful on to a small round of parchment paper after a teaspoonful of cooked sweetened apple. Bake in a hot oven, 425° F. for 10–15 minutes.

Plain Macaroons

½ cup ground almonds
4 tbs. rice ground in blender or
  mill

½ cup raw sugar
3 egg whites, lightly beaten

Mix almonds and rice with sugar and fold in egg whites. Shape into balls about 1½ in. across. Place on parchment paper on baking sheet and bake in slow oven at 300° F. for 10-15 minutes.

Merry Macaroons

2 eggs
½ cup raw sugar
1 cup rice flour
1 tsp. butter
  pinch of salt

1 tsp. vanilla (or almond)
essence
nearly 3 cups shredded
coconut

Beat eggs till they foam. Add sugar slowly and beat about 5 minutes till thickened. Add rice flour and salt slowly, then beat in butter, flavoring and coconut. Drop teaspoonfuls on to baking sheet. Bake in pre-heated oven, 325° F. for about 15 minutes or till brown round the edges. Cool lightly before removing.

Special occasions. Garnish when cool with dab of lemon curd or shelled and skinned peanuts.

Special Macaroons

½ cup raw sugar
½ cup blanched and ground almonds

2 egg whites
1 tbs. lemon juice
few whole almonds, blanched

Mix sugar and almonds. Beat egg whites to stiff peak. Stir into almond mixture. Add lemon juice. Drop in small portions on parchment paper on baking sheet and bake in slow oven, 325° F. for about 20 minutes. When nearly done, put half an almond on each center.

Corn Cakes

½ cup cornmeal
3 tbs. raw sugar
½ tsp. grated orange rind
1 egg, well beaten

2 tbs. cold water (approx.)
3 tbs. oil
⅛ tsp. cinnamon
powdered sugar

Blend all ingredients except cinnamon-sugar and oil. The mixture should be very light, but not runny—almost like a thick cake batter. Heat oil in a large, heavy frying pan. Drop mixture in pan by spoonfuls when oil is medium hot. Spread mixture lightly and cook till brown on both sides. Drain and dust immediately with a mixture of powdered sugar and cinnamon.

Almond Cones

4 tbs. butter or soft margarine
¼ cup raw sugar
½ cup ground almonds

3 tbs. rice ground in blender or mill
pinch of salt
1 egg

Beat butter to a cream. Add sugar, almonds, ground rice and salt. Mix well with beaten egg to form stiff paste. Place in small cones on oiled pan to bake in moderate oven at 350° F. for about 20 minutes.

Fruit Fingers (uncooked)

½ cup raisins
½ cup shredded fresh coconut
½ cup shelled peanuts
½ cup pitted dates
½ cup chopped raw apple

1 banana
dried milk powder as required
few drops of lemon juice

Put all ingredients except the milk powder through the meat grinder or blender and turn into bowl. Stir in enough dried milk powder to make a dryish mixture and mix thoroughly. Taste and add a few drops of lemon juice, if too sweet. Lay a piece of parchment paper on a flat dish and spread the mixture over it with a spatula smoothly. Cover with an equal-sized piece of parchment paper and press down well. Chill. Cut into fingers with a sharp knife or roll into walnut-sized balls.

Peanut Fingers (uncooked)

½ cup peanut butter (unhydrogenated)
½ cup honey
½ cup lightly roasted peanuts, ground

1 tsp. brewer's yeast
1-1½ cups powdered milk
½ cup raisins
2 tbs. soya flour

Blend all ingredients in bowl till consistency of pastry dough. Pat into strip about 1½ inches wide and ½ inch deep on parchment paper. Press down well. Chill and cut into fingers.

Peanut Butter Fingers (uncooked)

½ cup peanut butter
1 cup powdered milk
½ cup seedless raisins
½ lemon rind, grated

½ cup ground toasted peanuts or hazelnuts
1 tbs. soya flour
pinch of salt

Mix all together well. Spread on board and knead to a stiff dough, adding a little more soya flour if too moist. Pat out on parchment paper. Chill. Cut into fingers.

Rice Feathery Cakes

¾ cup rice flour   ¼ cup raw sugar, sieved
  pinch of salt   2 eggs
6 tbs. (¾ stick) butter   grated lemon rind

Mix rice flour and salt, and sift. Beat butter and sugar to soft
cream, stir in rice flour till well blended. Beat eggs thoroughly, grate in a little lemon rind and add, beating well, to
mixture. Three-quarters fill patty pans, sprinkle with a little
sugar on top, and bake about 10 minutes in moderate oven,
350°–400° F.

Ground Rice Strips

1¼ sticks butter or soft marga-   1 scant cup rice ground in
  rine   blender or mill
½ cup raw sugar   grated rind and juice of 1
1 dessertspoon molasses   lemon

Melt butter, sugar and molasses in pan over low heat, stirring
all the time. When melted, add ground rice, lemon rind and
juice and mix well. Spread over shallow oiled baking sheet
and bake at 400° F. for 25 minutes. Cut in strips while hot
but do not remove till cold as they break easily.

Rice Cookies

¼ lb. (1 stick) butter   ½ cup raw sugar
1½ cup rice flour   1 egg

Beat butter to cream, stir in rice flour and sugar, beat egg
thoroughly and moisten mixture with it to stiff paste. Roll out,
cut into small rounds and bake in a very slow oven at 225° F.
for 12–18 minutes. Makes about 18 cookies.

DESSERTS AND PUDDINGS

Apple Amber

1 lb (3 or 4 medium) apples	1 tsp. lemon rind, grated
½ cup raw sugar	2 eggs, separated
2 tbs. butter or soft margarine	⅝ cup milk

Core and cut up apples. Add ¼ cup sugar, butter and lemon rind. Cook in minimum of water till soft. Beat smooth with fork. Add beaten egg yolks and milk and mix well. Turn into oiled dish and bake in moderate oven, 325° F., until set firm—about 20 minutes. Remove and cool. Beat egg whites with ¼ cup sugar stirred in lightly till stiff. Pile on pudding and return to oven to set meringue at very moderate heat till pale gold only.

Serve hot or cold with cream or yogurt.

Apple Cream

¾ cup apple juice	2 tbs. honey
2 egg yolks	1 tbs. lemon juice
(reserve whites for batter or droppies)	

Mix all ingredients thoroughly in a bowl. Stand in a pan of warm water. Beat with rotary beater till creamy. If too thick, add a little more lemon juice. Chill.

Serve in individual glasses.

Apple Crumble

1 lb. (3 or 4 medium) cooking apples	1 stick butter or soft margarine
2 cloves	½ cup rice ground in blender or mill
½ cup raw sugar	1¾ cup dried coconut

Wash, dry, core and quarter apples. Put in a pie dish, add cloves and sprinkle of sugar. Rub butter into ground rice, stir in rest of sugar and coconut, and spread mixture over the apples. Bake in fairly hot oven, 375° F. for about 30 minutes. But do not over-bake or burn. Serve with top milk or yogurt.

Alternative fruits. Substitute blackberries, rhubarb, or pitted, stewed prunes, and reduce baking time by 10 minutes.

Apple and Raisin Rice

1½ lb. (4 or 5 medium) apples
¼ cup raisins
    rind and juice of 1 lemon

4 tbs. butter
2 cups Basic Rice (cooked)
¼ cup raw sugar

Core and cut up apples. Chop raisins and slice lemon rind. Butter pie pan. Put in layer of boiled rice, then layer of apples, sprinkling of lemon juice and sugar, a few raisins and a little rind. Repeat till all used. Last layer must be *rice*. Put rest of butter in small dabs on top and put in moderate oven. As soon as browning begins, cover with parchment paper and continue cooking till apples are done. Turn out on to dish. Serve hot with yogurt or custard.

Apple and Rice Custard

1½ lb. (4 or 5) cooking apples
4 tbs. butter
1¼ cups Basic Rice (cooked)
¾ cup raw sugar

2 eggs
1¼ cups milk
    pinch of cinnamon or grated
    lemon rind

Core and chop apples. Butter pie pan well and sprinkle over it a layer of cooked rice. Now put in half the apples mixed with half the sugar, the rest of the rice, and the rest of the apples and sugar. Beat the eggs well. Mix in the milk and cinnamon (or lemon rind). Pour this over. Bake at 375° F. for about 45–60 minutes, standing in baking dish of water to prevent curdling. Keep below boiling point.

Baked Apple Pudding

1 lb. (3 or 4 medium) cooking
   apples
1 lemon
2 tbs. water

2 eggs
¼ cup raw sugar
4 tbs. melted butter

Peel and core apples carefully and cut in small pieces. Drop them in pan with the juice and grated rind (yellow only) of lemon with 2 tbs. of boiling water. Simmer till soft. Beat eggs well and mix with the sugar and melted butter. Blend well with the apple. Turn into oiled pie pan standing in a baking dish containing enough water to reach halfway up the pan, and bake for 30 minutes at 325° F.

Apricot and Coconut Pudding

½ cup dried apricots
2 tbs. honey
   strip of lemon rind

1 cup shredded coconut
2 eggs
3¾ cups milk

Soak apricots overnight in boiling water to cover well. Cook gently with same water, honey and yellow strip of rind, till soft pulp. Remove rind. Oil pie pan. Put layer of coconut then layer of apricots, till all are used, with coconut on top. Beat eggs well, add milk and pour over. Stand pan in baking dish in a little water and bake till set at 350° F. Serve hot.

Apricot Rice (1) (uncooked)

½ cup dried apricots
2 cups Basic Rice
½ cup nuts, chopped coarsely

2 tbs. honey
   whipped top milk (raw or
   unhomogenized) or yogurt

Soak apricots overnight in boiling water to cover. Cut each in four and combine thoroughly in a bowl with all the other ingredients. Spoon into individual glass dishes. Top with whipped top milk or yogurt and chill thoroughly.

Apricot Rice (2) (baked)

1½ cups stewed dried apricots	⅓ cup raw sugar
3 tbs. raw rice	3 eggs
2½ cups milk	2 tbs. butter or soft margarine

Arrange apricots at the bottom of an oiled casserole. Add rice. Whisk together milk, sugar, and eggs and pour over the rice. Dot with butter and bake at 325° F. for 1½ hours.

Apricot Rice Mold

3¾ cups milk	¼ cups stewed apricot puree
3 tbs. rice ground in blender or mill	1 tbs. raw sugar

Bring milk to a boil. Sprinkle in ground rice. Simmer about 10 minutes. Strain apricot purée into the pan, add the sugar and mix well together. Pour into a ring mold which has been rinsed in cold water, cool and then chill. Turn out and fill center with apple puree or lightly stewed dried apricots.

Baked Banana Pudding (serves 6)

2 tbs. butter	¾ cup rice flour
3 tbs. honey	2 bananas
2 eggs, separated	

Cream butter and honey. Beat in egg yolks separately. Stir in rice flour and thinly sliced bananas. Whip whites stiffly and fold in. Pour mixture in one large or six small baking dishes. Bake large about 60–75 minutes and small 30–35 minutes at 350° F. Serve with yogurt, custard, top milk (raw or unhomogenized) or a sweet sauce.

Celebration Pudding

2 beaten egg yolks
6⅔ cups (1 lb.) seeded,
  chopped muscatels
1⅜ cups chopped raisins
1⅛ cups chopped dried
  bananas

¾ cup whole raisins
1 cup chopped walnuts
  grated lemon rind
  orange juice to moisten

Mix all ingredients to a stiff consistency, thinning with orange juice as necessary. Steam for 1 hour in buttered bowl. Serve hot with cream, yogurt or hard sauce.

Black Currant Cream (yogurt in disguise)

Raspberries, loganberries, red currants, ripe gooseberries or blackberries (using 1 cup tart cooking apple with 1 cup blackberries) may be used.

1 carton yogurt
2 tbs. clear honey or
  to taste

2 cups black currants cooked in
  minimum water or canned
4 almonds

Put yogurt and honey in blender and start motor. Add fruit gradually, blend till smooth. Scrape down sides with spatula and pour into dessert glasses. Garnish with almonds blanched and halved. Chill well before serving. Wash out blender with 1 cup milk for milk shake.

Fruit Juice Pudding (baked)

⅔ cup water
1¼ lbs. any soft fruit or
2½ cups orange juice un-
  sweetened

⅛ cup raw rice
1½-2 tbs. honey
  few drops vanilla

Bring water to boil, add fruit and boil till shape collapses. Blend in blender and strain to remove seeds, skins, etc.

`

Measure off 2½ cups. Put rice, honey and vanilla in baking dish. Pour juice over. Cover lightly and bake until set, at 300° F. Serve hot with raw cream or yogurt.

Fruit Froth

2 cups chopped apples, guavas, berries or any other suitable raw fruit
2 egg whites, stiffly beaten
a grating of lemon rind

honey to taste
N.B. Raw egg white steals biotin, but this method cooks it lightly.

Blend in blender or sieve the chopped fruit. Put in a pan and heat to boiling point. Cool slightly. Fold in egg whites, lemon rind grated and honey to taste. Cool gradually. Pile into individual fruit dishes and top with a dab of yogurt or whipped cream.

Lemon Mold

3-3½ cups water
grated rind and juice of 1 lemon
½ tsp. salt

½ cup raw sugar
1 cup rice
½ cup cream

Bring water to boil with lemon juice, rind, salt and sugar. Add washed rice and cook for 30 minutes. Turn into bowl to cool. Whip cream into rice, turn into mold rinsed previously in cold water. Chill. Turn out on dish and garnish with strawberries or lemon curd or surround with apple puree.

Mincemeat

½ lb. nut butter
1½ cups raisins, seeded and chopped
1 cup raw sugar or ½ cup honey
1½ cups sultanas

½ tsp. each nutmeg, mace, cinnamon, or 1 oz. mixed spices
1½ cups currants (optional)
3 cooking apples, chopped
grated rind and juice of 1 lemon

Mix all together very thoroughly in a bowl. Press into a jar. Cover closely and keep refrigerated. Eat without pastry in fruit dishes at Christmas time.

Orange Pudding

2 eggs, separated
¼ cup raw sugar
1 cup rice ground in blender or mill
1 cup milk

¾ cup orange juice
1 tbs. lemon juice
grated rind of 1 lemon
2 tbs. melted butter

Beat egg yolks, fold in sugar. Add rice and milk alternately. Then add juices, rind and butter. Beat whites until stiff and then fold in. Turn into greased pie pan and set in pan of warm water. Bake for 45 minutes in moderate oven, 350° F. When ready, the pudding should be crisp on top and more liquid underneath.

Rhubarb Whip (1)

4-6 stalks rhubarb cut in cubes
  boiling water to cover
2 tbs. powdered milk

1-2 cups fresh milk
½ cup raisins or chopped pitted dates

Pour boiling water on rhubarb. Let stand for 10 minutes, then drain off to reduce oxalic acid. Chill. Liquidize in blender with powdered and fresh milk to desired thickness and add raisins or dates gradually. Scrape out when smooth, strain and turn into individual glasses and chill. Top with dab of cream or yogurt or grated nutmeg.

Rhubarb Whip (2)

2 tsp. agar-agar, or
1 tbs. gelatin
2 cups cubed rhubarb

3-4 tbs. honey
4 blanched almonds

Soften agar-agar or gelatin in 2 tbs. cold water. Cook rhubarb lightly in water to cover with honey. Add gelatin to hot rhubarb and stir until dissolved. Chill until texture is semi-solid. Turn into bowl. Whip with rotary beater until doubled in volume. Pile into individual glasses or dishes. Chill again until firm. Top with a dab of cream or yogurt and 1 sliced blanched almond.

Pumpkin Pudding and Popcorn (hot) (1)

Cut up one small pumpkin in wedges, after removing seeds and membranes. Steam on rack over a little boiling water in a covered pan, till tender—about 15 minutes. Remove skin and mash smoothly with a little lemon juice and honey to taste. Turn into an oiled pie pan, dot with freshly popped corn and brown lightly in oven. Serve with top milk (raw or unhomogenized).

Pumpkin Pudding (2)

1½ cups pumpkin pulp (cooked)	4 tbs. honey
1½ cups milk cheese	pinch of salt
3 eggs	cinnamon

Liquidize in blender all ingredients except cinnamon. Pour into an oiled pan or individual custard cups, and sprinkle with cinnamon. Stand in pan of water and bake in slow oven, 300° F. for about 40 minutes till firm, or straw inserted comes out clean. Serve hot or cold with yogurt or top milk.

Pumpkin Pudding (3) South African

N.B. Adjust sugar to sweetness of pumpkin, which varies with variety.

2 lbs. pumpkin	2 eggs
½ cup raw sugar	grated nutmeg
½ cup milk	1 tbs. butter

Remove seeds and membranes of pumpkin. Steam till tender, about 15–25 minutes. Cool and peel. Drain well, mash in a bowl till quite smooth. Add sugar, milk and eggs beating lightly. Put in oiled pie pan and smooth over with back of fork. Grate nutmeg generously over surface and dot with butter. Bake at 350° F. about 30 minutes, but do not overbrown.

Pumpkin Puree (cold)

Cut up a large slice of pumpkin or about half a small one (after removing seeds and membranes) into small wedges. Set on a rack over a little boiling water in a pan and cover. Simmer till tender, about 15 minutes. (Reserve water for gravy, stew or soup.)

Remove skin, puree smoothly, adding a little honey to sweeten to taste. Pile into individual glasses, garnish with sprinkle of cinnamon, raisins or chopped nuts as desired. Chill. Serve cold with yogurt, or top milk sweetened with powdered milk.

Sweet Potato Tartlets

1 medium sweet potato	apple or pumpkin lemon curd
2 tbs. oil	to fill patty shell

Scrub sweet potato well and peel. Shred finely and sauté without browning in the oil pre-heated in a pan. Press firmly on the bottom and sides of oiled patty pans. Bake about 10 minutes in hot oven, 425° F. Cool. Serve filled with lemon curd made with apple or pumpkin.

Basic Baked Custard

3 eggs	crushed half bay leaf or piece
3 tbs. honey	of lemon rind
3 cups milk	

Blend eggs, honey and milk and add bay leaf or lemon rind

as desired. Pour into oiled pie pan. Set in baking tin containing water to prevent over-cooking and curdling. Bake at 375°
F. about 40 minutes. Serve hot or cold with sweet sauce or
lightly cooked fruit.

Coconut Mold

2½ cups milk (or soya milk)   2 tbs. honey
4 tbs. rice   1 cup dried coconut

Put milk, rice and honey in pan and simmer gently till rice is
soft and mixture thick. Stir in coconut. Turn into mold previously rinsed in cold water, and chill. Turn out and serve with
sweet sauce or stewed fruit.

Coconut Pudding

2 beaten eggs   1 cup shredded coconut
1 cup milk (or soya milk)   grated rind of 1 orange or
1 cup finely chopped raisins   lemon

Thoroughly mix all ingredients. Turn into oiled pie pan. Set
in shallow dish of water. Bake at 325° F. until set. Serve hot
or cold with cream or yogurt.

Date and Rice Pudding

2 tbs. rice   1 egg
4 tbs. boiling water   1⅞ cups milk (or soya milk)
1 cup dates, washed, pitted
   and chopped

Wash rice, drop into 4 tbs. of boiling water. Simmer till tender and all water is absorbed, adding a little more if required.
Put into oiled pie pan, add dates and mix well. Beat the egg,
add the milk, stir into dish, and bake, set in pan of water, in
moderate oven, 350° F. till nicely browned.

Baked Rice with Raisins

½ cup raisins
3¾ cups milk
2½ tbs. rice

1 tbs. butter
1 tbs. honey

Wash and pit raisins. Rinse pan and put in milk and rice. Simmer for 20 minutes. Grease pie pan, put in rice and honey, stir in raisins, and bake 45 minutes in moderate oven, 350 °F. Serve with rhubarb sauce.

Rice Cream

½ cup chilled yogurt
¼ cup powdered milk
  vanilla flavoring, or grated lemon rind
2 tbs. raw sugar
2 tbs. lemon juice

1 cup Basic Rice (cooked)
1 cup drained crushed pineapple, fresh or canned unsweetened
¼ cup broken walnuts or pecans

Put yogurt in bowl. Add and beat slightly the powdered milk, vanilla, sugar, lemon juice and rice. Add pineapple and nuts. Stir all the ingredients to combine thoroughly. Chill. Serve in dessert glasses. Garnish with half nut. Prepare less than two hours before serving.

Rice Jelly

3 tbs. rice
5 cups boiling water
  pinch cinnamon, 1 tsp. lemon juice or piece of vanilla pod

honey to taste

Wash rice, drop into boiling water with desired flavoring, and boil gently till the water gets thick and starchy. Strain off grains (reserving for thickening gravy, stew, etc.). Sweeten liquid to taste and turn into small molds rinsed out in cold water. Chill. Turn out when firm. Serve with rhubarb or banana sauce.

Ground Rice Molds

3 tbs. rice ground in blender or
   mill
2½ cups milk
   grated lemon rind or strip of
   lemon or other desired flavoring

3 tbs. honey
1 egg white

Mix rice smoothly with a little of the milk. Simmer the rest of
the milk with lemon rind. Leave to infuse a few minutes.
Strain on to rice paste, stirring well. Replace in pan and simmer gently, about 10 minutes. Add honey and leave to cool a
little. Whip egg white to a peak, then fold it in. Pour into
small molds previously rinsed in cold water and chill. Turn
out and garnish with dabs of lemon curd.

Ground Rice Custard

2 tbs. rice ground in blender or
   mill
3 ¾ cups milk

1 tbs. honey
2 eggs

Brush pan with oil, then simmer rice in milk over gentle heat
for 5 minutes. Turn out into a bowl. When cool stir in honey
and eggs well beaten. Bake in greased pie pan in very moderate oven, 325° F. till set firm. Serve sprinkled with cinnamon
or grated orange rind if liked, or with stewed fruit.

Rice Pancakes (sweet)

3 eggs
5–6 tbs. honey
1½ cups fresh milk

1 tsp. salt
1–3 cups Basic Rice (well
   cooked)

Blend eggs, honey, milk and salt. Beat rice into liquid mixture
till smooth, thick, creamy batter. Drop by tablespoonfuls on to
un-oiled hot griddle or heavy oiled pan. Brown lightly on

both sides turning with a spatula and serve hot with lemon wedges or apple puree, etc.

Queen's Pudding

4 tbs. rice
2½ cups milk
1 tbs. honey
1 tbs. butter

1 large egg or 2 small ones, separated
juice and rind of ½ lemon
2 tbs. raw sugar

Wash rice, put in pan with milk, honey and butter and simmer until tender. Cool. Stir in beaten yolk of egg and lemon rind grated. Turn into oiled pie pan and smooth down. Whip egg white until stiff, folding in lemon juice and sugar. Spread this over pudding with back of fork and brown in moderate oven at 325° F. Serve hot or cold.

Chestnut Cream

1 lb. chestnuts
1 tbs. honey

1¼ cups milk
grated lemon rind

Boil and peel chestnuts. Cook in top of double boiler with honey, milk and lemon rind until tender. Liquidize in blender or rub through sieve. Heap in individual glasses, chill and serve garnished with apple or pumpkin lemon curd or whipped top milk.

Chestnut Puree (sweet)

2 lbs. chestnuts
2½ cups milk
1 tsp. vanilla essence

½ cup raw sugar
⅔ cup water
⅔ cup cream (optional)

Make a diagonal cross on the flat side of the chestnuts and bake in the oven until the shells crack. Remove the shells and skin. Cover with milk, add the vanilla and cook until tender. Press through sieve while still hot. Dissolve sugar in water in a pan and cook until syrup thickens. Stir in with the chestnuts to make a moist mixture. Press through a sieve or ricer into individual glasses and garnish with a little whipped cream or yogurt.

Malay Rice Pudding

1 cup rice	2 tsp. butter or oil
3 cups water	½ tsp. turmeric powder
½ cup raw sugar	½ cup raisins

Cook all ingredients together in covered pan and boil about 30 minutes—till all liquid is absorbed and rice is tender, adding a little extra water if needed. Serve hot with cream or yogurt.

Cottage Cheese and Apple Cream

1½ cups cottage cheese	2 tbs. honey
2 dessert apples	8 blanched almonds or 2 walnuts
1 tbs. lemon juice	

Mash the cheese in a bowl. Wash but do not peel apples. Shred on a grater and cover with lemon juice. Add the honey, blend with the cheese and beat well with a fork. Heap in fruit dishes and garnish with blanched almonds or walnuts.

Rice Pudding (steamed)

3 tbs. rice	a grating of lemon rind
2½ cups milk	1 tbs. raw sugar
1 tbs. butter	

Wash rice thoroughly, put in top of double boiler with milk, butter, salt, a grating of lemon rind and sugar. Keep surrounding water boiling well until rice is swollen and tender, about 1–1½ hours. Stir occasionally to keep grains from sticking to the bottom. Pile up on hot dish and garnish with dried apricots soaked 24 hours or ring round with apple puree.

Cottage Cheese Whip

2 tbs. honey
2 egg yolks

1 cup cottage cheese
1 tbs. lemon juice

Beat honey and egg yolk with rotary beater in large bowl, till very foamy and light. Gradually add the cottage cheese and then lemon juice. Turn into individual dishes in a peaked shape and chill. Serve with apricot sauce, or rose cream in a sauce boat, or garnish with blanched almonds. (Rose cream is yogurt, tinted with beet juice.)

Cream Cheese Balls

1 cup cream cheese
  pinch of salt
2 tbs. honey
¼ cup chopped seedless raisins

¼ cup chopped blanched almonds or chopped peanuts

Mix all together. Shape into small balls. Chill. Serve as dessert.

Pashka Pudding (or cake)

2 cups cottage cheese
2 tbs. unsalted butter
2 tbs. powdered milk sifted
  with 4 tbs. raw sugar
  grated rind of 1 lemon
¼ lemon, finely chopped

4 cups sultanas or seedless raisins
4 tbs. blanched almonds or cashews
½ tsp. vanilla

Blend cheese and butter till smooth. Add rest of ingredients and stir well. Put a clean cloth over a colander. Pour the mixture over it and place a saucer on top as weight. Set colander on large plate and leave in refrigerator overnight. Turn on to cake dish, remove cloth, slice with sharp knife. Freeze any leftovers.

Junket (reinforced)

2 cups fresh milk
½ cup powdered milk
2–3 tbs. honey or raw sugar
1 tsp. essence of rennet

1 tsp. fresh grated orange or lemon rind (optional)
pinch of salt

Liquidize in blender or beat till smooth all the other ingredients except rennet with 1 cup of fresh milk. Add other cup of fresh milk and raise at least to blood heat (98° F.), but not over 110° F. Stir rennet for a few seconds only into warm mixture. Pour at once into individual glasses and do not move for about 10 minutes or till firm. Chill. Serve sprinkled with cinnamon, shredded coconut or chopped nuts, as desired.

Milk Jelly

2½ cups milk or soya milk
    thinly cut rind of 1 lemon
1 tsp. (heaped) gelatin

2 tbs. honey
2 eggs, separated

Heat milk with lemon rind in top of double boiler over boiling water. Stir in gelatin softened in 1 tbs. cold water and whisk till dissolved. Add honey and beaten egg yolks and cook gently a few minutes. Take out lemon rind. Let mixture cool slightly then fold in stiffly beaten egg whites. Leave to set in individual dishes. Chill. Decorate with whipped cream, apple or pumpkin lemon curd or chopped nuts as desired.

Zabaglione (without alcohol)

3 egg yolks
3 tbs. honey

3 tbs. apple juice, slightly warm

Beat together egg yolks and honey in a bowl till pale and fluffy. Put in top of double boiler (or stand bowl in pan of hot water), and add slightly warm apple juice. Beat over good heat for five minutes till mixture is like whipped cream. Remove from heat and continue beating for two minutes more. Pour into glasses and serve chilled.

Poached Egg Pudding

6 egg whites
  pinch of salt
¼ cup raw sugar
4 egg yolks, whole

2 tbs. Pumpkin or Apple Lemon Curd
4 blanched almonds

Whip egg whites, adding pinch of salt, to stiff peak. Beat in sugar. Put half of this into well oiled soufflé dish. Arrange egg yolks on this, surrounding each with pumpkin or apple lemon curd, and lay ½ almond on each. Cover with the rest of the whipped whites. Cook in moderate oven, 350° F. for about 25 minutes.

Quick Custard

1 egg, well beaten
¾ cup milk (or soya milk)
  small pinch of salt

1–2 tbs. honey
2 tbs. powdered milk (optional)

Beat together all ingredients. Put into large tea cup, cover and set in the open top of a boiling kettle. Steam until firm. (To thicken texture and increase food value, 2 tbs. of powdered milk can be smoothly stirred into the liquid milk first.)

Spanish Soufflé

1⅝ cups milk
  cinnamon to taste
¾ cup ground almonds or hazelnuts

4 tbs. raw sugar
6 egg yolks
2 egg whites

Heat the milk with the cinnamon. Pour gradually over the ground almonds in a bowl. Cream sugar and egg yolks till they froth, then add to the bowl. Beat egg whites stiffly and fold into the mixture. Pour into a buttered soufflé dish. Stand in a shallow pan of water and bake in a moderate oven, 325° F. about 25 minutes. Test by inserting a fine steel knitting needle from rim to center of dish. Ready if it comes out clean. If ready too soon, leave 5 minutes in oven with door ajar, but best take at once to table. (Cover with thin piece of parchment paper to prevent over-browning.)

N.B. Do not open oven door for first 15 minutes.

DRINKS

SAVORY

Carrot Milk Shake (serves 1)

1 large young carrot, grated   few drops lemon juice
½ cup milk

Liquidize all ingredients in juicer or blender till smooth. Strain, chill and serve.

Comfrey Cocktail

1 tomato
1½ cups young comfrey leaves, chopped
2 tbs. celery leaves, chopped
1 chopped shallot or very small onion
¼ cup young nettle leaves or chickweed

1 tbs. fresh basil leaves
1 apple, cored and chopped
1 or 2 mint leaves, chopped
water as required
seasoning to taste

Put the tomato in the liquidizer or blender. Put on the baffle and top leaving the center open. Start the motor and gradually drop in the other ingredients, except the water and seasoning. Place your hand over the open center to prevent splashing. Rest the motor for a moment. Turn on again and liquidize fully, adding sufficient water to make a drinkable consistency. Add salt or honey as desired. Strain before serving.

Tomato Juice

2 cups water
2 cups chopped tomatoes, fresh
or canned

1 shallot or very small onion
pinch basil or marjoram
dash of honey

Libuidize all ingredients in juicer or blender till smooth. Strain, reserving pulp for gravy, etc. and serve.

SWEET

Cold Lemon Tea (serves 1)

½ tsp. tea
1¼ cups boiling water

honey to taste
2 tbs. lemon juice

Pour boiling water on the tea. Let stand 3 minutes, strain and add honey and lemon juice, and chill. Serve in glass.

N.B. With this method there is no bitterness as when lemon slices are used with the pith on.

Sweet Lemonade (without sugar)

½ lb. seedless raisins
5 cups cold water

juice of 2 lemons, unstrained
1 tbs. honey

Liquidize raisins or grind very finely. Add water and bring to boil. Leave overnight. Next day, press through fine sieve. Add lemon juice and honey and mix well. Chill.

Carob—The Cocoa Substitute

Cocoa powder, since it has white flour added to it, is forbidden, but carob flour is permitted. This is the ground-up pod of the algarroba bean of Spain and Spanish America where it is fed to donkeys and horses and is also much appreciated by chewing children, and is known as "donkey's chocolate." It can be used as follows to take the place of cocoa or Ovaltine, etc.

Donkey's Chocolate (serves 1)

1-2 tsp. carob flour	scant cup milk (or soya milk)
2 tbs. cold water	honey or raw sugar to taste

Put carob flour in cup. Add water, mixing to smooth paste. Put milk in pan previously rinsed in cold water and bring to boil. Pour over paste and stir well. Return to pan and re-heat, stirring well. Add honey or raw sugar to taste, and a few drops vanilla essence if desired.

Soya Milk (1) (from beans)

1 cup soya beans	pinch of salt
4-5 cups cold water	1 tbs. honey (optional)

Put the soya beans in a large bowl (they swell to about 3 times the dry size), cover with water and leave in fridge 1 or 2 days changing the water several times. Drain, either chop or put in blender until very fine. Add about 5 cups of water and bring to a boil. Simmer gently about 15 minutes, remove and cool. Strain through a very fine sieve, preserving residue for stews, etc. Add salt and honey and use for drinks instead of cow's milk.

Soya Milk (2) (from commercial or pre-cooked flour)

1 cup soya flour	4 cups water

Put the water and soya in a bowl. Let stand for a couple of hours. Cover the bowl and place in a pan of boiling water. Cook for 20 minutes. Cool, strain through a fine sieve. Residue can be added to gravies, etc. Use instead of cow's milk.

Berry Milk Shake

1 cup strawberries, raspberries, blackberries, etc.
1 tbs. honey
1 tbs. lemon juice

pinch of salt
3–4 cups of fresh milk (or soya milk)

Liquidize or blend and chill. Serve in tall glasses.

Cinnamon Flip (serves 1)

1 egg yolk
1 tsp. honey

1¼ cups milk (or soya milk)
cinnamon or nutmeg to taste

Beat egg yolk and honey together. Warm milk and stir it in. Heat gently without allowing it to boil. Sprinkle with cinnamon and serve hot in a tall glass.

Egg Flip (serves 1)

1 egg yolk
1 tbs. honey
¾ cup milk (or soya milk)

A few drops vanilla essence or lemon juice to taste

Put egg yolk in bowl and beat well, adding vanilla, or lemon juice. Heat milk below boiling and stir in the honey. Pour over the egg, stirring well. Drink at once.

Horchata (orr-cha-ta) (Spanish favorite) or Chufa Shake (serves 1)

6-12 chufa nuts (*Cyperus esculenta*) (obtainable at health food stores)

1¼ cups water
2 drops almond essence
dash of honey, if desired

Liquidize all ingredients in blender or juicer, strain and pour into tall glass. Chill.

Soya Milk Shake (chocolate-colored)

4 cups soya milk (home-made)   ½ tsp. vanilla extract
4 tbs. molasses

Blend in blender. Chill and serve in tall glasses.

Spiced Soya Milk Shake

4 cups soya milk (home-made)   ½ tsp. grated or ground nutmeg
3 tbs. honey   ½ tsp. ground ginger
   generous pinch of salt

Blend in blender and chill. Serve in tall glasses.

Molasses Milk

3¾ cups milk or soya milk   2 tbs. top milk or light cream
2 tbs. molasses   powdered cinnamon

Heat the milk and stir in the molasses well. Pour into glasses,
add ½ tbs. top milk or cream to each and sprinkle with cinnamon. Serve hot or cold.

Molasses Milk (fortified)

1 cup fresh milk   1 tbs. molasses
4 tbs. powdered milk, dissolved   cinnamon or nutmeg to taste
   in 1 cup water

Blend in blender or whip with rotary beater in a bowl. Chill
before serving, or serve hot sprinkled lightly with cinnamon
or nutmeg.

FISH

All fish supply about the same amount of protein as meat,
are easily digestible, quickly cooked without elaborate recipes, provide some unsaturated fats (E.F.A.s), lead such active

lives that they have a high content of vitamin B complex, and have so far escaped dosage with hormones or whatever. In addition, ocean fish are excellent sources of iodine. So they are clearly a good buy and should be served at least once or twice a week either at breakfast or main meals. A common complaint from the kitchen is the odors which they can also provide. But this need not be. If temperatures in cooking are kept low and the hands are washed with a little vinegar, they can be blameless in this respect, as in others.

Fish Baked with Lemon

1 large lemon	1 clove garlic (optional)
1 cup water	2 tsp. mashed potato
1 tbs. butter	4 white fish fillets or steaks
1 small lemon	

Squeeze and strain juice from large lemon and add to cup of water in small pan. Grate in rind. Add half the butter, and bring slowly to boil. Add skin and finely chopped pulp of small lemon and, if desired, pulped garlic clove. Dissolve mashed potato in enough water to make a thin paste and pour into boiling mixture in pan. Stir till thickened and clear. Add second half of butter. Pour over fish pieces arranged in oiled dish. Cover with parchment paper and bake at 350° F. about 20 minutes.

Fish Baked in Milk

a little oil	milk to cover
4 fish fillets or steaks	sprinkle of paprika and salt
small onion, grated (optional)	

Brush an oven pan with the oil and lay fish in it, adding grated onion if desired. Just cover with milk, and cook at 375° F. about 15 minutes more or less, according to the thickness of the fish. Sprinkle with paprika and salt if desired before serving.

Curried Fish (without curry powder)

½ coconut
1 cup boiling milk
1 large cooking apple
1 large onion
2 tbs. oil
1 lb. steamed flaked fish
1 crushed bay leaf

2 cups Basic Rice
1 tsp. ground ginger
1 tsp. ground rice
1 cup water
1 small chili pepper
salt

Prepare coconut milk 1 hour before meal. Grate coconut into a bowl, pour boiling milk on it, cover and set aside. Wash and core apple and peel onion, reserving a large piece of clean outer skin. Chop apple and onion finely. Heat oil in pan. Put in fish, apple, onion and half of the bay leaf. Sauté gently till onion is brown. Mix together the rest of the bay leaf, 1 cup Basic Rice, ground ginger, ground rice and water and add with chili pepper, and onion skin, to other ingredients. Simmer gently for about 20 minutes. Remove onion skin and chili pepper. Strain off milk from grated coconut and stir in. Taste for salt. Serve ringed by the second cup of Basic Rice reheated.

Steamed Fish

4 fillets or slices of fish
½ tsp. oil
  sprinkle of paprika

1 tsp. lemon juice
sprinkle of salt

Brush oil over a soup or other deep plate. Lay fish on it and sprinkle with salt, paprika and lemon juice and cover with parchment paper. Set plate over large pan of boiling water and cover with similar plate or pan lid. Keep water boiling hard and cook about 20 minutes or till tender.

Fried Fish (without batter or breadcrumbs)

4 fish steaks

¼ cup cornmeal or rice or soya flour for dredging

Dry steaks well. Dredge with cornmeal, soya or rice flour and salt mixed. Heat oil in pan and fry slices over moderate heat till brown. Do not cover. Turn to brown other side. Serve with lemon wedges or Golden Sauce.

Broiled Fish Fillets

1½ lb. fish fillets   paprika to sprinkle
1-2 tbs. oil   salt to taste

Arrange fillets on wire rack or broiler. Brush with oil and sprinkle with paprika but not salt. Broil about 1 in. away if gas or 5 in. if electricity, leaving oven door open. Keep heat low. Turn after about 10 minutes and broil other side about 5–7 minutes. If fish is on broiling pan cook longer but do not turn. Sprinkle with salt to taste and serve with lemon wedges.

Fish Kedgeree

1 lb. cold steamed fish   1 tbs. oil
2 hard boiled eggs   ½ tsp. salt
2 cups Basic Rice   sprinkle of paprika

Flake fish, chop whites of egg finely and rub yolks through a sieve. Heat oil in a pan and put in fish, rice, whites of egg, salt and paprika. Stir till well heated through. Turn out on hot dish and shape into pyramid. Scatter sieved yolk over and serve.

Fish and Cornmeal Cakes

1 cup cooked, flaked fish   2 tbs. cornmeal for dredging
1 cup Basic Cornmeal (po-   3 tbs. finely chopped parsley or
  lenta)   chives mixed with melted
1 tbs. soya flour (optional)   butter
1 egg, beaten

Mix well first four ingredients in a bowl. Roll into walnut-size balls then flatten into cakes. Dredge with cornmeal. Broil till nicely brown, turning to broil other side. Serve with a little melted butter and finely chopped parsley mixed well together.

Fish and Onion Pie

1 lb. flat fish fillets
2 tbs. finely chopped parsley
½ cup finely chopped onion
  salt to taste

1 lb. potatoes (3 or 4 medium)
½ cup milk
2 tbs. butter or soft margarine

Wash fillets and cut in pieces. Lay a few pieces in oiled pie pan, sprinkle with chopped parsley and onion, and salt lightly. Continue with similar layers till all are used. Steam potatoes, rub through sieve, beat in butter, season to taste, and make a soft paste with the milk. Spread over the fish, ripple with back of fork, dot with remainder of butter and bake about 20 minutes at 375° F.

Fish Salad

½ lb. cold steamed fish
½ cup home-made mayonnaise
1 tbs. lemon juice

2 tbs. seedless raisins, finely chopped
1 head of lettuce
1 sweet red pepper (optional)

Flake the fish. Mix mayonnaise, lemon juice and raisins well. Toss fish in it and coat evenly. Chill. Wash and whirl dry lettuce. Set leaves around glass dish and pile fish in center to serve. Garnish with strips of sweet pepper.

Scrambled Fish

4 eggs
2 tbs. milk
  salt to taste

¼ lb. fish flaked (fresh or leftovers)
2 tbs. oil

Beat eggs just enough to mix white and yolk and stir in milk, adding salt as desired. Add flaked fish. Heat oil in pan, turn in mixture, and stir gently over very low heat till mixture thickens. Serve for breakfast or light supper with sautéed or jacket potatoes.

Baked Stuffed Herrings

1 shallot or small onion	¼ tsp. salt
4 sprigs parsley	1 egg, well beaten
1 cup Basic Rice	4 large herrings
1 tbs. oil	

Chop onion and parsley very finely. Mix with rice, oil and salt. Bind with egg. Split herrings, remove backbone and as many small bones as possible. Spread ¼ of mixture on each herring. Fold over and secure with strong thread. Place in oiled casserole and bake covered at 375° F. for 10 minutes, then uncovered for about 10 minutes longer.

Spiced Herrings

4 large herrings	¾ tsp. salt
2 tbs. oil	½ tsp. raw sugar
1 cup lemon juice	¼ tsp. ground ginger

Clean and split fish removing backbone and small bones. Lay in casserole. Mix together oil, lemon juice, salt, sugar and ginger. Pour over fish. Cover and bake at 400° F. about 25 minutes or till tender. May be eaten hot or cold.

Smelts

1 lb. smelts	sprinkle of salt
2 tbs. cornmeal for dredging	4 lemon wedges
1 tbs. oil	

Wash fish and dry well. Leave on heads and tails. Dredge with cornmeal. Heat large pan, brush with oil and arrange smelts on it either head and tail alternately or with heads at the edge and tails in center. Cook till half thickness looks opaque, then turn with spatula carefully and cook other side till nicely brown and crisp. Sprinkle with salt and serve at once with lemon wedges.

MEATS

Most cook books give plenty of recipes for using expensive cuts of meat but few supply enough recipes for using far the most valuable parts of the beast which are the organ meats. Liver, sweetbreads, kidney, heart and brains are excellent foods because they are the best sources among meats of the vitamin B complex, especially of folic acid, B_{12} and pantothenic acid, of minerals and of superior quality proteins. Liver used to be given only to dogs before World War I, drawing the acid comment of a nutritionist that this appeared to be one of the reasons why it was a country producing over one hundred breeds of splendid dogs but generations of young men suffering from every kind of degenerative disease, as revealed by the recruiting statistics. Those who value their health eat liver (or Marmite, if vegetarians) and the other organ meats at least once or twice a week.* So a great many different ways of serving them are included here.

Since the price of meat continues to rise, recipes using the cheaper cuts, either as they are or ground are also given.

Beef Cake

1 onion, chopped fine	1 cooked carrot
1 tbs. oil	1 turnip or sweet potato, cooked
1 lb. ground beef	and mashed
1 tbs. chopped parsley	1 egg yolk
salt to taste	

* Unfortunately, liver and kidney, being filters, concentrate the dubious residues from modern farming and those unable to obtain these from organic sources (i.e. using no pesticides, antibiotics or hormones) may prefer to get their folic acid from the foliage (i.e. leaves) of raw green vegetables and vitamin B_{12} from the yeast extract Marmite.

Toss onion in hot oil, till tender without browning. Add beef and cook 3 minutes. Add parsley and season with salt. Oil a casserole and cover the bottom with rows of sliced carrot. Spread half meat mixture in layer over this. Cover with mashed turnip or sweet potato and egg yolk beaten together. Then add rest of meat in a layer. Cover and bake in fairly hot oven, 375° F. for 15 minutes. Cool slightly. Turn out on warm dish and serve with a green cooked vegetable, or salad.

Beef Chop Suey

3 tbs. oil	water
3 medium-sized onions, chopped	1-2 tbs. molasses
4 stalks celery, sliced	2 tbs. soya flour
¾ lb. ground beef	2 tbs. cold water
2½ cups mung bean sprouts (optional)	½ cup sliced mushrooms
	2 cups Basic Rice

Heat oil in pan and sauté the onions until tender. Add celery and cook 2 minutes longer. Add beef and cook over high heat 2 minutes. Remove beef and set aside. Add sprouts and enough water to barely cover. Bring to boil and simmer, covered, 15 minutes. Combine molasses, soya flour and water. Stir into bean sprout mixture. Add mushrooms and beef. Re-heat and serve over Basic Rice.

Beef and Rice Loaf

1 lb. ground beef	½ cup Basic Rice
1 large carrot, grated	½ cup stock or water
1 onion, grated	½ cup powdered milk
1 egg, beaten	1 cup canned or fresh tomatoes
1 tsp. salt	

Blend all ingredients together. Put into oiled bread pan. Bake at 350° F. for 1 hour. Or steam in covered bowl standing in pan of boiling water. Serve hot or cold garnished with chopped chives or parsley.

Beef and Potato Loaf

2 lbs. ground beef
1 cup tomatoes, sieved or put through blender
1 onion, finely chopped
2 cups finely shredded raw potatoes

1 tbs. chopped parsley
1 carrot, grated
2 eggs, lightly beaten
1 tsp. salt

Mix all ingredients together and pack into an oiled 9 × 5-inch loaf pan. Bake 30 minutes or until done at 375° F.

Herb Meatcakes

1 lb. ground roundsteak or sirloin
2 tbs. chopped chives

1 tsp. dried thyme
1 egg, beaten
2 tbs. rice or soya flour

Mix all together in bowl very well and shape into thin, flat cakes. Coat with rice flour or soya flour. Broil, bake or sauté in oil until nicely browned on both sides.

Steamed Meat Roll

¾ lb. ground roundsteak
6 slices bacon, chopped
1 small cup Basic Rice
1 tsp. mixed herbs

1 carrot, grated
salt to taste
1 egg, beaten

Mix all ingredients well and bind with beaten egg. Pack into large rimless greased canning jar or oven-proof bowl. Top with parchment paper secured by rubber band. Steam 2–2½ hours. Chill. Slip out onto dish and cut in slices. Serve hot garnished with watercress or parsley or use cold for picnic sandwiches.

Sausages

1 egg
1 raw onion
1 tsp. salt or 2 slices cooked
chopped bacon

1 lb. ground beef
mashed potato to thicken
rice flour or cornmeal
2 tbs. oil

Beat the egg well in medium bowl. Grate in the onion. Add salt and stir in beef. Add enough mashed potato to form a firm dough. Spread on rice or cornmeal-floured board and roll out 1 in. thick. Cut into strips, then roll in the palms into finger-long sausages. Roll in rice flour and brown in hot oil on all sides without covering the pan. Serve hot for breakfast or other meals, or cold, to be eaten with the fingers for picnics.

Chopped Meat with Cabbage

2 tbs. oil
1 lb. chopped meat
1 large onion
1 carrot
1 parsnip
2 scant cups vegetable water

salt to taste
1 raw potato, grated
1 cabbage, shredded
2 tbs. butter
1 tsp. crushed caraway seeds
(optional)

Heat oil in pan and fry meat 3 minutes, stirring constantly. Set aside. In same pan fry onion, carrot, parsnip lightly. Add water and salt and grate in raw potato. Simmer till just tender. Sprinkle on meat and heat up. Meanwhile wash, dry and shred cabbage. Steam on rack or minimum boiling water, 5-7 minutes. Turn out, mix in butter and seeds (if used). Make ring of cabbage on serving dish and fill center with meat.

Mushroom Beefburgers

1 egg
1 lb. ground beef
1 cup mushrooms, chopped
pinch of salt

1 tbs. soya flour
1 tbs. minced onion
1 tsp. oil

Beat egg and use to bind all other ingredients beaten together. Divide into 8 flat cakes. Brush lightly with oil and
broil until golden on both sides. Serve with broiled tomatoes
and mushrooms, and garnished with watercress sprigs.

Oriental Beef (or lamb)

1 large onion	¼ tsp. turmeric powder
1 minced clove of garlic (op- tional)	2 cloves
	4 finely chopped tomatoes
2 tbs. oil	½ lb. fresh or frozen peas
1 lb. chopped beef or lamb	1 tbs. lemon juice
¼ tsp. salt	

Sauté onion (and garlic) in oil until golden. Add meat and
seasonings. Stir over low heat about 5 minutes. Add tomatoes,
peas and lemon juice. Cook gently until all liquid is absorbed. Serve over Basic Rice ringed by watercress.

Ground Beef Stroganoff

1 lb. ground beef	salt to taste
2 tbs. oil	pinch of raw sugar
½ lb. fresh mushrooms, chopped fine	1 tbs. lemon juice in ¼ cup milk or ½ cup sour cream

Break up beef with a fork. Toss in hot oil in a pan till
browned, about 3 minutes. Add mushrooms and simmer 10
minutes. Sprinkle with salt and pinch of raw sugar. Stir in
sour cream or lemon juice and milk and re-heat, but do not
boil. Sprinkle with plenty of chopped parsley. Serve surrounded by Basic Rice or Emerald Potato and green salad.

Stuffed Onions

2 tbs. rice
1 tbs. oil
¼ lb. ground beef
¼ lb. chopped bacon
1¼ cups stock or salted water

1 sweet pepper (small), de-
  seeded and chopped fine
¼ tsp. paprika
4 large onions

Fry rice in oil for 1 minute, then add rest of ingredients except onions. Cook till all liquid is absorbed. Remove outer skin
of onions and scoop out centers with teaspoon (reserve for
some other dish). Stuff with meat mixture. Set in casserole.
Cover and cook at 400° F. for 1 hour. Reduce to 350° F. for
further ½ hour.

Ham and Rice Balls

1 tbs. oil
1 small onion or shallot,
  chopped fine
6 oz. finely chopped cooked
  ham

½ cup Basic Rice
1 tbs. chopped parsley or sage
  pinch of salt
1 egg
  ground rice for dipping

Brush pan with 1 tbs. oil and sauté onion till light brown. Mix
together ham, rice, parsley and salt. Add to onion and stir till
hot. Beat egg and stir in, continuing stirring till thickened,
then spread on a plate. When cool shape into balls or sticks,
roll in ground rice, spread out separately on plate and set
aside. Heat 2 tbs. oil in pan and sauté till brown. Serve hot
with gravy or Golden Sauce.

Meat-Stuffed Apples

4 large cooking apples
1 onion, grated
  salt to taste

1 lb. chopped meat
2 tbs. oil

Wipe clean, cut off tops of apples and scoop out flesh, leaving

firm shell. Remove cores and chop flesh, mix with grated onion and meat and add salt. Sauté in oil lightly, then use to
stuff apple shells. Replace tops as "lids." Set in a pan containing a little water and bake at 350° F. for 1 hour.

Cornmeal Scrapple (serves 6)

2 lb. fresh pork hocks, cut up	1½ cups uncooked cornmeal
5 cups water	½ tsp. sage
1 onion studded with 2 cloves	⅛ tsp. mace
salt to taste	bacon drippings for frying

Place pork in pan with the water. Bring to boil and skim off
scum. Add onion studded with cloves, and salt. Cover and
simmer gently 2 hours, or until meat falls off bones. Strain off
broth and measure 5 cups, adding water if necessary. Remove
meat from bones, discard bones and chop meat finely. Heat
broth to boiling and while stirring, gradually pour in cornmeal. Cook, stirring, 15 minutes. Add chopped meat, sage,
mace and salt to taste. Pour into an oiled 2 lb. loaf tin and allow to cool. To serve, heat bacon drippings in a heavy pan
and fry thick slices of the scrapple until browned on both
sides.

Paella

¾ cup oil	2 medium tomatoes
2 cups cooked, diced chicken	1 small sliced green pepper
4 cooked prawns	salt to taste
1 sliced sweet red pepper	2 cups rice
¾ cup cooked peas	pinch of saffron
¼ cup sliced olives	

Use a large, heavy pan that can come to table. Heat oil and
fry chicken, prawns, sweet pepper, peas, olives, tomatoes and
green pepper and sauté gently about 10 minutes. Add salt and
rice and continue cooking and stirring for 5 minutes. Pour in 5
cups boiling water and continue cooking till liquid is ab-

sorbed, and rice is soft, about 20–25 minutes. Dissolve saffron in teaspoon of hot water and stir in. Serve hot in same pan.

Golden Rice and Leftovers

1 cup raw rice
2 tbs. oil
2–3 cups water (boiling)
   pinch of basil
1 tsp. salt
3 pieces onion outer skin

1 minced garlic clove (optional)
1 cup diced cooked beef, heart, tongue, kidney, sweetbread, lamb or flaked fish, etc.

Wash rice rapidly. Pat thoroughly dry and fry in oil at high heat, stirring often, and cook till golden brown. Add slowly the salted boiling water, seasoning, outer skin of onion and garlic and simmer about 20 minutes or till tender, but not mushy. Just before ready, remove onion skin and stir in 1 cup of diced meat. Serve when heated through, with tossed green salad or plain watercress in bowl. If liked, garnish with ripe olives or toasted peanuts or almonds.

Meat Kedgeree (leftovers)

1 finely chopped shallot or small onion
1 tbs. oil
1 cup coarsely chopped cooked meat

1 cup cooked rice
2 hard-boiled eggs
   grated nutmeg
   salt to taste
1 tsp. finely chopped parsley

Fry onion or shallot lightly in the oil. Add the meat and cook for a moment. Add the rice, whites of eggs coarsely chopped, grated nutmeg and salt. Stir till thoroughly heated. Serve hot arranged in a mound on a hot dish garnished with parsley and yolks of eggs rubbed through sieve and kept warm.

162

Beef Roulades

1 lb. flank or roundsteak	1 egg yolk, beaten
4 tbs. Basic Rice	powdered milk
1 medium carrot, grated	2 tbs. oil
1 medium onion, grated	1 cup vegetable or plain water
½ tsp. salt	

Pound meat well, then cut in thin strips about 4 in. by 3 in. Mix rice, grated carrot, onion and salt with the beaten egg yolk and add enough powdered milk to make a firm paste. Spread a layer of this on each slice of beef, then roll up and tie firmly with coarse thread. Heat oil in pan and fry rolls till lightly brown. Add vegetable water, cover, and simmer gently for 1¾–2 hours, or till tender, adding more fluid if required. Cut off thread, arrange with the gravy in center of hot dish and ring with Emerald Potatoes.

Potato Puffs (meat leftovers)

2 cups mashed potatoes	rice flour to dust board
2 eggs	2 cups finely chopped meat
2 tbs. powdered milk	leftovers
salt to taste	2 tbs. oil

Mix firm paste of potatoes, egg, powdered milk and salt. Roll out on board dusted with rice flour. Cut into rounds with a saucepan lid. Put some meat on one half and fold over the other half like a puff. Pinch or nick neatly all round. Heat oil in pan. Fry until light brown. Turn and brown the other side. Serve with home-made tomato sauce or melted butter and chopped parsley.

Headcheese (Brawn)

½ pig's head	pinch each of marjoram, basil
2 pig's feet	and thyme
1 crushed bay leaf	2–3 tsp. salt

Since these heads have been carefully cleaned and chopped at the slaughterhouse they are little work to prepare. Wash well and put the head and feet in a large pan and cover with cold water. Bring to a boil and simmer about 4 hours or till meat falls off bones. Set head in a colander over a dish and broth in a bowl to chill overnight, making them easier and less greasy to deal with. Remove all the bones carefully and cut the tongue, brains, skin and all the meat with a large knife into neat small cubes. Skim fat off the broth, then heat broth gradually in a pan with the salt, bay leaf and herbs, adding the jellied meat, and bring to a boil. Taste for seasoning. Simmer about 15 minutes. Turn into one or more bowls or bread pans and leave to chill till firm. Serve cold either sliced or in wedges with potato salad and watercress.

To Prepare and Pre-Cook Brains

The old-fashioned way was to soak for a long time and then boil with plenty of water which was thrown away with the valuable minerals and vitamins. Instead:

1. If able to use at once (which is preferable as brains are highly perishable) wash under running water, remove skins and fibers, dry well, slice or dice in small cubes and cook as desired.
2. If they are for breakfast next day, say, wash and skin them, then either flatten between two plates, or press into ice tray, and keep refrigerated till next day.
3. To pre-cook, steam on rack above minimum of water till firm, about 15 minutes.

Brains and Bacon

1 lb. pre-cooked brains   4 slices bacon

Cut brains in 4 or more portions and fry them with bacon.

Serve for breakfast with Creamed Potatoes sprinkled with chopped parsley.

Brain Cakes

2–3 tbs. oil	1 tsp. salt
1 lb. uncooked brains, prepared and diced	2 eggs
water to cover	cornmeal for dredging
1 crushed bay leaf	sprinkle of paprika
	1 shallot or small chopped onion

Heat 1 tbs. oil in pan and sauté brains lightly. Add water, bay leaf and chopped onions. Cover and simmer gently about 20 minutes or till brains are firm. Remove and chop finely, adding salt and beaten eggs. Return to pan and heat till mixture thickens. Cool, form into small round cakes, dredge with cornmeal and fry in remaining oil till lightly brown. Sprinkle with paprika and serve with potatoes and green vegetables or salad.

Creamed Brains with Cheese

1 cup milk	½–1 tsp. salt (depends on cheese)
1 tbs. powdered milk	
1 lb. brains, prepared and diced	4 tbs. cheese, grated
	2 tbs. parsley, finely chopped

Mix powdered milk smoothly with fresh, and bring to boiling point. Drop in diced brains and simmer till brains are tender, about 15–20 minutes. Stir in salt, turn out on to dish, sprinkle with grated cheese and parsley and serve with Sautéed Potatoes and yellow or green vegetable.

Brains in Disguise (for brains haters)

½ lb. brains, prepared but uncut	3 tbs. water
1 hard-boiled egg	1 tbs. lemon juice
	1 tsp. salt

Just cover brains with water and lemon juice and simmer gently till firm, about 20 minutes. Chill and chop finely. Shell egg and chop white similarly. Mix well together, and stir into kedgeree, pilau, salad, etc., where the brains will pass as white of egg. Sieve yolk and scatter over the surface.

Brains with Tomatoes and Rice

2 tbs. oil
1 onion, finely sliced
1 cup tomatoes, cut up finely
½ cup Basic Rice (cooked)
½ cup vegetable water or stock

1 tbs. soya flour
1 lb. brains, pre-cooked and diced
sprinkle of salt

Heat oil in pan, sauté onion and tomatoes, cover and simmer for 10 minutes. Add rice, vegetable water and soya flour. Stir in diced brains and sprinkle of salt. Heat thoroughly and serve.

Savory Hearts

2 calf or 4 lamb hearts
2 tbs. oil
1 cup vegetable stock or water
½ bay leaf
½ cup sliced onions

½ cup sliced carrots
½ cup chopped celery
raw potato, grated, or ground rice for thickening
salt to taste, parsley

Remove fat and sinewy parts from hearts. Cut into 8 ½ in. slices across the grain. Heat oil in pan and brown. Add water and bay leaf. Cover and simmer gently about 1–2 hours or till tender. Prepare and add the onions, carrots and celery. Cover and simmer about 10 minutes. Thicken with some finely grated raw potato or a little ground rice. Stir well and simmer for 5 minutes. Sprinkle lightly with salt and chopped parsley.

Roast Hearts with Nut Stuffing

4 large onions
4 lamb hearts
3 tbs. oil
4 tbs. Basic Rice
1 tsp. grated lemon rind
    pinch of salt

4 tbs. chopped nuts
    (hazel or peanut)
1 beaten egg
1 cup stock
1 tbs. chopped parsley

Peel onions and steam on rack 30 minutes. Wash hearts and cut off all fat and tough pieces, including membranes. Make stuffing by mixing together 1 tbs. oil, rice, lemon rind, salt and nuts, adding enough egg to bind. Stuff into hearts and tie up with strong thread to keep stuffing in place. Brown hearts in 2 tbs. oil. Arrange in ovenproof dish, surrounded by onions, pour oil from pan over these and add stock. Cover and cook in fairly hot oven, 400° F. about 75 minutes, or till tender. Scatter with chopped parsley before serving hot. Serve any leftovers sliced as cold meat.

Sautéed Hearts with Lemon

2 tbs. oil
1 small onion, chopped fine
2 calf or 4 lamb hearts
2 tbs. powdered milk

juice of ½ lemon
2 tbs. chopped parsley
salt to taste

Heat oil in a pan and fry onion till browned. Remove. Slice hearts thinly and sauté in same pan, cooking about 4–5 minutes on each side. Mix the powdered milk, lemon juice, and fried onion thoroughly. Pour mixture over the slices and coat them well with it as they re-heat. Sprinkle lightly with chopped parsley and salt and serve at once.

Kidneys in Apple Juice

3 kidneys (veal)
    a little milk
½ cup green onions, chopped

3 tbs. oil
½ cup apple juice
    sprinkle of salt

Remove fat from kidneys, trim off hard portion, slice thinly and leave to soak in a little milk for 1 hour. Sauté the onion in the oil for 3 minutes. Remove the kidney slices from milk and dry on toweling. Add to the pan and cook quickly 2–3 minutes, browning on each side. Add apple juice to pan and boil it up fast, blending juices and onion. Pour this sauce over kidneys. Add sprinkle of salt and serve on heated dish surrounded by Basic Rice or Emerald Potatoes.

Kidney and Mushrooms

4 lamb kidneys, halved
2 tbs. oil
1 onion cut in rings
½ cup mushrooms, sliced

½ tsp. lemon juice
1 tsp. soya flour
4 tbs. stock or water
½ tsp. salt

Sauté kidneys (after cutting out membranes) in hot oil for 2 minutes. Add onion and mushrooms and sauté for another minute. Add rest of ingredients, mixing well. Cover and simmer gently for 8–10 minutes. Sprinkle with salt and serve scattered over Basic Rice.

Kidney and Beans

2 tbs. oil
1 onion, chopped
2 tbs. butter beans,
  soaked overnight to cover in
  refrigerator, then cook 2–3
  hours till nearly tender with

1 bay leaf and 2 cloves
4 tomatoes
1 tsp. molasses
  pinch of salt
1 lb. beef kidney

Heat oil and cook chopped onion in it till tender and golden. Add beans, tomatoes, salt and molasses. Skin kidney and cut in small cubes, then add and brown lightly all over. Bring to boil and simmer gently at low heat, 350° F. till beans are quite tender.

Kidney and Beef Leftovers

1½ cups leftover brown gravy
1 unpeeled, scrubbed potato, grated
1 carrot, grated
1 onion, sliced fine

pinch of mixed herbs or marjoram, thyme and parsley
1 bay leaf, crushed
1 tsp salt
½ lb. leftover roast beef or heart
½ lb. lamb or beef kidney

Heat gravy, add prepared vegetables and seasonings and cook till tender. Dice beef and add. Remove hard membranes from kidneys and cut into small cubes. Stir into stew and cook for 3–5 minutes longer. Serve ringed by Basic Rice or Emerald Potatoes.

Broiled Lamb Liver

1 lb. lamb liver
1 tsp. oil

1 tsp. lemon juice

Trim liver and cut in ½ in. slices. Brush with oil, sprinkle with lemon juice and place on rack under broiler. Cook at low heat only, letting it just cook through, and brown lightly before turning to brown other side.

Chicken Livers and Rice

6 cut-up chicken livers
1 cup onion, chopped
2 tbs. oil
1 cup canned or cooked tomatoes
½ tsp. brown sugar

3 bacon slices, broiled and chopped
2 cups Basic Rice
pinch of basil
stock or water to moisten

Sauté livers and onion lightly in oil. Stir in rest of ingredients. Cover and simmer 10 minutes. Serve over Basic Rice reheated.

Savory Liver Strips Sauté

2 tbs. oil
1 large onion, thinly sliced
1 lb. liver, cut in thin strips

pinch of salt
sprinkle of paprika

Heat oil in pan and sauté onion till golden. Set aside. Sauté liver strips in same pan but cook 3 minutes only. Return onion to pan and cover for 1 minute before removing. Sprinkle with salt and paprika before serving.

Liver Sticks

1 lb. pig liver
½ lb. fresh belly of pork
1 large onion, chopped fine
    sprinkle of dried sage or
    a couple of fresh leaves
    salt to taste

2 eggs, beaten
½ tsp. grated nutmeg
    Basic Rice
    oil for utensils
    a little stock or gravy

Mince liver and pork coarsely, put them in a heavy pan brushed with oil, with chopped onion and sage. Season with salt to taste. Cook over low heat, 250° F., about 30 minutes, to brown all over, stirring occasionally to prevent burning. Pour off juices and mix meat with beaten eggs, nutmeg and enough Basic Rice to make a stiff but easy-to-handle mixture. Re-season if necessary after tasting. Shape into small sticks. Lay them side by side in an oiled, oblong casserole. Pour stock over them and cook in moderate oven, 350° F. for about 50 minutes. Add drained-off juices 5 minutes before serving with watercress.

Malay Curried Chicken Livers
(no curry powder)

3 tbs. oil
1 shallot or small onion, chopped
¾ lb. chicken livers
1 tsp. salt
1 tbs. ground ginger

1 tbs. allspice
2 tbs. sultanas or seedless raisins
1 cup Basic Rice (cooked with onion skin in water)

Heat oil in pan, fry onion about 10 minutes or until brown. Add livers and cook 3 minutes longer. Mix salt, ginger, allspice and raisins and put into pan. Simmer 2 minutes more and serve scattered over re-heated Basic Rice. Serve with green salad.

Sautéed Liver Slices

1 lb. beef liver
2 tbs. oil

paprika or cornmeal, for dredging

Trim liver and remove membranes. Cut into ½ in. slices. Dredge with paprika or cornmeal and sauté in oil not more than 3 minutes on each side.

Liver and Beef Loaf

½ lb. liver, cut in slices
½ lb. beef, cut in slices
2 tbs. oil
1 onion
1 stick of celery with its green leaves

¼ cup Basic Rice (cooked)
¼ cup powdered milk
1 egg, lightly beaten
1 tsp. salt
1 raw tomato pureed
pinch of mixed herbs

Dredge the liver and beef in powdered milk. Heat the oil and sauté the slices quickly. Set aside. Put onion and celery through the meat grinder. Turn into the pan used for sautéing the meat. Cover and stew 8 minutes. Meanwhile, grind the liver and beef and add to the vegetables with the Basic Rice, the rest of the powdered milk, egg, salt, tomato and herbs. Mix thoroughly, put in a loaf pan well brushed with oil and bake in a moderate oven, 350° F. about 40 minutes. Serve hot or cold.

Liver and Prunes

1 lb. calf liver, trimmed and thinly sliced
1-2 tbs. powdered milk to coat
2 tbs. oil
1 tbs. onion, chopped

1 tomato, peeled, seeded and chopped
4 tbs. prunes, soaked overnight, drained and chopped

Dredge liver in the powdered milk. Heat oil in heavy pan and brown slices quickly on both sides, about 5 minutes. Add onion and tomato and simmer 5 minutes longer. Add prunes and heat thoroughly. Serve with Basic Rice.

Baked Liver and Rice

6 tbs. rice
1 cup milk
1½ cups water
1 small onion, chopped fine

½ lb. calf liver, chopped
4 tbs. sultanas or raisins
½ tsp. marjoram
½ tsp. molasses (optional)

Wash rice and put in large pan with water and milk. Bring to boil, then simmer 5 minutes. Mix in rest of ingredients. Pour into oiled fireproof dish and bake at 400° F. about 60 minutes, till brown and crisp on top.

To Prepare and Pre-Cook Sweetbreads

Do not parboil in a lot of water in the old-fashioned way but steam gently on a rack above a minimum of water about 10-15 minutes. Allow to cool then trim off fat, skin and membranes.

Creamed Sweetbreads

1 tbs. oil	1 tbs. cornmeal, soya or rice
1 cup milk	flour
1 lb. sweetbreads, pre-cooked	1 tsp. salt
and cubed	2 tbs. chopped chives
1 small onion, grated	

Brush pan with oil, pour in milk and bring to boil. Drop in sweetbreads and grated onion and simmer gently about 5 minutes. Stir in meal or flour and keep stirring for 5 minutes. Add salt, sprinkle with chopped chives and serve. (This recipe can also be used for brains.)

Broiled Sweetbreads

1 lb. sweetbreads, pre-cooked	1 tsp. paprika
but uncut	sprinkle of salt
1 tbs. oil	

Cut whole sweetbread in half lengthwise. Brush with oil, sprinkle well with paprika, set on rack under broiler and cook slowly about 10 minutes till brown. Turn and cook about 5 minutes longer to brown other side. Sprinkle with salt and serve for breakfast (or other meal as desired) with Steamed Potatoes.

Sautéed Sweetbreads

1 tbs. oil	cornmeal or rice flour for
1 lb. sweetbreads, pre-cooked	dredging
or raw	1 tsp. salt
	sprinkle of paprika

Heat oil in pan. Cut sweetbreads in bite-sized pieces. Roll in seasoned meal or flour and sauté in hot oil at moderate heat, turning till golden on all sides and cooking about 15–20 minutes or till tender. Serve with Emerald Potatoes.

Savory Sweetbreads

2 tbs. oil
1 small onion, grated
1 cup tomatoes (or
  mushrooms), chopped

1 lb. sweetbreads, raw and
  trimmed
1 crushed bay leaf
1 cup water or vegetable water
1 tsp. salt

Heat oil in pan and sauté grated onion and tomatoes. Add the sweetbreads uncut with bay leaf and water. Cover and simmer gently for 25 minutes or till tender. Sprinkle with salt. Serve with Creamed Potatoes and cooked green leaf vegetable or watercress.

MISCELLANEOUS

Batter for Fish, Fritters, etc. or Droppies

4 tbs. rice flour or cornmeal
  pinch of salt
2 tsp. oil (corn, peanut or sunflower)

2 tbs. lukewarm water (about)
1 egg white

Mix flour and salt with oil and water to make a coating of dropping consistency. Beat egg white stiffly and fold in lightly just before use, or else leave in refrigerator for 1 hour. Makes small flat drop biscuits on griddle or heavy frying pan, or batter for fritters, etc.

Milk Cheese (1)

Best made with rennet since this retains the calcium. If milk is merely left to get sour, the calcium is dissolved into the whey. Of course, this should be drunk or used in cooking, but is usually discarded and the calcium lost.

5 cups skim milk, heated to
  lukewarm (100° F.)

1 tsp. essence of rennet
1 tsp. salt

Put milk into large pan and add rennet and salt. Stir well and leave to set. Place over very low heat, or in larger pan of hot water. Insert cooking thermometer and heat to 100° F. again. Line colander with clean double cheesecloth. Pour in curds, then gather up corners of cheesecloth and squeeze out the whey and scrape off curds. Add salt and stir well. Put in suitable dish and chill.

Milk Cheese (2) (simple method)

2½ cups milk   1 tbs. lemon juice

Bring milk to boil. Add lemon juice and bring to boil again to curdle milk. Turn into double cheesecloth draped over a bowl, then hang up the cheesecloth over the bowl to drain off the whey for a moist cheese, reserving for cooking. Leave to drain 2 hours. For a dry cheese, drape the cheesecloth over a large sieve set over a bowl and pressed down with a saucer with a weight on it. Try frying small strips of this with bacon or eat with apple or sprinkled on small potato fingers or droppies.

Chestnuts

Boiled chestnuts are equal in iron and vitamin B_1 (thiamine) content to whole wheat, and have a low fat, high starch content. Boil unshelled, starting in cold water, about 20 minutes or till tender, and drain well. Carry in small flat tin and include a small spoon. They are delicious eaten like a boiled egg held in the palm of the hand with a pinch of salt.

Instant Chutney (1)

2 medium-sized tomatoes, chopped
2½ cups freshly shredded coconut
1 finely chopped or grated onion
pinch of salt

grated nutmeg
1 cooking apple, grated
1 tbs. finely chopped raisins
½ tsp. lemon juice and grated rind of ½ lemon
pinch raw sugar

Mix thoroughly in a bowl. Serve with cold meats or rice dishes.

Instant Chutney (2)

2 raw cooking apples, finely chopped
2 tbs. chopped sweet peppers, seeded
2 tbs. onion, grated
2 tbs. raisins, pitted and quartered

1 tsp. salt
2 tbs. lemon juice
2 tbs. sugar
1 tsp. ground ginger (optional)
1 clove garlic, finely chopped (optional)

Mix thoroughly and serve with rice dishes or cold meats.

WARNING ABOUT SOYBEANS

The raw soybean contains anti-trypsin that must be fully cooked. Bought flour has been pre-cooked and can be used uncooked. Flour made from beans at home must be cooked at least 30 minutes before use. Whole beans need at least 3 hours cooking.

Soya Nuts (roasted)

½ cup soybeans
1½ cups water

1 tbs. oil
½ tsp. salt

Soak beans overnight in water and if possible place in freezing compartment of fridge overnight. Remove and simmer for 3 hours, adding more water if required. Pat thoroughly dry on toweling. Oil a heavy pan, drop in the beans and cook, stirring them until they are golden brown. Just before removing stir in the salt. Use instead of roasted peanuts, etc.

Soya Grits

Prepare soybeans as above but do not add oil or salt when roasted. Instead, cool and put through the coarse blade of the meat grinder or the blender for a couple of seconds, breaking each bean into 8 or 9 pieces. These can be eaten as a breakfast cereal with salt or honey to taste, or take the place of ground nuts.

Home-Made Soya Cheese (for milk intolerance)

1 cup full fat soya flour
1 cup cold water
2 cups boiling water

the juice of 2 lemons
½ tsp. salt
seasoning as desired

Make smooth paste of soya flour and cold water. Add to boiling water and cook 5 minutes. Add lemon juice. Remove and cool. When mixture curdles, strain through cheesecloth, over a colander. Put into a dish and season with paprika, chopped chives, parsley or any favorite herb or celery seeds. Chill before serving or at least set aside for 1 hour.

Potato Pastry (savory)

3 cups steamed or leftover potatoes
2 tbs. powdered milk

½ tsp. salt
1 egg, separated
1 tbs. fresh milk

Rub potatoes while warm (re-heat leftovers) through a sieve. Before they are quite cold add powdered milk and salt and mix well. Beat egg yolk well, add fresh milk and stir this into mixture. Spread this over any fish, meat or vegetable pie which must always be already cooked, and rough it in curves with a fork. Brush over with beaten egg white and bake till golden brown in hot oven, 425° F.

Apple and Banana Chutney (uncooked)

2 cooking apples, cored and chopped finely
1 banana, peeled and sliced thinly
1 onion, chopped very finely or grated

½ tsp. salt
1 tsp. lemon juice
2 tbs. seedless raisins, chopped finely
pinch ground ginger

Mix all ingredients thoroughly in bowl. Turn into glass dish and serve with cold meat and rice dishes.

Cornmeal Yorkshire Pudding

½ cup cornmeal
1 tsp. salt
½ tsp. marjoram (optional)

2 cups milk
4 eggs, beaten
1 tsp. oil

Make paste from cornmeal, salt, marjoram and ½ cup milk. Heat rest of milk in top of double boiler on direct heat. When it boils, add cornmeal paste. Stir till smooth. Place over hot water in double boiler. Cover. Cook gently till all liquid is absorbed. Remove. When lukewarm, blend in eggs. Oil large baking pan or individual ones, placed in pre-heated oven. Pour in mixture to half full. Bake at 350° F. for 10 minutes. Remove. Dot with remainder of oil. Return to oven and bake 15 minutes more.

Rice and Rosemary Stuffing

2 cups Basic Rice (cooked)
2 tbs. butter or oil
½ cup carrot, finely chopped

½ cup onion, finely chopped
½ tsp. salt
½–1 tsp. dried rosemary

Put rice in bowl, stir in well all other ingredients. Use to stuff fowl.

Rice and Prune Stuffing

8 raw prunes
water to cover
3 raw cooking apples

1 cup Basic Rice (cooked)
2 cloves, ground

Pit prunes and soak overnight. Chop finely and put in bowl. Core and chop apples. Add to prunes, stir in rice and cloves, mixing very thoroughly. Use to stuff heart or fowl.

Rice and Tomato Stuffing

1 tbs. oil
1 raw apple, grated
1 raw onion, finely chopped
1 raw tomato, cut up small

1½ cups Basic Rice (cooked)
1 tsp. basil
½ tsp. salt

Heat oil in pan and fry apple, onion and tomato lightly. Mix well with rice, basil and salt. Use to stuff poultry, heart, etc.

Rice and Chestnut Stuffing

1 or 2 onions
1 celery stalk and leaves
  bunch of parsley

chop finely, toss gently in 1 tbs. oil, then cover and cook 5 minutes

Remove and add to:

1 cup cooked rice
1 cup of stock or water
1 tsp. salt
  pinch of thyme, marjoram or basil

1 cup cooked chestnuts (boil unshelled, 20 mins. Drain well. Cut off skin while still hot and crumble coarsely)

Mix thoroughly and use to stuff chicken, heart, pork or turkey.

Rice and Vegetable Stuffing

2 cups carrots, grated fine
2 stalks celery, chopped fine
1 onion, grated
1 cup pumpkin or parsnip, raw, grated
2 apples, grated

½ cup roasted peanuts
½ cup raisins, chopped
1 tbs. parsley, chopped
½ cup Basic Rice (cooked)
1 tbs. sat
2 eggs, beaten

Combine all ingredients. Add a little milk if too dry. Use to stuff poultry.

SALADS FOR ALL SEASONS

According to Chambers 20th Century dictionary a salad is "a preparation of raw herbs (lettuce, endive, chicory, celery, romaine, watercress, onion, radishes, tomatoes, chervil, etc.) cut up and seasoned with salt, etc." showing that although cold potato and Russian salads are useful ways of using leftovers, they are not entitled to call themselves *salads*.

We can expand this list of "raw herbs" so as to provide a real salad daily throughout the year without paying exorbitant prices for any out-of-season ingredient. To use lettuce as the only green leaf makes for monotony and can be ruinous in winter, and there are not only many other green leaves which offer far better value, but many roots and fruit vegetables which can supplement them or take their place, to provide the vitamin C for which salads are so valuable.

Pigs going short of vitamin C because their food has been overcooked or contains none, show this by losing the curl to their tails. A pity perms don't react in the same way. What a health-and-beauty-building run that would cause on salads, which also give us vitamin A, folic acid, catalase and lysine, three essential nutrients largely destroyed by cooking.

Growing Green Salads Indoors

Spread a piece of thick white blotting paper or 4 thicknesses of paper towel on a flat dish or plastic tray. Dampen it well, sprinkle thickly with a single layer of seed—mustard, cress, alfalfa, etc. and set on a window sill. Water lightly every day. When the leaves are ready, cut off evenly with a sharp pair of large scissors.

"Wheat grass" is simply ordinary wheat grown the same way and cut before it gets too long and tough. Use in salads or as edible garnish for any dish, hot or cold. (The *grass is*, of course, *gluten-free.*)

Available for Salads

Spring

Leaves Mustard greens, spinach, lettuce, chives, parsley, mint, lemon balm, watercress, chickweed (*stellaria media*), dandelion (*taraxacum officinale*), seedlings from thinning rows (carrot tops, beet greens, radish tops).

Roots Scallion, radish.

Summer

Leaves Lettuce, red and white cabbage (best eaten raw), parsley, mint, lemon balm, watercress, chives, nasturtium leaves, arugula.

Flowers or fruit Cauliflower, broccoli, cucumber, peas, tomatoes, string beans, green pepper.
Roots Beet, leek, radish, carrot, onion.

Fall

Leaves Lettuce, cabbage, celery, endive, dandelion.
Flowers or fruit Tomatoes, broccoli, cauliflower.

Roots Beet, carrot, kohlrabi, parsnip, radish, yellow and white turnip, onion, Jerusalem artichoke.

Winter
Leaves Cabbage, endive, romaine, spinach.
Flowers or fruit Broccoli, cauliflower, apples.
Roots Carrot, beet, turnip, leek, onion, parsnip, Jerusalem artichoke.

Salad Preparations

How to use leaves
Pick freshly, wash rapidly but thoroughly, dry by whirling in salad basket or in clean dry cloth gathered up by the four corners and swished about till all moisture has gone. Tear soft leaves, and shred hard ones with sharp knife, put in deep bowl and with wooden servers or spoons incorporate chosen dressing till leaves are coated. Serve.

If gathered on warm day put in refrigerator for an hour or so in closed plastic bag before preparing. Chives, parsley, mint or lemon balm cut into small pieces with kitchen scissors can be sprinkled over or served in separate small bowl to be added according to taste of the individual.

Perhaps the most useful first spring leaves are the thinnings from a row of spinach which dares the weather that daunts the lettuce and keeps it back. Eaten very young, about 2 in. long, these are sweet and delicious, for the oxalic acid has not yet risen in them, it seems, judging by the flavor. Children like to dip individual leaves into personal tiny dishes of their favorite salad dressing.

How to use Flowers or Fruits
Broccoli and cauliflower need careful washing and drying. Flowerets can then be broken into easy-to-handle bits and served with small bowls of mayonnaise for each person to dip into, or else treated as leaves and coated with the desired dressing in a large bowl. Incidentally, cooked cauliflower has

a higher vitamin value than the raw material. As for tomatoes, agreeing with Clement Freud, that they are not compatible with lettuce, we eat those of our own growing with their thin skins merely washed and dried. Then sliced, sprinkled with a pinch of brown sugar and perhaps a touch of basil, on their own with spoons out of a bowl. If cucumbers are well washed they can be sliced with the peel still on and this prevents them from being indigestible. Sousing them with vinegar spoils the delicate flavor and we prefer them with lemon and/or oil and sprinkled with mint or parsley, but others may disagree. Green peas in their youth should never be cooked but make a delicious addition to any salad. Sweet peppers must have their very pungent seeds removed before use, and must not be confused with the hot variety, chili peppers, used in pickling and curries.

Roots

We store roots in dry peat very successfully and find them invaluable for winter salad. Beets, turnips and carrots can all be taken up, dried off and brushed clean of soil and then stowed between layers of dry peat in a covered box standing on canning jars if mice or rats are a possibility—they cannot climb up the glass. Raw shredded carrots are commonplace, but contain less food value than cooked carrots, though pleasant and popular. But raw shredded beets are better because they contain betaine which can double for choline (part of vitamin B complex) which is likely to be short if too little protein is eaten and is needed to help the body utilize fat. Cooked for ages and drowned in vinegar they lose half their charm. Scrub and if necessary peel, then shred.° This can be done on a square grater, available at all health food stores. Kohlrabi, onions, leeks—using about 3 in. of the green part— and spring onions can all be thinly sliced and served in separate bowls, since they are not to everyone's taste. I find that covering all the onion family in oil and refrigerating for, say,

° N.B. Prepare all salads as soon as possible before serving. If not possible, cover and place in refrigerator till needed.

half an hour removes the "repeater" action, and all grated, shredded and cut-up raw vegetables are best if tossed in a little oil to prevent oxidation and loss of vitamin C.

Wild saladings

The advantage of these is that they cost nothing and can be found when there is nothing yet available in the garden, or everything is still very expensive in the stores. Well washed chickweed (*Stellaria media*), choosing leaves which are large and tender before flowering begins, makes green sandwiches between slices of home-made meatloaf which children like as well as adults. Most French markets sell dandelion leaves for salad, but we have to look for our own *Taraxacum officinale,* though they are usually not far off. Choose young leaves for they get bitter in their old age.

Special warning

In the tropics or wherever there is danger of amoebic infection, it is recommended to dip prepared vegetables to be eaten raw in a solution of chloride of lime. Use 5 grams (⅙ oz.) to 5 cups of water. Then wash well in water that has been boiled to remove all trace of the chloride of lime.

Suggestions for Salads

1. Thinly sliced leek, using white and green parts, dessert apple shredded, and tomato sliced, with oil and lemon dressing.
2. Finely shredded raw beet and diced celery or diced or grated apple with mayonnaise dressing on bed of lettuce or watercress.
3. Finely shredded raw red cabbage with diced apple and celery with oil and apple juice dressing.
4. Shredded cabbage heart and shredded onion tossed in oil and orange or lemon juice.
5. Diced steamed potato and radishes with mayonnaise and mustard greens, or chopped chives or chopped mint.

6. Sprigs of broccoli flowers with oil and lemon dressing for dunking.
7. Very young spinach leaves tossed in 1 tbs. oil, *then* sprinkled with lemon juice.
8. Shredded cabbage heart in mayonnaise, garnished with raw carrot strips and olives.
9. Well-dried lettuce leaves torn in pieces and tossed in 1 tbs. oil, then sprinkled with lemon juice.

Salad Dressings

Oil and Lemon. 1 tbs. oil, 1 tbs. lemon juice and a grating of the rind, pinch of raw sugar or ½ tsp. honey and a pinch of salt, blended.
Oil and Orange. Equal parts oil and orange juice and a little peel grated, pinch of salt and honey to taste, blended.
Peanut and Honey. 1 tbs. peanut butter, 1 tsp. honey, 1 tsp. oil, 1 tbs. lemon juice, blended well.
Mayonnaise (egg). Put in blender 1 egg yolk, 1 tsp. honey, ¼ tsp. salt, juice of large lemon. Blend for a second or so, then gradually pour in oil till mayonnaise is thickness desired—about 1 cup suffices. Can be stored in fridge in screw-top bottle.

Eggless Mayonnaise

2 tbs. soya flour (pre-cooked)	1 cup oil
2 tbs. water	juice of ½ lemon
¼ tsp. salt	3 tbs. minced parsley

Make a smooth paste of soya, water and salt in a bowl, stand it in pan of hot water, and let it heat. Slowly beat in oil with rotary beater. Remove from heat when thick and add lemon juice and minced parsley. Beat till smooth and thick.

Winter Lettuce and Sprout Salad

2 celery stalks, chopped fine
2 cups mung sprouts
2 tbs. peanuts, chopped
juice of ½ lemon
pinch of salt

2 tbs. oil
1 tsp. honey
lettuce—a crisp variety like romaine

Arrange celery, sprouts and peanuts in salad bowl. Use blender or rotary beater to make dressing of lemon juice, salt, oil and honey. Stir into other ingredients in bowl. Surround with lettuce leaves, previously washed and dried and refrigerated in covered container. Serve at once.

Summer Cucumber Salad

1 cucumber
1 tbs. salt
5 tbs. yogurt or fresh cream

2 tsp. tarragon, chopped
1 small lettuce

Slice cucumber finely and sprinkle with salt. Let liquid drain for several hours. Wash off surplus salt and pat dry. Mix in bowl with yogurt and tarragon, and fringe with lettuce leaves.

*Potato Salad with Cheese

2 large waxy potatoes
1½ cups Dutch cheese, diced
2 carrots, grated
1 small onion
4 tbs. oil
2 tsp. lemon juice

pinch of salt
pinch of raw sugar
1 tbs. cream or yogurt
4 hard-boiled eggs
1 tomato
chopped parsley or basil

Steam potatoes over minimum of water till cooked. Peel while warm and dice. Dice cheese same size. Grate carrots and onion. Blend oil, lemon juice, salt, sugar and cream or yogurt. Rub salad bowl with cut side of garlic clove or omit if not liked. Pour dressing in bowl and stir in the potatoes, cheese,

° N.B. Potato salad should not be kept overnight. It decomposes easily.

onion and carrots. Garnish with sliced eggs and sliced tomatoes and sprinkle with chopped parsley or dried basil, as preferred.

SAUCES (without flour)

SAVORY

Foam White Sauce

2 egg whites, beaten to a peak   3 tbs. hot milk
   pinch of salt   chopped chives or parsley
   onion juice to taste

Sprinkle salt into beaten egg white and grate in onion juice.
Gradually pour on the hot milk while beating well until it
thickens. Add chopped chives or parsley. Use for vegetables
instead of white sauce.

Golden Sauce

1 egg yolk, well beaten   pinch dried herbs (optional)
   pinch of salt   or chopped parsley or chives
½ cup hot milk

Beat egg yolk in a bowl. Add salt. Stand in pan of hot water.
Pour on hot milk gradually and stir gently until sauce thickens smoothly. Serve hot with vegetables, instead of white
sauce. Add herbs or parsley or chives before serving if
desired.

Golden Cheese Sauce

2 egg yolks   salt to taste
4 tbs. finely grated cheese   2 tbs. butter

Beat egg yolks with grated cheese and salt. Melt butter in top of double boiler or bowl over pan containing boiling water, add mixture and stir until it has thickened enough. Thin with a little milk if necessary. Serve with vegetables, fish, hot hard-boiled eggs, etc.

Savory Sauce

1 tbs. onion juice	small pinch of grated nutmeg
1 tsp. crushed celery seeds or grated celery stalk	1 tbs. nutritional yeast
4 tbs. oil	pinch of salt

Blend all ingredients in blender and serve cold.

Tomato Sauce

4 ripe tomatoes, fresh or canned	pinch of salt
1 shallot or small onion	pinch of raw sugar

Slice the tomatoes and onion and cook them until soft in just enough water to prevent burning. Cool. Stir in salt and sugar to taste. Sieve and serve hot or cold.

Lemon Sauce (sweet or sour)

½ cup water	½ cup milk or powder
1 tbs. lemon juice	3 tbs. honey or pinch of salt

Blend water and lemon juice in large bowl. Beat with rotary beater. Gradually sprinkle in milk powder, constantly beating. When mixture has thickened, add honey or salt a little at a time. Continue beating until mixture stands up in peaks.

SWEET

Apricot Sauce

⅓ cup dried apricots   1 tbs. dried milk powder
   water to cover

Pour boiling water over apricots to cover well and leave overnight. Put in blender with milk powder or rub through sieve
and blend in. Should be of a thick cream consistency. Use
with plain puddings.

Hard Sauce (no alcohol)

½ cup sieved raw sugar   4 tbs. butter
½ cup powdered milk   3 tbs. lemon juice

Mix sugar and milk powder well together in a bowl till
smooth. Beat in lightly warmed butter and lemon juice. Chill
and serve with hot pancakes or Celebration Pudding.

Peanut Sauce

½ cup peanut butter   ½ cup fresh milk
   (unhydrogenated)

Blend till quite smooth. Serve as sauce for plain puddings,
adding a little honey if desired.

Rhubarb Sweet Sauce

1 cup raw young rhubarb, cut   2 tbs. powdered milk
   in cubes   2–3 tbs. honey

Liquidize all ingredients together until smooth. Serve with
plain puddings.

Molasses Sauce

½ cup molasses   juice of 2 lemons
2 tbs. powdered milk or soya   1½ tbs. oil or butter
    flour

Heat molasses. Beat in rest of ingredients. Serve hot with pancakes or waffles.

SOUPS

Canned and dehydrated soups are OUT on a gluten-free diet because they are thickened by white flour, the cheapest filler. But this does not mean no home-made soups, which can be honest-to-goodness foods, NOT commercially profitable non-foods.

They range from the raw and chilled in summer, to the hot and lightly cooked in winter, so conserving natural values, flavor and color, and they take little time to prepare. As a starter on a cold night they set the digestive juices flowing with their delicious scent and appearance. As a stirrup cup for departing guests facing the darkness after a party, they have the price-less advantage over the conventional "one for the road" of warming the very cockles without the risk of making anyone too "high" to be safe on the highway as a driver.

Soup Stock (To be used in place of water or milk in recipes)
Following the thrifty French we can prepare soup stock by extracting vitamins and minerals from bones and scraps of meat. Simmering is the usual procedure, at about 180° F., but in fact a higher temperature is preferable for bones since they contain no vitamins to be destroyed and the best method is to cook them in a pressure cooker for 30 minutes. Failing this, it is best to boil at 212° F. for a couple of hours adding some salt to extract the juices.

However, there is no need to use anything but vegetable leftovers and discards. Collect any coarse outer leaves of cabbage, broccoli, spinach, lettuce or any other green leaves usually thrown away when preparing salads or cooked vegetables, also pea pods, stalks of cabbage, celery and so on, with green tops of leeks and onions, wash thoroughly, and put into the refrigerator in a plastic bag with any vegetable parings from well washed vegetables. When ready to make soup, chop well, cover with water and boil slowly for only 15 minutes to extract flavors and as many minerals and vitamins as possible. Strain off the liquid and allow to cool. Use what you require for the soup you have selected, and store the rest in screw-topped jars in the refrigerator. It has been demonstrated that boiling for only 4 minutes draws out magnesium, iron, manganese, potassium, sodium and phosphorus into the water used and during the 15 minutes suggested, the greater part of the minerals has been transferred to the stock. Incidentally, the nutritive value of any soup can be raised by adding a little soya flour which does not alter the taste but thickens it slightly.

Lima Bean Soup

1 cup shelled lima beans past their first youth
1 large onion, cut up
2½ cups water, lightly salted, or vegetable stock

bunch of fresh or pinch of dried herbs
1 potato, cut up
milk to thin to desired thickness

Drop the beans in the boiling water with the onion, herbs and potato. Cook until beans are tender. Remove and cool. Blend in blender and strain or put through sieve. Add milk and reheat short of boiling point, then serve.

Quick Onion Soup

2 large onions
1 tbs. oil

1½ pints of vegetable stock or milk
grated cheese

Sauté onions cut into thin rings in oil till they are transparent.
Add stock or milk, drop in a piece of well washed onion skin
which gives a rich golden color and should be removed before serving, and heat gently, keeping below boiling point.
Serve in bowls with plenty of grated cheese.

Parsnip Soup

1 medium parsnip	3¾ cups water or vegetable
2 tbs. oil	stock
2 tbs. chopped onion	½ cup milk
washed onion skin to color	chopped chives
1 small potato, cooked	

Peel and dice parsnip. Heat oil and add parsnip and onion.
Cover and simmer gently for 10 minutes. Do not allow to
brown. Add onion skin, potato and water. Simmer till the
parsnip is tender. Liquidize in blender with milk added, to
desired thickness. Taste for seasoning but keep flavor mild.
Reheat, and sprinkle with chopped chives. (Roasted soya
beans can be added in place of bread croutons.)

Pea Soup (dried peas)

1 cup dried split peas	1 clove (optional)
3¾ cups water or beef stock	1 tsp. raw sugar
½ lb. (2 medium) potatoes,	1¼ cups milk
scrubbed and cut up	salt to taste
1 small onion, chopped	mint, finely chopped
1 small carrot, cut up	

Wash peas well discarding dark ones which float. Put in bowl,
cover with cold water or stock and leave 24 hours, refrigerated if possible. Put in pan with same water (minerals and vitamins have soaked into it) and simmer about 1¾ hours, adding more water as it boils away. Now add potatoes, onion and
carrot, clove and sugar and continue simmering till all are
soft, which will be about 15 minutes. Remove clove. Rub re-

mainder through sieve. Return to pan, add milk and salt. Reheat short of boiling or it will curdle. Sprinkle with mint.

Pea-pod Potage

2 lbs. fresh young pea pods   1 sprig of mint
    pinch of salt and raw sugar   1¼ cups milk
1 onion (small) or 3 shallots

Wash the pods and drop them into enough seasoned boiling water to cover. Peel and chop onion and add. Boil until softish. Allow to cool in bowl then add mint. Liquidize in blender and strain through a sieve to remove the fibers. Add milk and heat to below boiling point and serve. (The mint not only adds flavor but color.)

Pumpkin Soup

1½ lb. pumpkin   pinch of salt and bunch of
1 potato   herbs if desired
    seasoned water to cover   1¼ cups milk

Remove seeds and rind and cut pumpkin in cubes, scrub and cut up potato, but peel if the skin is dark. Boil together in seasoned water to cover until potato is cooked. Remove and cool, then blend in blender or put through a sieve. Add milk, heat to below boiling point and serve.

Quick Thick Rice Soup

1 tbs. oil   5 cups stock or water
1 stalk celery with leaves, diced   salt to taste
1 small carrot, diced fine   1 cup Basic Rice
1 leek, diced fine   chives, finely chopped

Heat oil and sauté vegetables in it, about 5 minutes. Add stock or vegetable water and salt. Simmer for 5 minutes, then stir in rice. Heat and serve sprinkled with chives.

Carrot Soup

5 cups stock or water	1 onion
½ lb. carrots	salt to taste
1 small potato	

Bring stock or water to boil in a pan. Scrub carrots and potato well, peel onion and shred them all on a grater gradually into the boiling liquid. Keep at boiling point for a moment. Cover and lower heat and cook gently until tender. Add salt to taste and serve in bowls.

Leek Soup

3¾ cups stock or water	1 tbs. rice ground in blender or
4 leeks	mill
1 shallot or small onion	1 cup milk
1 sprig each thyme and parsley	

Bring water or stock to boil. Trim and wash leeks very thoroughly. Peel shallot or onion. Cut all in small pieces and drop into boiling water. Add herbs and cover. Lower heat and cook gently about 10–15 minutes. Cool and sieve or liquidize in blender, then return to pan. Stir ground rice into milk and stir into pan, continuing to stir until it has boiled for 5 more minutes. Season to taste before serving.

String Bean Soup

(Use beans too stringy and old to eat as vegetable)

2½ cups water	1 large potato, raw
salt to taste	1¾ cups milk
1 cup string beans, cut up	

Bring water and salt to boil. Drop in string beans. Grate in the raw potato and boil till beans are tender. Remove and cool. Liquidize and strain off fibers, or rub through sieve.

Add milk and re-heat short of boiling and serve.

Soya Soup

1 tbs. oil	2 tbs. soya flour (pre-cooked)
1 onion, chopped finely	5 cups vegetable stock or water
1 tomato, chopped finely	salt to taste

Heat oil and sauté onion and tomato lightly. Make paste with soya flour and a little of the liquid. Stir into rest of liquid, pour over onion and tomato mixture. Simmer 7–10 minutes, stirring frequently. Add salt if desired before serving.

Scotch Broth (millet, not barley)

½–1 lb. end of lamb roast	½ turnip
(omit if vegetarian)	½ celery stalk
7½ cups cold water or stock	1 tbs. whole millet
½ onion	salt to taste
½ carrot	1 tsp. parsley, finely chopped

Cut meat in small pieces, put into pan with water or stock and simmer gently about 2½ hours. Dice prepared vegetables and add to broth, with millet. Continue simmering about 30 minutes or till millet is tender. Strain and return broth to pan. Cut meat in very small pieces, carefully removing any fragment of bone from vegetables and millet and return all these to the broth. Re-heat, and season to taste before serving sprinkled with chopped parsley.

Spinach Soup

1 lb. spinach	2½ cups milk
2½ cups water	good pinch of salt
1 large potato	pinch of grated nutmeg
1 small onion	

Wash spinach thoroughly in many waters to remove any grit. Put in large pan with the water. Add the potato, well-scrubbed and diced, and onion finely chopped. Simmer until potato is tender. Remove and cool. Liquidize in blender or rub through a sieve. Return to pan, add milk, salt and grated nutmeg. Re-heat without boiling and serve.

Tomato Soup

1 small onion	pinch of basil
1 tbs. oil	2½ cups stock or water
1 lb. tomatoes (fresh or	1¾ cups milk
canned)	salt to taste
1 medium potato	

Peel and chop onion. Heat oil in pan and sauté onion lightly. Cut up tomatoes and potato and add with basil. Pour on stock or water and simmer about 15 minutes or till potato is tender. Cool and liquidize in blender and strain or rub through sieve. Return to pan, add milk and salt to taste and re-heat without boiling.

Quick Vegetable Soup

2 tbs. oil	1 sprig each marjoram, thyme
1 lb. carrots	and parsley and ½ bay leaf
1 small parsnip	1¼ cups milk
2 medium onions	1 tbs. parsley, chopped
2½ cups stock or water	salt to taste

Heat oil in pan and grate in finely the carrots, turnip, parsnip and onions. Sauté together lightly. Add stock and herbs tied in muslin. Simmer gently for a few minutes until tender. Remove herbs, add milk, salt to taste and re-heat. Add finely chopped parsley just before serving.

Mixed Vegetable Soup

Have boiling salted water ready in a pan. Throw in cut-up onion, carrots gently brushed and cut lengthwise, torn-up outer leaves of cabbage, sprouts, or broccoli, cut-up potato and any bits of vegetable in season. Five minutes before it is cooked throw in a large handful of cut-up parsley. It can be mashed up when ready. Serve thick with plenty of grated cheese, ringing the changes with milk, stock or Marmite. Eat it fresh.

Summer Soup (1) (uncooked, served cold)

1 lb. canned tomatoes or	¼ cucumber
1 lb. fresh tomatoes chopped in	¼ onion or 2 shallots, chopped
1 cup of water	1 clove garlic (optional)
½ bell pepper with seeds re-	1 tsp. raw sugar or molasses
moved (preferably red)	salt to taste

Wash vegetables thoroughly, peeling onion and garlic only, then drop all ingredients into a blender or use a Mouli machine to blend, adding more water if too thick. Taste and season, if required. Chill in refrigerator and serve in bowls. (This may also be heated in a pan with the lid on and served hot.)

Summer Soup (2) (uncooked, served hot)

1 small sweet pepper (red or green)	1 small apple
1 tomato	1 oz. blanched almonds
1 carrot	½ cup mashed potato
1 stick of celery	milk

Remove seeds from the sweet pepper, then wash and cut up with the other vegetables and pass all ingredients through blender or meat grinder. Add milk to dilute and allow to stand for 2 hours. Heat gently, keeping below boiling point, and serve in bowls.

SPREADS (in place of jams)

Apple Lemon Curd

½ lb. cooking apples
1 cup raw sugar
    juice and grated rind of 1½ lemons

2 eggs
4 tbs. butter

Cook apples lightly and puree or sieve when cool. Add sugar, lemon juice and grated rind. Beat in eggs and mix very thoroughly. Melt butter gradually in a pan first brushed with oil to prevent sticking. Add apple mixture and continue cooking and stirring for about 30 minutes. Cool, then seal in warm jars like jam.

Kidney Spread

½ lb. beef kidney, cooked and minced
1 raw onion, finely grated
¼ tsp. dried marjoram or thyme

½ tsp. salt
4 tbs. cottage cheese
    yogurt as required

Blend all ingredients gradually adding enough yogurt to make the mixture spread. Turn into screw-top glass jar and chill. Keep refrigerated. Serve between leaves of lettuce or on potato toast or plain droppies.

Liver Spread

1 tbs. oil
½ lb. liver, diced and trimmed of membranes and blood vessels
1 onion, chopped

½ tsp. salt
1 tbs. soya flour
    milk or stock as needed
1 sprig parsley
    pinch of marjoram or oregano

Heat oil in pan and sauté liver on both sides lightly. Set aside. Sauté onion in same pan. Cool. Put all ingredients one after the other into blender, adding enough stock to make a smooth paste and blend. Turn into small glass dish and chill. (If no blender, this can be pounded to a smooth paste with a pestle and mortar. Different herbs or flavoring can be used to suit individual tastes.) Eat in lettuce sandwiches or on droppies.

Piquant Spread

½ cup cottage cheese
¼ cup fresh milk or soya milk or
    1 tbs. powdered milk in ¼ cup
    water

2 tsp. grated raw onion juice or
    chopped chives
    paprika, salt or celery seed to
    taste

Soak cheese in fresh milk, add onion juice, then blend in blender or beat thoroughly with egg beater. Add seasoning to taste. Press into screw-top jar and chill. Use as spread on toasted potato slices or rice droppies, etc.

Pumpkin Lemon Curd

4 lb. pumpkin (seeds removed)
1 cup water
4 lb. raw sugar

2 sticks (½ lb.) butter
6 lemons

Peel, chop and simmer pumpkin 15–20 minutes. Drain and rub through a sieve. Stir in sugar and butter. Grate rind of lemons into the mixture. Squeeze in juice and pulp discarding pips and pith. Boil for 5 minutes and allow to cool slightly. Turn into warm jars as for jam. Sets on cooling.

Potted Meat Spread

¼ lb. leftover heart, etc., diced
    small or minced
1 onion, chopped roughly, raw
1 tbs. soya flour (commercial,
    i.e. pre-cooked)

½ tsp. sea salt
    sprig of parsley, chopped
    finely

Blend all ingredients gradually. Moisten with a little melted butter, oil or home-made mayonnaise. Press into glass dish and chill. Serve with plain droppies, potato toast or between lettuce leaves.

Shrimp Spread

20 fresh shrimp, boiled	grated nutmeg
1 tbs. butter	1 tsp. melted butter
sprinkle of paprika	

Peel and chop shrimps, pound in a mortar or bowl; beat together butter and paprika and grated nutmeg. Add pounded shrimps and mix well. Press into small glass dish or jar and cover with 1 tsp. melted butter and parchment paper. Put weight on top and chill for 24 hours.

VEGETABLE AND FRUIT COOKING
(for best nutritional value)

The rules for preparing vegetables and fruits are simple and few but important. It is so easy to be a killer in the kitchen, murdering the enzymes, vitamins and minerals committed to our care and necessary for the health of the household. Here is a list of the essential rules and the reasons for them:

Rule	*Reason*
1. Leave on roots, tops and outer leaves in gathering or buying. Cut off just before washing.	Delays wilting, and vitamin values are increased until the onset of wilting, when they decline.
2. Wash rapidly and thoroughly under the cold tap.	Soaking, or using warm water causes loss of vitamins B and C.
3. Drain quickly then pat fruits and roots dry with Turkish towelling. Dry leafy ones by whirling in a bag made of this or an old pillow slip.	This prevents minerals, water-soluble vitamins B and C and flavors passing into the water as readily as sugar or salt.

4. Keep in a plastic bag, or other closed receptacle in refrigerator until required for salad or cooking.

Prevents attack by oxygen and enzymes causing loss of vitamins A, C and E.

5. Keep all requiring storage in a cool dark place.

Light and warmth can steal much riboflavin, folic acid and vitamin C.

6. Avoid peeling as much as possible. Scrub well with nylon nail brush.

Many valuable nutrients lie in and under the skin.

7. Never discard liquids from cooking. Save for use in soups and gravies.

These contain extracted minerals and vitamins.

COOKING VEGETABLES

Boiling vegetables is an insult to plant and palate. It should never be inflicted on either. Methods of preserving flavor, appearance and food value include the following:

1. Pressure cooking absolutely accurately according to the instructions issued with the utensil. Over-cooking very rapidly occurs causing unpleasant odors leading to flatulence and indigestion from the breakdown of sulphur, destruction of vitamin B complex as well as vitamin C, and loss of flavor through expulsion of aromatic oils and damage to proteins.
2. Waterless cooking (so-called). This in fact requires a couple of tablespoons of water heated to boiling point to fill the utensil with steam to drive out the oxygen. The vegetable or fruit is then dropped in gradually. When the material is heated through, heat is lowered to prevent the escape of steam, and the natural water content is sufficient to complete the cooking.
3. Steaming in a steamer or on a rack in a pan. Vegetables are left unpeeled and uncut if possible, to prevent too many minerals and water-soluble vitamins dissolving into the water below, which should in any case be kept and used in gravy or soup.

4. Sautéing in a covered pan. 1–2 tablespoons of oil are heated, well dried and chilled vegetables are shredded freshly with a sharp knife, dropped in and well tossed to coat them with the oil and seal the surfaces against oxygen. When heated through they should be covered and cooked at lower heat about 5–10 minutes.

5. Broiling, after brushing with oil, heating rapidly to heat through, then turned to ensure crispness and to prevent shriveling.

6. Frying well dried and chilled vegetables cut up and dropped into deep hot oil has the advantage that cooking time is short and only oil and the natural juices are used, but it is not recommended for frequent use and the oil must not be re-used.

7. Baking either in or out of jacket for onions or potatoes has the disadvantage of slow initial heating and long cooking with subsequent loss of vitamin C and more still if jacket is removed by peeling and exposure to oxygen. This can be overcome to some extent if surfaces are brushed with oil, or if vegetables are first steamed, and only finished in pre-heated oven.

8. Quick cooking in milk. This has become our favorite method for all green stuffs as well as root crops. Milk, like oil, acts to prevent dissolution of minerals and vitamins and has a wonderfully sweetening and digestive effect on even quite elderly and coarse green leaves of cabbage (red and white), cauliflower, broccoli, chard, kale, spinach, turnips, radishes and also such sulfur-rich things as onions. This is the method which I owe to Adelle Davis, though I have added a preliminary brush with oil on the bottom of the pan to keep the milk from sticking which it does so easily if one turns one's back. After applying the oil, pour in ½ to 1 cup of milk, replace cover and bring to the steaming point. Meanwhile, shred vegetables with a sharp knife or cut up small if a root, drop in, replace cover, shake well to coat all surfaces with the milk, keep heat up for a few seconds to heat through, then lower to simmering and leave

5–7 minutes. If all the milk has not been absorbed pour it off to add to gravy or soup, and serve the vegetable as it is.

N.B. Always sprinkle with a pinch of sea salt just before serving instead of at the beginning of cooking which drains out the juices and flavors, and garnish with paprika, chopped fresh herbs, a dash of oil or butter, or a grating of onion as liked.

COOKING FRUIT FOR DESSERT

All fruits except quinces are best eaten ripe and raw. However, if you must cook some, it saves vitamins and minerals *not* to stew slowly and long, *not* to cook unripe fruit with masses of sugar, guaranteed to steal vitamin C.

Use only fully ripe fruit when the natural sugar content is at its highest, cook lightly and shortly, without sugar, just before serving with a jug of top of the milk containing a level tablespoon of powdered milk well stirred into it. The additional milk sugar (lactose) not only sweetens, but aids the absorption of calcium, which is decreased by the addition of cane or beet sugar. Alternatives are honey diluted with water, or yogurt, or else to add a few chopped raisins or dates when cooking or serve with a boiled custard sweetened with honey.

PRESERVED AND CANNED FRUIT

Preserved fruit is not, of course, raw fruit but a useful way of using surplus summer fruit in winter. If put up at home, there is no need for any sugar at all, just water. All *canned* fruits, unfortunately, as well as commercially preserved fruits are heavily sweetened with white sugar and should be avoided; the higher the grade the higher the amounts of sugar.

POTATOES

Learn to respect the common potato. Although it is predominantly a carbohydrate food, its protein is ranked as superior to those found in the cereal grains. So "a liberal amount of potatoes in the diet is preferable to its equivalent in cereals" (Mattice, M. M., *Bridges Food and Beverage Analysis*, Henry Kimpton, London, 1950). In fact, potato proteins have been revealed as a very good source of the essential amino acids, and except for histidine as much higher than whole wheat (Hughes, B.P., *Brit. J. Nutr.*, 12, 188–95, 1947), and numerous nutritional and "balance" experiments with potatoes as the sole source of protein have consistently proved the high value of the protein content (Schuphan, Werner, *Nutritional Values in Crop Plants*, Faber and Faber, 1965). So anyone on a gluten-free diet is losing nothing, but in fact gaining in nutritional value, by using potatoes in place of bread, biscuits, breakfast cereals and so on.

But of course this does *not* mean *chips with everything*. There are far better ways of serving them (see recipes which follow). Avoid deep-fried potatoes when eating out in restaurants (even in Chinese ones where liquid oils are used), because hydrogenated fats are the cheapest and are always used. Unfortunately, all fats are re-used time and time again and this practice has been found to produce an anti-vitamin A factor, destroying part of the vitamin A activity of foods eaten at the same time (Peacock, P. R., *Brit. Med. Bull.*, 4, 364, 1947).

Warning

However, one warning regarding potatoes must now be given, as it was from the House of Commons by Sir Keith Joseph, Minister of Health, in September 1972, that damaged, discolored or diseased potatoes should be discarded. This warning is based on the hypothesis of Dr. James Renwick (*New Scientist*, 2, 11, 1972) that if such potatoes are eaten during the first month of pregnancy an unknown factor in such blighted potatoes may cause such serious birth defects as spina bifida and anencephaly. A controlled clinical test of potato-avoidance in women at high risk has been suggested, but this could take up to five years. In the meantime, heed the warning and discard all diseased, damaged and discolored potatoes, but use good ones lavishly.

Jacket Potatoes Baked in a Pan

Select long slim ones. Scrub thoroughly and dry with toweling. Brush all over with oil. Put in a pre-heated pan with 2 tbs. oil—replace lid and keep heat fairly high for 5 minutes to heat them through. Lower heat and simmer gently for 20–30 minutes, till tender when pierced by fork to let out steam. Leave off lid for last 5 minutes.

Potatoes Baked under Broiler

Scrub required number of potatoes and dry with towelling. Brush with oil and place on baking sheet under moderate broiler. Leave about 15 minutes then turn to heat through. Transfer to moderate oven, 350° F. and cook about another 15 minutes or till tender when pierced by fork to let out steam.

Jacket Potatoes Baked in Oven

Place potatoes prepared as above in hot oven, 450° F. and cook about 45 minutes, or till tender when pierced.

Baked Potatoes with Lemon Curd (apple or pumpkin)

Use organically grown potatoes to get the best flavor. Parboil in jackets. Cut off skin on top and scoop out a little from the middle. Fill cavity with lemon curd, replace the "cover" and bake until tender when the curd flavor will have spread through the potato. Eat for a snack or light supper.

Potatoes Steamed

Drop required number of scrubbed, unpeeled small potatoes or large ones cut to size into ½ cup of boiling water, or place on rack above boiling water. Replace lid and cook about 15–20 minutes or till tender. Peel, holding with fork when slightly cooled, return to pan to heat up and sprinkle with salt to taste, and a little chopped parsley mixed with melted butter or oil.

New Pototoes Baked

Scrub and dry well small new potatoes, place them on oiled baking pan and either bake in oven or on top of the stove for about 20 minutes shaking a couple of times to turn them over. Serve sprinkled with salt, oil and paprika.

Potatoes Oven-Fried

Scrub required number of potatoes and chill. Do not peel but cut into thin sticks. Pat dry, toss in a bowl with 1–2 tbs. oil. Put into hot oven, 450° F. in a baking pan and leave about 8 minutes, lower heat and cook till tender. Sprinkle lightly with salt before serving.

Broiled Potato Slices

Select large waxy potatoes. Scrub well, but do not peel. Chill. Cut in thin slices. Brush both sides with oil and arrange on oiled baking sheet under broiler. Cook about 5 minutes or until nicely brown, then turn and cook another 3 to 5 minutes until brown on the other side. Sprinkle lightly with salt and serve. Buttered hot, these can be spread with any savory spread such as Marmite and eaten for snacks instead of buttered toast.

206 GOOD FOOD, GLUTEN FREE

Potato Sticks

Scrub potatoes thoroughly without peeling. Over a couple of layers of paper towels shred the potatoes coarsely with a potato peeler or on a grater to make sticks from ¼-inch to ⅛-inch thick. Cover with more paper towels and leave to absorb the moisture. Place in an oiled pan and bake until crisp in a hot oven, 425° F. Sprinkle lightly with salt.

Potatoes Creamed

Use either small new, or old potatoes, whole, or cut large ones into similar sizes. Rub off skins or peel lightly. Drop them into a pan containing about 1 cup of milk. Replace lid and simmer about 10–15 minutes or till tender, and most of milk has been absorbed. Sprinkle lightly with salt. Serve sprinkled with grating of onion or finely chopped chives or parsley.

Emerald Potatoes

Scrub and chill then cut in 1-in. chunks, 4 large unpeeled potatoes (peeling only if pedantic about whiteness). Simmer in ½ cup of hot milk in a closed pan about 10 minutes or till soft. Heat ricer well over the pan, press potatoes through ricer into pan, add 2 tbs. finely chopped parsley and 2 tbs. top milk and beat with fork till well mixed in. Taste for seasoning with salt and serve at once. Or steam above boiling water till tender, then treat in same way (N.B. adding the parsley makes up for the vitamin C lost in ricing and beating).

Potato Salad

Salad should consist of raw vegetables, so this is a misnomer but a popular name for the dish and a pleasant way of serving them as a cooked vegetable or of using leftover steamed potatoes. Steam above a small amount of boiling water about 4 large waxy scrubbed unpeeled potatoes. Chill, then peel and dice them. Mix well with ½ cup home-made mayonnaise, sprinkle with chopped chives, mint or parsley or scallions. Serve on bed of watercress or ringed by lettuce or mustard and cress. (N.B. Do not keep overnight, as potato salad soon decomposes.)

Shredded Potatoes (quick cooked)

Shred over paper towels, then pat dry, 4 thoroughly chilled, scrubbed unpeeled potatoes. Heat 4 tbs. oil in a pan and drop in potatoes. Keep heat high, turn frequently and cook till golden brown, about 5–8 minutes. Sprinkle with salt and a dash of paprika. If liked, a little shredded onion may be cooked with the potatoes.

Steamed Unpeeled Potato Leftovers

Keep in refrigerator overnight. Slice thinly and heat up in ¼ cup hot milk or leftover gravy, sprinkle with chopped chives and serve.

Potato and Cheese Pan Roast

6 medium potatoes, raw   2 tbs. oil
½ cup cheese, grated   salt to taste
1 onion, finely chopped

Scrub potatoes well and steam unpeeled till nearly cooked. Peel and grate them coarsely. Mix with cheese and salt. Fry onion in hot oil till golden. Stir in potato mix. Press mixture down well in pan and cook over low heat till brown and crusty below taking care not to burn. Turn over on to hot round dish, serving with a crust uppermost. A poached egg may be arranged on each quarter as a breakfast dish.

Sautéed Potatoes

2 tbs. oil   sprinkle of salt or kelp
3 or 4 medium-sized potatoes

Heat oil in pan. Cut potatoes in thin slices and drop into pan. Toss well to cook until lightly brown, about 5 minutes if pre-cooked and 5 to 10 minutes longer if you are using raw pota-toes. Sprinkle with salt or kelp and serve.

VEGETARIAN DISHES

As vegetarians rely largely on delicious and nutritious whole-meal bread at most meals, and wholemeal flour in much of their cooking, they are accustomed to eat much more rye, oats, wheat and barley than meat eaters and likely to feel more deprived than most of us of these four grains and their products.

However, they, above all, should avoid replacing them by gluten-free flour or cornflour, but should instead use whole rice, whole corn and whole millet and soya.

There seems to be no separate record of how many vege-tarians are celiac, multiple sclerosis or schizophrenia sufferers. But for those who are, a special warning is due. Today, wheat gluten (cheaper than corn, which is mostly fed to stock), is widely included in made-up vegetarian foods in order to put up the protein content with this filler, leftover, presumably when white flour has been made gluten-free for the special use of celiacs. Recalling that healthy volunteers who were given 100 grams (about ¾ cup) of gluten daily for no more than 10 weeks, developed mild symptoms of celiac disease (Levine, R. A., et al., Am. J. Clin. Nutr., 14, 142, 1964), one wonders whether vegetarians may not run into trouble if they too reach the stage of eating ¾ cup of gluten daily.

In any case, any vegetarian on a gluten-free diet would be well advised to give up all commercial made-up foods (unless they carry a guarantee that they only contain corn protein, which is permissible) and rely entirely on home-made dishes from known ingredients.

Indeed, as meat and fish get more and more expensive, non-vegetarians could do worse than sample some of the savory vegetarian recipes which follow.

VEGETARIAN

Apple and Coconut Curry (no curry powder)

Basic Rice as desired, cooked with onion skin to color yellow
2 tbs. oil
2 onions, finely chopped
2 cups tomatoes, finely chopped
1 tbs. raisins
1 tsp. molasses
1 tsp. ground ginger
1 tsp. allspice
2 cooking apples cored and chopped
1 cup shredded coconut

Heat oil. Fry onions and tomatoes until tender. Add raisins, molasses and spices and stir well. Cook for 1 minute. Add apples and coconut and cook for 5 minutes. Scatter over Basic Rice, re-heated, and serve.

Butter Bean Pie

1½ cups butter beans, pre-cooked
½ cup finely chopped onions or leeks
½ cup finely chopped celery
¼ cup chopped peanuts
2 eggs, beaten
½ cup milk
salt or kelp to taste
1 cup mashed potatoes
1 tbs. butter

Mix the butter beans, onions, celery, nuts, eggs, milk and salt in a bowl thoroughly. Turn into an oiled pie pan and press down evenly. Cover with potatoes, smooth over with knife and dot with butter. Bake in moderate oven, 350° F. for about 40 minutes or until surface is well browned.

Basic Soybeans

After soaking soybeans according to the basic preparation procedure described on page 82, they may be cooked in one of two ways:

In a pressure cooker for 15 to 30 minutes at 15 pounds pressure, or

Cook, covered, in water for about 3 hours, skimming the foam from the beans when they begin to boil. Cook at low heat and replace water when necessary.

Savory Soybeans

2 tbs. oil
1 large onion, finely chopped
1 cup tomatoes, finely chopped
1 tsp. salt or kelp

1 tsp. molasses
2 cups Basic Soybeans
2 tbs. chives, chopped

Heat oil in pan and saute onions and tomatoes until tender. Add salt, molasses and soybeans, cover and heat well. Serve garnished with chopped chives.

Carrot and Chive Cutlets

2 cups Basic Rice
2 tbs. chopped chives
1 large carrot, grated fine
2 tbs. peanuts, chopped fine
2 tbs. powdered milk

½ tsp. salt or kelp
1 egg, beaten
cornmeal to coat
2 tbs. oil

Mash rice with fork until quite smooth. Mix in chives, carrot, peanuts, powdered milk and salt. Shape into cutlets, set aside on plate to dry. Dip in egg and coat with cornmeal. Heat oil in pan and fry cutlets until lightly browned on both sides.

Carrot and Rice Loaf

2 cups raw carrot, grated
1 cup celery, grated
½ cup unhydrogenated peanut butter

1½ cups Basic Rice
4 tbs. soya flour
2 eggs, lightly beaten
salt or kelp to taste

Mix carrot, celery, peanut butter and rice. Then blend in the soya flour. Pour beaten eggs over mixture and stir well, adding salt or kelp to taste. Turn into oiled casserole and bake at 325° F. about 50 minutes or till set.

Savory Soya Loaf

2 cups Basic Soybeans (cooked)
1 cup onion, shredded
1 cup celery, shredded
1–2 tbs. vegetable water or water

½ cup Basic Rice (cooked)
½ tbs. oil
sprinkle of paprika

Mash up the soybeans in a bowl. Add and mix well onions, celery and liquid. Pack into a pie pan, smooth down and spread Basic Rice over the surface. Brush with oil, sprinkle with paprika and bake in moderate oven, 350° F. about 30 minutes until nicely brown.

Vegetable Casserole

1 cup raw potato, shredded
2 cups shredded raw carrot
1 cup onions, finely sliced
1 cup Basic Rice (cooked)
2 tbs. soya flour

1 tsp. salt or kelp
pinch of raw sugar
1 cup raw tomato juice
(reserve pulp for stews, etc.)

Blend all ingredients thoroughly in bowl to make wettish mixture. Add a little water if too dry. Turn into oiled casserole, cover tightly, and bake about 30 minutes in a moderate oven, 350° F.

Mixed Vegetable Cutlets

2 onions
2 carrots
1 potato
½ cup peanuts, finely ground

½ cup powdered milk
½ tsp. salt or kelp
2 eggs, well beaten
2 tbs. oil

Mince onions, carrots and potato fine or shred fine on grater. Combine with peanuts, powdered milk, salt and eggs. If mixture is not dry enough add powdered milk. Spread out on a plate and chill for 30 minutes. Shape into cutlets. Heat oil in pan and fry cutlets until well browned, turning to brown other side, or brush with oil and broil till brown on both sides.

Peanut and Potato Loaf

3 cups mashed potatoes
1 onion, chopped and sautéed in oil
1 cup celery or carrot, chopped
1 cup peanuts, minced

grated nutmeg
3 tbs. parsley, finely chopped
1 egg, beaten
1 tsp. salt or kelp

Mix all ingredients thoroughly, adding a little milk or water if too dry. Turn into oiled loaf pan. Bake at 350° F. for 30 minutes. Serve hot with grated cheese or chill and serve in thin slices as open sandwiches without bread, with choice of spreads.

Potato and Cheese Soufflé

3 or 4 medium potatoes
3 eggs, separated
1¼ cups cheese, grated

good pinch paprika
pinch of salt or kelp
3 tbs. light cream

Scrub potatoes and steam unpeeled until tender. Sieve or put through ricer. Beat egg yolks into potato in a bowl, then beat in the cheese, seasoning and cream. Beat egg whites until stiff and fold them in. Bake in soufflé dish in fairly hot oven, 400° F. for about 25-30 minutes. Serve immediately.

Potato Droppies (Savory)

4 chilled unpeeled potatoes
1 small onion

1 tbs. rice flour
1 tsp. salt or kelp

Grate or shred finely potatoes on to a dish towel and squeeze dry. Place in a bowl. Add grated onion, rice flour and salt and mix well. Drop by spoonfuls into hot oil in a pan. Sauté till well browned on both sides. Serve with chopped parsley and butter blended.

Rice and Cheese

1 egg
1 cup milk
1 small onion, chopped finely
2 cups Basic Rice

½ cup cheese, grated
salt, depending on saltiness of cheese
½ tbs. oil

Beat egg lightly, then beat in milk. Add rest of ingredients except oil, and mix thoroughly. Brush casserole with oil. Turn mixture into it and bake in moderate oven, 350° F. till set.

Rice Flake Croquettes

½ cup onions, chopped
1¼ cups hot water
½ lb. rice flakes
2 tbs. ground nuts (peanuts, soya, hazel, etc.)
2 eggs, well beaten

salt to taste
grated nutmeg
a little chopped parsley or marjoram
paprika

Cook onions in oil or butter until soft. Pour the water on the flakes in a bowl, add the other ingredients and mix thoroughly. Form into croquettes. Sprinkle with paprika to assist browning, and fry in a pan with a little hot oil until nicely brown.

Rice and Parsley Cheese

2 tbs. oil
1 onion, chopped
1 clove garlic (optional)
1 cup rice
2 cups water or vegetable water, hot

½ tsp. basil or marjoram
3 tbs. parsley, finely chopped
good pinch of turmeric
½ cup cheese, grated

Heat oil and sauté onion and garlic if used. Add rice and cook
3 minutes stirring constantly. Grains should all be golden.
Add basil, tumeric and parsley to hot water and pour 1 cup
of this on rice. Cover and let simmer, add remaining cup of
water gradually, till it is all absorbed—about 30–40 minutes.
A few minutes before serving, add half the cheese. When
lightly melted remove from heat, add rest of cheese and serve.

Rice Patties

1 cup Basic Rice (cooked)   a little powdered milk
1 tbs. oil

Combine ingredients, using enough milk powder to bind.
Shape into patties and arrange in oiled baking pan. Sprinkle
with paprika. Broil till each side is browned.

Savory Rice

2 small onions   1 tsp. salt
2 tbs. oil   7½ cups vegetable water
2½ cups rice   nutmeg, chives and parsley

Sauté chopped onions in oil, add cleaned rice, salt and vegetable water on a low heat and cook for 30–40 minutes—a longer
cooking time and more water may be needed. When ready,
add nutmeg, chives and parsley. Serve with more fried onions
and tomato sauce (home-made).

Savory Rice Cutlets

3 medium potatoes   1 tsp. Marmite
2 tbs. oil   ¾ cup milk
1 cup Savory Rice   1 egg, beaten
1 onion, grated   2 tbs. ground rice
    pinch of salt or kelp

Steam the scrubbed, unpeeled potatoes till tender. Meanwhile, heat oil in pan, add the rice, grated onion, salt, Marmite, and milk, and stir till it boils. Leave to simmer gently about 15 minutes. When potatoes are cooked, peel and mash smoothly, then add to the mixture. Beat well together, then spread out on an oiled surface. Cut in any shape desired when cold. Roll in egg and ground rice and fry till golden brown. Serve with plenty of chopped parsley in melted butter.

Soya Flat Cakes

2 cups soybeans (well cooked)   1 egg
1 onion, grated   salt to taste
   soya flour to dredge

Mash soybeans well in a bowl, grate in peeled onion and stir thoroughly. Add the egg beaten lightly and salt. Form into small flat cakes. Dredge in the soya flour and cook in an oiled baking pan in moderate oven 350° F. until brown, turning to brown other side.

Millet and Mushroom Stew

2 tbs. oil   4 cups water
1 large onion, chopped   ½ tsp. salt
½ cup mushrooms, sliced   ½ tsp. basil
1 cup raw millet

Heat the oil and sauté onion and mushrooms about 7 minutes. Add the millet, water, salt and basil. Cover and simmer gently 45 minutes or longer until the millet is tender. Serve at once.

Carrot Fingers Toasted

4 large carrots   3 tbs. boiling salted water
1 tbs. oil

Scrub carrots well and cut in four, lengthwise. Brush saucepan with oil, add boiling water, and drop in carrot fingers.

Cover tightly and simmer gently about 10 minutes. Add a
drop more water if needed to prevent burning. Remove, pat
dry with toweling, brush with oil and place on oiled baking
pan, and cook in moderate oven, 350° F. about 10 minutes, or
place under moderate heat and broil until toasted.

Cheese Dumplings

7 tbs. butter	½ cup rice flakes
3 eggs	pinch of salt
½ cup cottage cheese	pinch of saffron
2 cups milk	

Cream butter in bowl, add well-beaten eggs, cottage cheese,
milk, rice flakes, salt and saffron. Mix well and add more milk
if too solid or more flakes if not firm enough to form
dumplings with hands. Drop into boiling salted water. When
they rise to the top, they are ready. Serve with braised onions
or tomato puree or horseradish sauce.

Cheese and Potato Pancake

2 onions, sliced	1 cup cheese, grated
2–3 tbs. oil	good pinch of salt
4 cooked potatoes, sliced	4 eggs, whole

Sauté onions in hot oil till tender, add potato slices and
cheese, sprinkle with salt, press down in pan and fry till
golden. Turn to brown other side. Cover with plate, reverse
pan and slip pancake on to warm dish. Fry 4 eggs lightly and
place on top.

Savory Cheese and Potato

6 steamed potatoes, slightly un- dercooked	2 tbs. oil
⅔ cup cheese, grated	1 onion, finely chopped

Peel potatoes, grate coarsely and mix with cheese. Heat oil in pan and sauté onion till golden brown. Mix in potato and cheese, press down well in the pan and cook over low heat till well browned below. Turn on to dish. Garnish with chopped parsley or chives.

Cheese and Rice Rolls

1 cup cheese, shredded	salt to taste
1½ cups Basic Rice (cooked)	1 egg
2 tbs. onion, grated	1–2 tbs. oil
2 tbs. parsley, chopped	

Mix together all ingredients except oil. Form into rolls or fingers. Roll in powdered milk, cornmeal or ground rice. Sauté in oil till nicely brown.

Basic Omelet (enriched)

¾ cup fresh milk	4 eggs
2 tbs. powdered milk	1 tsp. salt

Blend in blender or beat well together fresh and powdered milk. Add eggs and salt, beating lightly. Pour into heated frying pan brushed with oil. Cover and heat slowly about 8 minutes. Loosen edges with spatula, and fold to center, letting uncooked egg run to sides of pan. Recover and heat 5–8 minutes. Fold over alone or over desired filling. Cover and serve as soon as heated through.

Spanish Omelet (to be eaten cold)

3 or 4 medium unpeeled potatoes	pinch of salt
1 bunch spring onions	6 eggs
1 small, sweet pepper	2½ eggshells of cold water
	2 tbs. oil

Dice potatoes in ½ in. cubes. Skin and halve onions if they are large. Open sweet pepper, remove seeds and shred. Break eggs into bowl, add water measured in half-eggshell (as handy measure). Season eggs and beat with a fork just enough to break and mix yolks and whites. Heat oil in pan and fry potatoes slowly till nearly tender, add onions and pepper and fry till all are light brown and tender. Pour egg mixture on to vegetables and cook the omelet, stirring it to start with over fairly brisk heat until it sets solid. Chill. Pack between plates or in flat container and serve cut in wedges for picnics.

Egg Pilau

1 onion, chopped
1 clove garlic, minced (optional)
4 tbs. oil
1 cup rice
2–3 cups hot water
½ tsp. allspice, ground

½ tsp. cinnamon
3 cloves
1 tsp. salt
4 tbs. blanched almonds or peanuts
2 eggs, hard-boiled

Sauté onion (and garlic, if used) in oil. Add rice and cook till transparent, stirring constantly. Pour hot water over spices and salt and add ½ cup of this to pan of rice. Cover and simmer gently, adding rest of liquid till all is absorbed and rice is tender, about 30–35 minutes. Stir in sliced almonds or peanuts and raisins and garnish with chopped egg.

Savory Steamed Eggs

3 eggs
2 scant cups milk or home-made soya milk
2 tbs. oil
1 tsp. sea salt

1 tbs. finely chopped chives or green part of scallions or young leeks
paprika

Beat the eggs in a large bowl with rotary beater. Add other ingredients and beat again well. Pour into a deep casserole.

Cover. Place in steamer, or rack, over boiling water in a saucepan, and cook steadily but not too vigorously for 20 minutes. Sprinkle with paprika and serve.

Basic Lentils

2 cups water or stock   1 tsp. salt
1 cup lentils

Bring water to boil. Add lentils slowly so as not to stop boiling. Cover and simmer 30 minutes or till tender. Add salt.

Lentil Flatties

⅔ cup lentils   pinch of thyme
1¼ cups water   ⅔ cup cooked rice
1 onion, chopped   1 egg, beaten
1 tomato, peeled, seeded and   2 tbs. ground rice or powdered
  juiced   milk
1 tbs. oil   2 tbs. oil for frying
½ tsp. salt   chopped parsley in butter

Wash and cover lentils with water. Leave overnight. Add onion, tomato, oil and seasoning, cover pan and simmer 2 hours. Stir in rice and keep stirring about 10 minutes till mixture is stiff. Cool. Form into flat cakes. Dip in beaten egg, roll in ground rice or powdered milk, and sauté in oil till brown on both sides. Serve with chopped parsley blended with butter.

Lentil and Millet Casserole

2 cups Basic Lentils (cooked)   pinch nutmeg
1 cup Basic Millet (cooked)   4 tbs. parsley, minced
1 egg, beaten   ½ tsp. salt
2 tbs. oil   pinch of thyme and marjoram
2 onions   sprinkle of paprika
1 clove garlic (optional)   stock or water to moisten

Blend all ingredients, adding just enough liquid to make firm

consistency. Turn into oiled casserole and sprinkle with paprika. Bake in fairly hot oven, 375° F. about 30 minutes.
Serve with home-made tomato or savory sauce.

Savory Cornmeal with Roasted Onion

1¼ cups water	1 tbs. butter or oil (i)
2½ cups milk	1 onion, finely chopped and
good pinch of salt	roasted
1 cup (scant) cornmeal	2 tsp. butter (ii)

Boil water, milk and salt, add cornmeal, then butter (i) and
stir. Cook for about 20–30 minutes. Serve with butter (ii) and
roasted onion.

Polenta Savory Droppies

1 cup cornmeal	1 egg, beaten
1 tbs. soya flour	1 cup cheese, grated
3 cups water	salt to taste

Stir cornmeal and soya into 1 cup of liquid. Blend to paste.
Bring to boil rest of liquid in top of double boiler over direct
heat. When boiling add meal mixture. Stir till smooth. Place
over hot water in double boiler. Cover. Cook gently till all
liquid is absorbed. Remove. Leave to cool till lukewarm. Stir
in smoothly beaten egg, salt and grated cheese. Drop spoonfuls on oiled baking sheet. Broil until brown on both sides.

Baked Millet Savory

1 onion	1 tsp. mixed herbs
⅓ cup whole millet	2 eggs
2 cups cheese, grated	1½ cups milk or soya milk
pinch of salt	

Peel the onion, cut up and cook in a pan with the millet in
water so that all is absorbed by the time the millet is cooked.

Add the grated cheese, seasoning, beaten eggs and milk. If a little too much water is used in cooking the millet, reduce milk. The mixture should be a thick pouring consistency when placed in a greased baking pan. Bake in a moderate oven, 350° F. for 30–40 minutes, until golden brown.

Millet Mix

5 cups stock
1 cup millet, uncooked
1 tsp. salt

3 tbs. mixed herbs
6 hard-boiled eggs

Bring stock to boil. Add millet slowly. Stir in salt and herbs. Simmer till millet is tender. Add hard-boiled eggs halved. Heat through. Serve garnished with cress, watercress or parsley sprigs.

Millet and Mushroom Casserole

4 tbs. oil
1 lb. mushrooms, chopped
2 onions, chopped

1½ cups raw millet
5 cups hot water or stock

Sauté mushrooms in oil 5 minutes. Set aside. Sauté chopped onions till browned and set aside. Toss millet in same oil and stir well till all grains are coated. Remove. Mix with mushrooms and onions and pour hot liquid over the mixture. Turn into an oiled casserole. Cover and bake in moderate oven, 350° F. about 60 minutes, adding a little more liquid if needed. Sprinkle with chopped chives or parsley before serving.

Millet and Onion Cheese Casserole

½ cup whole millet
2½ cups water
2 large onions
  salt to taste

dried herbs to taste (sage, marjoram or thyme)
1¼ cups milk
2–2½ cups cheese, grated

Place millet in water and cook 30-40 minutes, till tender and all water is absorbed. Peel onions, chop finely and stir in with salt and herbs, add the milk and most of the grated cheese. Place in a shallow oiled dish, sprinkle top with rest of cheese and bake in moderate oven, 350° F. about half an hour till top is golden brown.

Millet Pilau (1)

2 tbs. oil
1 large onion, chopped
1 large tomato, chopped
1 cup mushrooms, chopped

1 cup Basic Millet (cooked)
2 tbs. raisins
1 cup sour cream or top milk

Heat oil in pan and sauté gently onion, tomato and mushrooms. Stir in millet and raisins and continue cooking gently till all liquid is absorbed. Stir in some cream or milk and serve.

Millet Pilau (2)

1 cup millet, raw
1 tbs. oil
¾ cup water
1 tsp. salt

1–1½ tbs. onion juice
    small crushed cloves of garlic
    (optional)

Wash millet thoroughly then dry carefully. Heat oil in a large pan and add the millet. Fry till golden over medium heat, turning grains occasionally. Pour in water, allow to steam up, and add salt, onion juice and crushed garlic. Cook gently till all water is absorbed, when the grains should appear separate and dry. Flavor with fresh herbs, borage or basil, finely chopped scallions, or thin slices of raw button mushrooms. Stir and heat through well. Serve at once.

Millet Soufflé

1 cup milk
4 eggs, separated

2 cups Basic Millet (cooked in milk)
½ cup cheese, grated

Combine milk and egg yolks and cooked millet. Blend in cheese. Beat whites stiffly and fold in. Turn into oiled soufflé dish or individual baking dishes. Bake at 350° F. about 20 minutes.

Baked Chestnut and Onion Pie

1 lb. chestnuts
6 medium onions
1–2 tbs. oil for frying

a little rice flour or mashed potato to thicken
a little milk

Boil chestnuts till tender—about 20–30 minutes. Remove skins. Peel and chop onions finely and fry in the oil. Stir the rice flour or mashed potato into some of the milk and pour this over the onions, stirring all the time, and adding the rest of the milk. Pour into a casserole. Add the chestnuts and mix together. Cover and cook in the casserole in moderate oven, 350° F. till thoroughly heated. Serve with greens or a salad.

Steamed Vegetable Loaf

2 tbs. oil
1 cup tomatoes, chopped fine
1 cup onions, chopped fine
¼ cup peanuts, chopped fine
2 eggs, beaten
2 tbs. soya flour

2 tbs. powdered milk
¼ cup vegetable or plain water
grated nutmeg
½ tsp. salt
½ tsp. basil or marjoram
1 tbs. parsley, minced

Heat oil and sauté tomatoes and onions lightly. Blend with rest of ingredients. Turn into oiled pudding mold. Cover tightly. Steam 1½ hours. Set aside for 10 minutes, then turn

out. Chill. Serve in slices. Or keep in mold, chill and take for
outdoor meal, cutting in wedges or slices.

Uncooked Nut Savory

1 tomato, put through blender	salt to taste
1¼ cup coconut, shredded	1 tsp. chopped marjoram or
1 tsp. onion, grated fine	basil (dried or fresh)
⅔ cup hazel nuts, ground	mashed potato to stiffen

Pour tomato over coconut shreds and leave to be soaked up
for a few minutes. Beat with fork and add rest of ingredients,
adding enough mashed potato to make a stiff mixture. Press
into an oiled bowl, cover and chill. Serve sliced with jacket
potatoes and a green salad. Keeps 1–3 days.

Baked Walnuts and Cheese

1 tbs. oil	½ lemon
2 onions, chopped	pinch of salt or more, de-
1 cup walnuts, minced	pending on saltiness of cheese
1 cup hard cheese, grated	paprika to sprinkle
2 eggs, beaten	

Sauté chopped onion in hot oil till transparent. Add all other
ingredients and mix well. Taste for seasoning. Turn into oiled
loaf pan and sprinkle with paprika. Bake at 350° F. about 30
minutes. Serve with plain yogurt lightly salted.

Nut and Millet Rissolés

½ cup whole millet	1 tsp. mixed herbs
1 large onion	salt to taste
2 tbs. oil	grated nutmeg
⅔ cup nuts, minced fine or	milk or beaten egg
ground	powdered milk, cornmeal or
¼ cup mashed potato	ground rice for coating

Cook millet in salted water to cover till tender and water is absorbed. Peel and grate onion or chop very finely. Cook a few minutes in oil in separate pan. Add to millet when cooked with rest of ingredients. When cool, form into small rissolés. Dip in milk or beaten egg, and roll in powdered milk, cornmeal or ground rice. Sauté in hot oil till brown all over. Serve hot with green vegetables or cold with salad.

Savory Rice Rounds

¾ cup rice washed carefully	2 tbs. oil
½ tsp. salt	1 egg, beaten
2½ cups milk	ground rice or cornmeal for
¼ cup cheese, grated	dipping

Cook the rice and salt in the milk slowly in a pan for about 30 minutes or until it resembles thick porridge. Stir in the grated cheese. Spread the mixture thinly out on a flat surface, brushed with oil, and leave it till cold. Cut into small rounds or squares, dip in the beaten eggs, then in the ground rice or cornmeal and fry in the oil. Eat hot.

Risotto (1)

1 cup rice (washed)	1 tbs. oil
2 cups water, salted, or well-flavored stock	½ tsp. molasses
	4 tbs. cheese, grated
1 onion or 2 shallots, finely chopped	paprika to garnish

Heat oil in pan, add onion or shallots, and sauté about 5 minutes. Add water (or stock) and molasses and bring to a boil. Drop in rice gradually, cover and cook gently till rice is tender and all fluid is absorbed, adding more if necessary to prevent burning. Stir in cheese and serve at once, garnished with paprika.

Risotto (2)

2 scant cups rice   5 cups water or stock
2 tbs. oil   1 tbs. butter or oil
2 small onions, chopped fine   ½ cup cheese, grated
1 tsp. salt   parsley for garnish

Wash rice, pat dry on towel. Heat oil and fry rice until slightly yellow. Add onions, salt and water. Cover and simmer about 30 minutes until rice is tender and all water is absorbed, adding more if needed. Stir in butter or oil. Heap up on dish, sprinkle with grated cheese on top and garnish with parsley.

RECIPE INDEX

Almond cones, 124
Amber, apple, 127
Apple
  amber, 127
  and banana chutney, 177
  and coconut curry, 209
  cream, 127
  crumble, 127-128
  lemon curd, 197
  macaroons, 123
  meat-stuffed, 159-160
  pudding, baked, 129
  and raisin rice, 128
  and rice custard, 128
Apple juice, kidneys in, 166-167
Apricot
  and coconut pudding, 129
  rice, 129, 130
  rice, mold, 130
  sauce, 188

Bacon and brains, 163-164
Balls
  cream cheese, 141
  ham and rice, 159
  peanut butter, 121
Banana
  and apple chutney, 177
  pudding, baked, 130
Batter, 173
Beans
  and kidneys, 167
  See also specific kinds
Beef
  burgers, mushroom, 157-158
  cake, 154-155
  chop suey, 155

leftovers and kidneys, 168
  and liver loaf, 170-171
  oriental, 158
  and potato loaf, 156
  and rice loaf, 155-156
  roulades, 162
  stroganoff, ground, 158
Berry milk shake, 147
Biscuits, 105-109
Black currant cream, 131
Blender bread, cornmeal, 110
Brains
  and bacon, 163-164
  cakes, 164
  creamed, with cheese, 164
  in disguise, 164-165
  preparation of, 163
  with tomatoes and rice, 165
Brawn, 162-163
Bread(s), 109-111
  corn and millet, 109-110
  cornmeal blender, 110
  cornmeal quick, 110-111
  rice and soya flour, 111
Breadless sandwiches, 111-112
Breakfasts, 112-115
Brown nougat, 118
Butter bean pie, 209

Cabbage, chopped meat with, 157
Cake(s), 115-117
  beef, 154-155
  brain, 164
  cheese, 115
  corn, 124

227

Cake(s) (*cont.*)
  fish and cornmeal, 151-152
  fruit, 117
  milk cheese, 116
  pashka, 141-142
  potato, 116
  rice and corn, 116
  rice feathery, 126
  sponge, 117
Candy, 117-121
Canned fruits, 202
Carob, 145-146
Carrot
  and chive cutlets, 210
  fingers toasted, 215-216
  milk shake, 144
  and rice loaf, 210-211
  soup, 193
Casserole(s)
  lentil and millet, 219-220
  millet and mushroom, 221
  millet and onion cheese, 221-222
  vegetable, 211
Celebration pudding, 131
Cheese
  baked walnuts and, 224
  cake, 115
  casserole, millet and onion, 221-222
  with creamed brains, 164
  droppies, 105
  dumplings, 216
  milk, 173-174
  milk, cakes, 116
  and millet droppies, 106
  and potato pancake, 216
  and potato pan roast, 207
  with potato salad, 185-186
  and potato, savory, 216-217
  and potato soufflé, 212
  and rice, 213
  rice and parsley, 213-214
  and rice rolls, 217

sauce, golden, 186-187
soya, 176
Chestnut(s), 174
  cream, 139
  and onion pie, 223
  puree, 139-140
  and rice stuffing, 178
Chicken livers
  Malay curried, 170
  and rice, 168
Chive, and carrot cutlets, 210
Chop suey, beef, 155
Chopped meat with cabbage, 157
Chufa shake, 147
Chutney
  apple and banana, 177
  instant, 175
Cinnamon flip, 147
Coconut
  and apple curry, 209
  and apricot pudding, 129
  drops, 122
  mold, 136
  pudding, 136
  pyramids, 122
Cold lemon tea, 145
Comfrey cocktail, 144-145
Cones, almond, 124
Cookies, 122-126
  rice, 126
Corn
  cakes, 124
  crisps, 112
  and millet bread, 109-110
  muffins, southern, 105
  and rice cake, 116
  spoonbread, 110
Cornmeal
  blender bread, 110
  and fishcakes, 151-152
  fried slices, 113
  quick breads, 110-111
  savory, with roasted onion, 220
  scrapple, 160
  Yorkshire pudding, 177

Cottage cheese
  and apple cream, 140
  whip, 141
Cream
  apple, 127
  black currant, 131
  chestnut, 139
  cottage cheese and apple, 140
  rice, 137
Cream cheese balls, 141
Creamed
  brains with cheese, 164
  potatoes, 206
  sweetbreads, 172
Croquettes, rice flake, 213
Crumble, apple, 127-128
Cucumber salad, 185
Curried chicken livers, Malay, 170
Curried fish, 150
Curry, apple and coconut, 209
Custard
  apple and rice, 128
  baked, 134-135
  ground rice, 138
  quick, 143
Cutlets
  carrot and chive, 210
  mixed vegetable, 211-212
  savory rice, 214-215

Date and rice pudding, 136
Desserts, 127-144
Donkey's chocolate, 146
Dressings, salad, 184
Drinks, 144-148
Droppies, 173
  cheese, 105
  millet, 106
  millet and cheese, 106
  polenta savory, 220
  potato, 107-108
  rice and nut, 106
  rice plain, 109
Drops, coconut, 122

Dumplings, cheese, 216
Egg(s)
  baked in potatoes, 112
  flip, 147
  pilau, 218
  poached, pudding, 143
  savory steamed, 218
Eggless mayonnaise, 184
Emerald potatoes, 206

Fingers
  carrot, toasted, 215-216
  fruit, 125
  nut crunch, 120
  peanut, 125
  potato, 115
Fish, 148-154
  baked with lemon, 149
  baked in milk, 149
  batter for, 173
  broiled, 151
  cornmeal cakes, 151-152
  curried, 150
  fried, 150-151
  kedgeree, 151
  and onion pie, 152
  salad, 152
  scrambled, 152-153
  steamed, 150
Flat cakes, soya, 215
Flatties
  lentil, 219
  potato, 107
Flip(s)
  cinnamon, 147
  egg, 147
Foam white sauce, 186
Fondant
  modelling, 119
  nuts, 119
Fritters, batter for, 173
Fruit
  cake, 117
  cooking of, 202
  fingers, 125
  froth, 132
  preserved and canned, 202

Fruit juice, pudding, 131-132
Fruities, 120
Fudge, peanut butter, 121

Golden cheese sauce, 186-187
Golden rice and leftovers, 161
Golden sauce, 186
Greens, salad, 180-181
Grits, soya, 176
Ground beef stroganoff, 158
Ground rice
    custard, 138
    molds, 138
    strips, 126

Ham and rice balls, 159
Hard sauce, 188
Headcheese, 162-163
Hearts
    roast with nut stuffing, 166
    sautéed with lemon, 166
    savory, 165
Herb meatcakes, 156
Herrings
    baked stuffed, 153
    spiced, 153
Honey
    and peanut dressing, 184
    toffee, 121
Horchata, 147

Irish potato scones, 108

Jelly
    milk, 142
    rice, 137
Johnny cakes, 110-111
Junket, 142

Kedgeree
    fish, 151
    meat, 161
Kidney(s)
    in apple juice, 166-167
    and beans, 167
    and beef leftovers, 168
    and mushrooms, 167
    spread, 197
Kisses, lemon, 122

Lamb
    liver, broiled, 168
    oriental, 158
Leek soup, 193
Leftovers
    beef, and kidneys, 168
    golden rice and, 161
    in meat kedgeree, 161
    potato, steamed unpeeled,
        207
    in potato puffs, 162
Lemon
    curd, apple, 197
    curd, baked potatoes with,
        204
    curd, pumpkin, 198
    kisses, 122
    mold, 132
    and oil dressing, 184
    sauce, 187
    tea, cold, 145
Lemonade, sweet, 145
Lentil(s)
    basic, 219
    flatties, 219
    and millet casserole, 219-
        220
Lettuce and sprout salad, 185
Lima bean soup, 190
Liver
    and beef loaf, 170-171
    broiled lamb, 168
    chicken, Malay curried, 170
    chicken, rice and, 168
    and prunes, 171
    and rice, baked, 171
    sautéed, 170
    savory sauté, 169
    spread, 197-198
    sticks, 169
Loaf
    beef and potato, 156
    beef and rice, 155-156
    carrot and rice, 210-211
    liver and beef, 170-171
    peanut and potato, 212
    savory soya, 211

Loaf (*cont.*)
  steamed vegetable, 223-224

Macaroons
  apple, 123
  merry, 123
  plain, 123
  special, 124
Malay curried chicken livers, 170
Malay rice pudding, 140
Mayonnaise, 184
  eggless, 184
Meat(s), 154-173
  apples stuffed with, 159-160
  breadless sandwiches, 111
  cakes, herb, 156
  Kedgeree, 161
  roll, steamed, 156
  See also specific meats
Milk
  cheese, 173-174
  cheese, cakes, 116
  jelly, 142
  shake, berry, 147
  shake, carrot, 144
  shake, spiced soya, 148
Millet
  baked savory, 220-221
  basic, 114
  and cheese droppies, 106
  and corn bread, 109-110
  droppies, 106
  and lentil casserole, 219-220
  mix, 221
  and mushroom casserole, 221
  and mushroom stew, 215
  and nut rissolés, 224-225
  and onion cheese casserole, 221-222
  pilau, 222
  soufflé, 223
Mincemeat, 132-133
Mixed vegetable cutlets, 211-212
Mixed vegetable soup, 196
Modelling fondant, 119

Molasses
  milk, 148
  sauce, 189
  toffee, 118
Mold(s)
  appricot rice, 130
  coconut, 136
  ground rice, 138
  lemon, 132
Mrs. Johnny's Johnny Cakes, 110-111
Muesli, popcorn, 114-115
Muffins, southern corn, 105
Mushroom(s)
  beef burgers, 157-158
  and kidneys, 167
  and millet casserole, 221
  and millet stew, 215

Nougat, brown, 118
Nut
  crunch fingers, 120
  and millet rissolés, 224-225
  and rice droppies, 106
  savory, 224
  soya, 175-176
  stuffings, with roast beef, 166
  toffee, 120-121

Oil
  and lemon dressing, 184
  and orange dressing, 184

Omelet
  basic, 217
  Spanish, 217-218
Onion(s)
  and chestnut pie, 223
  and fish pie, 152
  and millet cheese casserole, 221-222
  roasted, with savory corn-meal, 220
  soup, quick, 190-191
  stuffed, 159
Orange
  and oil dressing, 184
  pudding, 133

Oriental beef or lamb, 158
Oven-fried potatoes, 205

Paella, 160-161
Pan roast potato and cheese, 207
Pancake(s)
  cheese and potato, 216
  rice, 138-139
Parsley and rice cheese, 213-214
Parsnip soup, 191
Pashka pudding, 141-142
Pastry, potato, 176-177
Patties, rice, 214
Pea-pod potage, 192
Pea soup, 191-192
Peanut
  fingers, 125
  and honey dressing, 184
  and potato loaf, 212
  sauce, 188
Peanut butter
  balls, 121
  fingers, 125
  fudge, 121
Pie
  butter bean, 209
  chestnut and onion, 223
  fish and onion, 152
Pilau
  egg, 218
  millet, 222
Piquant spread, 198
Poached egg pudding, 143
Polenta, 113
  savory droppies, 220
  slices, 113-114
Popcorn, 114
  muesli, 114-115
  pumpkin pudding and, 134
Potage pea-pod, 192
Potato(es), 202-208
  baked, 204, 205
  baked eggs in, 112
  baked, with lemon curd, 204
  and beef loaf, 156
  cake, 116

and cheese pan roast, 207
and cheese pancake, 216
and cheese soufflé, 212
creamed, 206
droppies, 107, 212-213
droppies, savory, 107-108
emerald, 206
fingers, toasted, 115
flatties, 107
leftovers, steamed unpeeled, 207
oven-fried, 205
pastry, 176-177
and peanut loaf, 212
puffs, 162
salad, 206-207
salad, with cheese, 185-186
sautéed, 207-208
savory cheese and, 216-217
scones, 108
shredded, 207
sliced broiled, 205
steamed, 205
sticks, 206
warning about, 203-204
wedges, 108
Potted meat spread, 198
Preserved fruits, 202
Prune(s)
  and liver, 171
  and rice stuffing, 178
Pudding(s), 127-144
  apricot and coconut, 129
  baked apple, 129
  baked banana, 130
  celebration, 131
  coconut, 136
  cornmeal Yorkshire, 177
  date and rice, 136
  fruit juice, 131-132
  orange, 133
  Pashka, 141-142
  poached egg, 143
  pumpkin, 134-135
  Queen's, 139
  rice, 140
Puffs, potato, 162

Pumpkin
  lemon curd, 198
  pudding, 134-135
  puree, 135
  soup, 192
Puree
  chestnut, 139-140
  pumpkin, 135
Pyramids, coconut, 122

Queen's pudding, 139
Quick breads, cornmeal, 110-111

Raisin(s)
  and apple rice, 128
  with baked rice, 137
Rhubarb
  sweet sauce, 188
  whip, 133-134
Rice
  and apple custard, 128
  apple and raisin, 128
  apricot, 129, 130
  apricot, mold, 130
  baked with raisins, 137
  basic, 115
  and beef loaf, 155-156
  and carrot loaf, 210-211
  and cheese, 213
  and cheese rolls, 217
  and chestnut stuffing, 178
  chicken livers and, 168
  cookies, 126
  and corn cake, 116
  cream, 137
  cutlets, savory, 214-215
  and date pudding, 136
  feathery cakes, 126
  flake croquettes, 213
  golden, and leftovers, 161
  ground, custard, 138
  ground, molds, 138
  and ham balls, 159
  jelly, 137
  and liver, baked, 171
  and nut droppies, 106
  pancakes, 138-139
  and parsley cheese, 213-214

  patties, 214
  plain droppies, 109
  and prune stuffing, 178
  pudding, steamed, 140
  and rosemary stuffing, 177-178
  rounds, savory, 225
  savory, 214
  soup, thick, 192
  and soya flour bread, 111
  and tomato stuffing, 178
  with tomatoes and brains, 165
  and vegetable stuffing, 179
Risotto, 225-226
Rissolés, nut and millet, 224-225
Roll(s)
  cheese and rice, 217
  steamed meat, 156
Rosemary, and rice stuffing, 177-178
Roulades, beef, 162

Salad(s), 179-186
  dressings, 184
  fish, 152
  greens for, 180-181
  potato, 206-207
  potato, with cheese, 185-186
  preparations for, 181-183
  summer cucumber, 185
  winter lettuce and sprout, 185
Sandwiches, breadless, 111-112
Sauce(s), 186-189
  apricot, 188
  foam white, 186
  golden, 186
  golden cheese, 186-187
  hard, 188
  lemon, 187
  molasses, 189
  peanut, 188
  rhubarb sweet, 188
  tomato, 187
Sausages, 157

Savory
    cheese and potato, 216-217
    cornmeal with roasted onion, 220
    drinks, 144-145
    droppies, polenta, 220
    hearts, 165
    liver strips sauté, 169
    potato droppies, 107-108
    rice, 214
    rice cutlets, 214-215
    rice rounds, 225
    sauces, 186-187
    soya loaf, 211
    soybeans, 210
    steamed eggs, 218
    sweetbreads, 173
Scones, Irish potato, 108
Scotch broth, 194
Scrambled fish, 152-153
Scrapple, 160
Shake(s)
    chufa, 147
    See also Milk shake(s)
Shredded potatoes, 207
Shrimp spread, 199
Smelts, 153-154
Soufflé
    millet, 223
    potato and cheese, 212
    Spanish, 143-144
Soup(s), 189-197
    carrot, 193
    leek, 193
    lima bean, 190
    mixed vegetable, 196
    onion, 190-191
    parsnip, 191
    pea, 191-192
    pumpkin, 192
    quick vegetable, 195
    soya, 194
    spinach, 194-195
    stock for, 189-190
    string bean, 193-194
    summer, 196-197
    thick rice, 192
    tomato, 195

South African pumpkin pudding, 134-135
Southern corn (maize) muffins, 105
Soya
    cheese, 176
    flat cakes, 215
    flour and rice bread, 111
    grits, 176
    loaf, savory, 211
    milk 146
    milk shakes, 148
    nut toffee, 118
    nuts, 175-176
    soup, 194
Soybeans
    basic, 209-210
    savory, 210
    warning about, 175
Spanish omelet, 217-218
Spanish soufflé, 143-144
Spiced herring, 153
Spiced soya milk shake, 148
Spinach soup, 194-195
Sponge cake, 117
Spoonbread, corn, 110
Spread(s), 197-199
    kidney, 197
    liver, 197-198
    piquant, 198
    potted meat, 198
    shrimp, 199
Sprout and winter lettuce salad, 185
Stew, millet and mushroom, 215
Sticks
    liver, 169
    potato, 206
Stock, soup, 189-190
String bean soup, 193-194
Stroganoff, ground beef, 158
Stuffings, 177-179
    nut, 166
Summer cucumber salad, 185
Summer soup, 196-197

Sweet drinks, 145-148
Sweet lemonade, 145
Sweet potato tartlets, 135
Sweet sauces, 188-189
Sweetbreads
  broiled, 172
  creamed, 172
  preparation of, 171
  sautéed, 172
  savory, 173

Tartlets, sweet potato, 135
Tea, cold lemon, 145
Thick rice soup, quick, 192
Toffee
  honey, 121
  molasses, 118
  nut, 120-121
  soya nut, 118
Tomato(es)
  juice, 145
  with rice and brains, 165
  and rice stuffing, 178
  sauce, 187
  soup, 195

Vegetable(s)
  casserole, 211
  cooking of, 199-202
  cutlets, mixed, 211-212
  loaf, steamed, 223-224
  and rice stuffing, 179
  soup, mixed, 196
  soup, quick, 195
Vegetarian dishes, 208-226
  breadless sandwiches, 111

Walnut
  baked, and cheese, 224
  wonders, 119
Wedges, potato, 108
Whip
  cottage cheese, 141
  rhubarb, 133-134
White sauce, foam, 186
Winter lettuce and sprout
  salad, 185

Yorkshire pudding, cornmeal,
  177

Zabaglione, 142-143

SUBJECT INDEX

Arthritis, rheumatoid, 39-40
Autism, 40-41
Axelrod, Julius, 35

Babies
  feeding charts for, 71-74
  packing food for, 87-88
  preparing solids for, 68-70
  weaning of, 67-68
Bag lunches, menu for, 103
Bed-time drinks, 104
Bicknell, Franklin, 56
Breakfasts, menu for, 102-3
Breaks, menus for, 103
Breathing exercises, 32-33
Brewer's yeast, 57-58
Burkitt, Denis, 50

Campbell, G. D., 10, 50
Cantor Lectures (McCarrison), 50
Carbohydrates, complete vs. refined, 50-52
Celiac disease,
  and fingerprints, 5
  diet deficiencies in, 45
  history of, 9-16
Children
  feeding chart for, 75
  food for parties for, 84-86
Clausen, J., 24
Cleave, T. L., 10, 50
Cold meals, packing of, 87
Crawford, Michael, 56n

Davis, Adele, 24, 50, 67, 83
Davison, Professor, 24n

Dermatitis herpetiformis, 11, 17-18
di Sant Agnese, P. A., 13
Diabetes, 17
Dicke, W. H., 10, 11
Diets
  Haas's, 59
  low residue, 9
Dohan, F. C., 35, 36, 38
Drinks, bed-time, 104

Eating out, 86
Electric hot plate, 104
Ennals, David, 34
Enteritis, 40-41
Evening meals, menu for, 95, 97, 99, 101, 104
Exercises for multiple sclerosis, 28-33
Fats and oils, 9, 23-24, 27, 40, 54-56, 70, 79
Feeding charts
  for babies, 71-74
  for children, 75
Flour, 39, 48, 55
Forbidden foods, 46-48
French language, menu terms in, 89-91
Freud, Sigmund, 34
Fruit and vegetables, 25, 45, 53-54, 153-155

Gee, Samuel, 9
General hints, 80-82
Gluten-free diet, 44-77
  foods forbidden on, 46-48
  for infants and children, 65-77

recommended foods on, 49-58
results to be expected from, 59-61
second-best foods avoided on, 48-49
Gluten, toxic constituent in, 11

Haas, S. V., 59
Hemmings, Mrs. Gwynneth, 37
Henry Doubleday Research Association, 2, 27
Hoffer, A., 38-39
Hot meals, packing of, 87
Hot plate, electric, 104
Hughes, Margaret, 27

Idiopathic staetorrhea, 12
Intestinal symptoms, 11-12
Italy, eating in, 92-93

Kwashiorkor, 20

Lunches, menus for, 103
Lymington, Viscount, 78

Magnesium, 24-25
and celiacs, 10
Main meals, eaten out, 86
McCarrison, Sir Robert, ix, 50
McDougall, Roger, 27
Menus
adapting to other people's, 102-104
children's party, 84-86
for packed meals, 87
menaces in French, 89-91
minimum trouble, 102-104
seasonal, 94-101
Milk
intolerance to, 19-20
powdered skim, 58
substitutes, 66, 146
Millar, J. H. D., 79

Minimum trouble menus, 102-104
Multiple sclerosis, 22-34

National Health Service, British, 4

Obesity, 44
Observer, 5-6
Osmond, H., 39

Packed meals, picnics, 87-88
Painter, N. S., 50
Paneth cell deficiencies, 14
Parties, children's, 84-86
Pauling, Linus, 34
Potatoes, 59, 61, 202-208
Price, Weston, 50
Proteins, complete, 52-53

Recommended foods, 49-58, 78-80
Refined carbohydrates, 50-52
Regional enteritis, 40-41
Rheumatoid arthritis, 39-40
Ridges, Pauline, 41
Rose, Mary Schwarz, 50

Scandinavia, eating in, 93
Schizophrenia, 34-39
Second-best foods, avoidance of, 48-49
Shatin, R., 26, 39-40
Skin diseases, 17-18
Snacks, 86, 87
Soybeans, 57, 58, 66, 82
Spain, eating in, 91-92
Spring menus, 94-95
Summer menus, 96-97
Supplements, 56-58
brewer's yeast as, 57-58
powdered skim milk as, 58
soybeans as, 58
yogurt as, 58

Taylor, Geoffrey, 50
Traveling, 88-89

Vegans, 66
Vegetables and fruit, 25, 45, 53-54, 153-155
Vegetarians, 208
Vitamins, 33-34, 38, 45-46

Winter menus, 100-101
Weaning charts, 71-74

Yeast, brewer's, 57-58
Yogurt, 58
Yudkin, John, 50